D1263954

RICHMOND HILL
PUBLIC LIBRARY

JUN 2   2009

CENTRAL LIBRARY
905-884-9288

BOOK SOLD
NO LONGER R.H.P.L.
PROPERTY

Sight Hounds

Sight Hounds

*Their History,
Management and Care*

JULIETTE CUNLIFFE

SWAN·HILL
PRESS

Dedication

To the memory of my first two Afghan Hounds, Ami and Moses,
who taught me how much there is to love about the
Sight Hound breeds, and to my Whippets and Deerhounds
that have followed them.

RICHMOND HILL
PUBLIC LIBRARY

JUN 2 2009

CENTRAL LIBRARY
905-884-9288

Copyright © 2006 Juliette Cunliffe

First published in the UK in 1992 by Popular Dogs Publishing Co Ltd under the title
Popular Sight Hounds

This updated edition published 2006
by Swan Hill Press, an imprint of Quiller Publishing Ltd

British Library Cataloguing-in-Publication Data
A catalogue record for this book is available from the British Library

ISBN 1 904057 78 0
     978 1 904057 78 9

The right of Juliette Cunliffe to be identified as the author of this work has been asserted
in accordance with the Copyright, Design and Patent Act 1988

The information in this book is true and complete to the best of our knowledge. All
recommendations are made without any guarantee on the part of the Publisher, who also
disclaims any liability incurred in connection with the use of this data or specific details.

All rights reserved. No part of this book may be reproduced or transmitted in any form or
by any means, electronic or mechanical including photocopying, recording or by any
information storage and retrieval system, without permission from the Publisher in
writing.

Typeset by Phoenix Typesetting, Auldgirth, Dumfriesshire
Printed in England by Biddles Ltd., King's Lynn

Swan Hill Press

An imprint of Quiller Publishing Ltd
Wykey House, Wykey, Shrewsbury, SY4 1JA
Tel: 01939 261616 Fax: 01939 261606
E-mail: info@quillerbooks.com
Website: www.swanhillbooks.com

CONTENTS

'I have sometimes thought of the final cause of dogs having such short lives, and I am quite satisfied it is in compassion to the human race; for if we suffer so much in losing a dog after an acquaintance of ten or twelve years, what would it be if they were to live double that time?'

SIR WALTER SCOTT, APRIL 1822

PREFACE

Writing about something of which one is fond is always a pleasure and I hope that those of you who are interested in the Sight Hound breeds will derive enjoyment from reading the following pages. Sight Hounds and dog books have shared my home for many years and I consider those of us currently involved and interested in these breeds fortunate to have access to so much well-documented information from early writers, including the work of artists, which enables us actually to see the hounds of years gone by.

There are, however, many inconsistencies in the spelling of dogs' names in early source material. For my part, I have made every endeavour to use the most usual spelling to avoid confusion.

I found it absorbing when putting together this book to see how the various breeds have influenced one another and, in some instances, have been incorporated in breeding programmes in order to re-establish or to improve a breed. It is my earnest hope that readers will not restrict themselves only to the chapter on their own particular breed, for there is much to interest them in the information on the other breeds within this select 'group'. My grateful thanks to the Kennel Club's library staff and to the Kennel Club itself, for having allowed me to include Breed Standards. The late Clifford Hubbard was always such a help and inspiration to me, and it has been good to work again with editor John Beaton, with whom I first came into contact some sixteen years ago.

Whenever I have a new book in my hands I am always anxious to move on to the heart and substance of it and so, on the assumption that you very probably feel the same way, I shall not delay you further. Should you not already have one of the Sight Hounds lying at your feet as you read, I hope that if and when you do so you will give each other as much pleasure as my own hounds have given me for the last thirty years.

JULIETTE CUNLIFFE

ACKNOWLEDGEMENTS

All photographs are by Carol Ann Johnson unless credited otherwise.
The Breed Standards on pages 33, 62, 99, 124, 153, 177 and 201are copyright of the Kennel Club and are reproduced with their kind permission.

IMPORTANT NOTE

Many of the Sight Hound breeds were traditionally used for hunting and coursing and whilst this is still legal in many countries of the world, readers should make sure that they are fully aware of the law as it applies in England, Wales and Scotland where restrictions apply to hunting with dogs. If they are in any doubt whatsoever they should seek legal advice.

When the author writes about coursing as it is today this only refers to countries where it is still legal.

ONE

THE MOST POPULAR
SIGHT HOUNDS

THE GROUP of dogs classified as Sight Hounds can just as easily be called Gaze Hounds or, indeed, from the natural history point of view, the Greyhound group.

Before we go back into the realms of antiquity, let us begin by defining exactly what a Sight Hound is, for it is quite distinct from any other of the groups of *Canis familiaris*. Sight Hounds cannot strictly be included with the true hounds, which hunt by scent, because they largely use sight to hunt their prey and they all possess a lean, powerful body, a deep chest and long legs, giving them both stamina and speed. They are cursorial animals, meaning that they are adapted to finding prey in open country and over-taking it by superior speed and endurance. As a result the distribution of this group of hounds has always been in regions where there is open countryside so that their special form of hunting can be used effectively: North Africa, the Arabian countries, Afghanistan and Russia, and for many centuries in Scotland and Ireland.

The most commonly accepted ancestor of the Sight Hound is *Canis lupus pallipes,* the Asiatic Wolf, which could most certainly have produced a cursorial form from which descended *Canis lupus Arabs*, the Desert Wolf of Arabia, and the Sight Hounds. A further reason for believing that the Asiatic

Figure 1   10th Century coursing hounds

1

Figure 2   Possibly the earliest representation of the Egyptian dog – pre-dynastic

Figure 3   Egyptian Greyhounds on grave of Ptahhetep Sakkara circa 2500BC

Figure 4   A Pharaoh spearing a lion 1735–1350 BC

Wolf is the ancestor of the Sight Hounds is that no other wolves are known to have existed in the areas where dogs of Greyhound type originated.

Large parts of the Sahara were once relatively well watered and supported plentiful herds of animals, making them excellent hunting grounds for the Sight Hound. Mohammed permitted dogs of the chase and the animals captured by them were allowed to be eaten provided that the name of Allah was uttered as the dogs were slipped to give chase.

Fortunately, for those of us who study dogs, the Ancient Egyptians knew the art of writing, and so we have pictures and the names of many of their dogs. The dogs of Ancient Egypt much resembled our hounds of the present day. It is clear that dogs were held in great veneration in those times, especially in Cynopolis where they were paid divine honours, being depicted on tombs as the symbol of the 'Divine Being'. In fact the inhabitants of the city were obliged to provide a specific amount of food for the dogs therein, and once there was even a war between them and their

3

Figure 5 Egyptian with hounds on leash.

neighbours, triggered off when one of them ate a dog from Cynopolis.

Sirius, the dog star, the brightest star in the sky, was venerated by all Ancient Egyptians. The country depended on the annual overflow of the Nile and the rising of this star in bright, glowing colours marked for them the New Year, and was a sure indication that the Nile would soon flood. It has been said that the dog was worshipped in Ancient Egypt because it assisted Isis in her long search for Osiris's body, which was eventually found in a tamarisk tree. Despite being highly esteemed, the dog did not, however, rank with the bull or the ibis in the eyes of the Egyptians.

Figure 6 Embalmed dog in various stages of undress

Figure 8   Dog depicted on an Ancient Egyptian tomb, *c.* 3000 BC.

Figure 7   Mummy of a dog.

The dog was mourned at death and it was not unknown for Egyptians to fast and shave their heads. The deceased dog was carefully embalmed, wrapped in linen and placed in a special tomb. The mourners wailed loudly and beat themselves as a token of their grief.

Among the paintings in his tomb, four dogs are represented at the feet of Antefa II (3000 BC). As an example of the high regard in which hounds were held, an official during the Middle Kingdom *(c.* 2040–1786 BC) described himself as 'a dog who sleeps in the tent, a hound of the bed, whom his mistress loves'.

The Hebrews loathed the dog and there are very few passages in the Bible which compliment the species *canis*. It is possible that this hatred dates from the Exodus and was a reaction against the Egyptian veneration of the dog. Thus they were taught to regard the dog with loathing so they should not fall into the error of worshipping it as a false idol as their former taskmasters had done. However, King Solomon in the Book of Proverbs (30:31) refers to the hound as one of four things which 'go well and are comely in going'.

Sight Hounds were known to the Greeks, who depicted this graceful animal in their decorative metalwork, carvings in ivory and stone and as parts of the designs on terracotta oil bottles, wine-coolers and vases. In most cases they are depicted with prick-ears but occasionally the rose ear is shown. Homer praises the dogs used in the hunt in several places, and

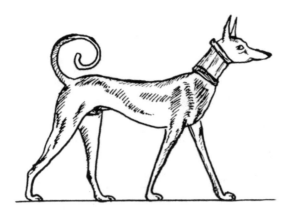

Figure 9 Dog from the tomb of Antefa II, 3000 BC.

indeed the chase, classed next to the gymnasium, was, in fact, one of the most important sports of the Greek heroes, for it was by the chase that they trained themselves for war. Hunting without dogs was, for the Greeks, a poor sport and because of this they paid much attention to their breeding. The Greeks principally chased the hare and wild boar, for which dogs from India, Crete and Sparta were deemed especially good and were hunted side by side. The Greyhound was one of three large dogs used by the Greeks, the others being the Mastiff and the Molossian Hound. Socrates speaks of snares and nets being 'everywhere prohibited', so it was evidently considered unsporting to use such methods.

Arrian, the Greek historian, lectured on coursing and in AD 124 described thus a Greyhound bitch:

> I have myself bred a hound whose eyes are the greyest of grey. A swift, hard-working, courageous, sound-footed dog, and she proves a match at any time for four hares. She is, moreover, most gentle and kindly-affectioned, and never before had I a dog with such a regard for myself. When I am at home she remains close by my side, accompanies me on going abroad, follows me to the Gymnasium, and while I am exercising myself sits down near me. If she has not seen me for a short time she jumps up repeatedly, by way of salutation, and barks with joy at greeting to me. At meals she pats me with one foot and then the other, to remind me that she is to have her share of the food.
>
> She has also many tones of speech – more than I ever knew in any dog – pointing out in her own language what she wants.

How little the Sight Hound has changed over the centuries! Clearly Arrian was considerate to his hounds for he also writes, 'Nothing is so helpful as a

Figure 10   Egyptian dogs from a tomb at Beni Hassan, 2200–2000 BC.

soft, warm bed. It is best of all if they can sleep with a person, because it makes them more human, and because they rejoice in the company of human beings.'

How much we can learn from Arrian whose 'Treatise on the Greyhound', incidentally, lay undiscovered for many years in the library of the Vatican for it had been mistaken for the better known manuscript 'Cynegeticus of Xenophon', Flavius Arrianus' pen-name being 'Xenophon'. It was eventually translated and was first published in English in 1831. Amongst his many words of wisdom are these:

> Now I myself shall tell you by what means you should judge the fast and well-bred ones . . . First, then, let them stand long from head to stern . . . Let them have light and well-knit heads . . . Let the neck be long, rounded and supple . . . Broad breasts are better than narrow, and let them have shoulderblades standing apart and not fastened together . . . loins that are broad, strong not fleshy, but solid with sinew . . . flanks pliant. . . Rounded and fine feet are the strongest.

A Roman Consul is probably writing about Irish Wolfhounds when, in a letter to his brother, he thanks him for the present of seven 'Scottish dogs which were shown at the Cirensian games, to the great astonishment of the people who could not judge it possible to bring them to Rome other than in Iron cages, like lions and tigers, so fierce were they'. Porters at the doors of Roman houses always had a dog and pictures of them were often painted outside the house or laid in mosaic just inside the front door.

One of the most famous marble canine sculptures, now housed in the British Museum, dates back to the second century AD and is of two seated Greyhounds. They are quite remarkably similar to the hounds we know today. In AD 500, in the south-west counties of Wales, we hear that 'two white-breasted brindled greyhounds' ran beside Prince Kilburgh, the son of Kilhith, as he travelled to Arthur's Court. They wore broad collars set with rubies and they 'sprang about him like two sea-swallows'.

The Arabs, and especially the Bedouin, have always favoured their hounds. Around the tenth century a Bedouin is reported to have praised a ruler by likening him to a dog: 'You are like a dog in maintaining a loyal friendship and like a he-goat in confronting difficulties.' For centuries the Sight Hound was the only animal permitted to sit beside the master and guests in a Bedouin household. In the seventh century, Ibn Umar made comment to a Bedouin with his dog, asking what he had with him. 'He who is grateful to me and keeps my secrets,' came the reply, to which Ibn Umar responded, 'Then take good care of your friend!'

Abu Nuwas, an Arabic poet who died shortly after the turn of the ninth century and was an important exponent of hunting songs, wrote of 'fine hounds' being highly prized, protected and given both training and names. Lines composed by him and translated from the Arabic read thus:

> I will sing the praises of a hound whose owners'
> Good fortune is assured by his strenuous effort.
> All the good things have come from him;
> His master is always his slave.
> At night the master brings him nearest to his bed;
> If he is uncovered, his master puts on him his own coat.
> He has a blaze and his legs are white;
> His excellent conformation is pleasing to the eye.
> What fine jaws he has! What a fine muzzle!
> Gazelles are really in trouble when he is hunting!
> What a fine hound you are, without equal!

There is much early Arab literature relating to Sight Hounds and indeed the teachings of the Qur'an are in favour of training hounds for the chase.

In Ireland, Bran, the dog of Fionn MacCoul, was led on a collar of beaten gold, attached to a great chain wrought in silver. Gifted with a remarkable foreknowledge of evil he was a 'ferocious, small-headed, white-breasted, sleek-haunched hound, having the eyes of a dragon, the claws of a wolf, the vigour of a lion, the venom of a serpent'. When they went to the chase it was said that Bran, always in the forefront, was accompanied by three thousand hounds and a thousand knights or more, each attired in a silken shirt, green doublet and a fine purple mantle. The great Bran was said to have died by following a hart which plunged into a lake. Bran seized the hart as she rose to the surface whereupon she changed into a woman and dragged him down with her. In memory of the event, the cliff from which they leapt is called Coegg-y-Bran. Irish dogs are still called after Bran for it is a name considered to be lucky for both hound and hunter.

A description of Bran, given as a translation by Father Hogan, runs thus:

> Yellow legs had Bran,
> Both sides and her belly white;
> Above her sides a speckled back,
> And two crimson ears, very red.

Throughout the centuries it would seem that hounds fared better than many other dogs for there was a complaint in the Middle Ages that the hounds had to be fed 'on bread and butter like a Christian', and this at a time when bread and butter were not easily come by for most people.

Finally it is interesting to note that seven was the number of hounds most usually used when making lordly gifts. A brace was only considered suitable in comparatively recent times.

Confusion over breed names

What confounds the researcher into the history of breeds is the variety of the names that have been given to them over time. This difficulty is often exacerbated by inaccurate translation having been made in the past and by authors using information without sufficiently full research.

To provide some insight into some of the problems involved, Buffon considered that the Irish Wolfhound and all the breeds of Greyhound, as well as the Great Dane and Albanian Dog, were simply variations of the 'matin' which he depicts as something resembling a pied lurcher. Confusion arose over the years due to the fact that several translators consistently translated 'matin' as 'Irish greyhound', whereas this is not always an accurate translation at all. Barr, translating Buffon in 1792, for reasons best known unto himself, sometimes translated 'matin' as 'Irish greyhound' and sometimes as 'shepherd's dog'. The two breeds today are poles apart!

Coursing

One of the reasons that dog and man combined their respective skills was so that together they might hunt more effectively and thus began the breeding of dogs with a conformation which would enable them effectively to bring down local game, providing an important part of the family diet.

Hounds which pursue their quarry by sight rather than smell are, indeed, coursing breeds and were developed to a large extent in the Middle East where there were wide open spaces and where rapid reactions, speed and stamina were needed to catch quarry. Even as early as 4000 BC there was a competitive and sporting element in coursing and this eventually led to codes of practice being introduced, which we know about from Arrian's writings in the second century AD. He says, 'The true sportsman does not take out his dog to destroy the hares, but for the sake of the course and the contest between the dogs and the hares, and is glad if the hare escapes.'

One of the principal reasons why many of the Sight Hound breeds have remained true to type over the centuries is that some have continued to be used for the work for which they were originally bred.

Coursing under rules in Great Britain

Not until the reign of Queen Elizabeth I was coursing conducted under established rules in Great Britain, the rules being drawn up by the Duke of Norfolk. The sport increased quickly in popularity and by 1776 the first coursing club had been established at Swaffham. Four years later, in 1780, the Ashdown Park Meeting came into existence, followed in 1805 by the Newmarket Meeting. A stud book was commenced in 1858 when the National Coursing Club was established and laws were drawn up for the regulation of coursing meetings. The Greyhound used in coursing differs, however, from the Greyhound seen today in the show-ring, the latter generally being considerably larger. The coursing fraternity said that although a 'good big one' would always have an advantage over a small hound, they considered it difficult to find the former and most of the chief winners of the Waterloo Cup have been comparatively small.

There are two types of coursing in Great Britain, walked up and driven, or static, although in both the principle is the same. In the former the coursers walk in a line with the slipper usually in the centre of the line. When a hare is put up the slipper will run forward and slip the brace of hounds. In static coursing the hares are driven forward past the slipper by beaters, the slipper usually being in the natural run of the hares but behind cover.

The rules state that the hares must have been at liberty on their own

Figure 11 Coursing at Swaffham *(Sporting Magazine)* 1793

ground for at least six months and when coursing it is not permitted to restrict the hares' running in any way at all. A slipper licensed to the National Coursing Club will also only slip to a good strong-running hare and will usually give it a minimum of 80 yards. Mounted on a horse, the judge follows the course to award points for the first dog to the hare (the run-up), for turning the hare and for deflecting it (the wrench). It is interesting to note that it is said to be rare that a point is awarded for a kill and there was one famous coursing judge, Jack Chadwick, who said that he could not ever remember awarding a point for such. Indeed, only about 20 per cent of the hares coursed are actually brought down by the hounds and under the rules of coursing people known as 'dispatchers' are obliged to ensure that any hare brought down, if not already dead, is dispatched without delay. Actually, when the dogs have brought down a hare they usually lose interest in it, so the hare is not torn apart as many people believe. The majority of hares killed at coursing meetings are used for human consumption.

The meetings are run as knock-out competitions, the winner of the first course meeting the winner of the second, and so on until an outright winner is determined. Stakes are run over one, two or three days, the largest of them being the renowned Waterloo Cup, now a three-day stake for sixty-four dogs.

I have not myself been involved in coursing meetings, but it is said that hares are not distressed by being coursed and that if they escape the hounds they will immediately return to the occupation they were involved in beforehand, be it eating or sleeping. Their apparent lack of concern seems to spring from the fact that they are a preyed-upon species and so coursing by dogs may not seem an unnatural or unusual occurrence.

It is often said that hares are released for coursing but this is now not so, for the release of hares has not been permitted in England for the last hundred years or so . Prior to that there was, indeed, something known as Park Coursing in which hares were released. In 1976 the House of Lords Select Committee found that no unnecessary suffering is caused to the hare by coursing.

The Hunting Act 2004

The Hunting Act 2004 came into force early in 2005, bringing with it an enormous amount of understandable controversy which hit the news head-lines in a big way, and took up many hours of valuable Parliamentary time which many people believe could have been better spent on other issues. It prohibits all hunting of wild mammals with dogs in England and in Wales, except where carried out in accordance with the conditions of an exemption. Hare coursing is banned, making it an offence for a person to participate in, attend or knowingly facilitate a hare coursing event.

For the purposes of the Act the word 'hunting' has what is described as 'its ordinary English meaning', which includes searching for wild mammals, chasing them, or pursuing them for the purpose of catching or killing. This is applicable both to a person hunting alone with a dog, or with others. It is an offence for a person knowingly to allow his land to be used for unlawful hunting.

The maximum fine for an offence is £5,000, but the magistrates' court also has power to make an order against a convicted person for the forfeiture of any relevant dog, vehicle or hunting article.

Exemptions
There are exemptions, subject to hunting taking place on land that belongs to the hunter, or when express permission has been given to use the land for that purpose by the occupier or, in the case of unoccupied land, by the person to whom the land belongs. Permission may also be given by a constable, in the case of recapture or rescue of a wild animal.

Dogs may be used to hunt rats or rabbits, to retrieve a hare that has been shot, or to flush a wild animal from cover, thereby enabling a bird of prey to hunt it. There are various rules regarding stalking and flushing out and for 'gamekeepers' exemption', which, in the main, have no particular relevance to the Sight Hound breeds mentioned in this book.

Showing and Kennel Club regulations

Many different breeds of Sight Hound are now to be found on the show-bench around the world, and many of them, though by no means all, are now exhibited in Britain. Their Kennel Club (KC) registration figures vary greatly, and in many cases a high proportion of the dogs registered with the KC are exhibited at shows, as opposed to being kept purely as pets.

The number of breeds found in Britain over recent years has grown rapidly and at the time of publication the following Sight Hound breeds are recognised by the KC: Afghan Hound, Basenji, Borzoi, Deerhound, Greyhound, Ibizan Hound, Irish Wolfhound, Pharaoh Hound, Saluki, Sloughi and Whippet. There are now other Sight Hound breeds in the UK, including the Cirneco del Etna which already has breeding programmes underway so this, and several other of the magnificent breeds that fall into this category, will also be covered briefly later in this book.

As the world grows smaller with the facility of air transport, more of us have the opportunity to travel to other countries to see Sight Hounds and to appreciate their beauty, elegance and many other remarkable attributes. How lucky we are!

TWO

THE AFGHAN HOUND

An Afghan Hound is distinctive in any company on account of
his looks, which most would describe as being eccentric.
A. CROXTON SMITH OBE

SIMILARITIES between the Afghan Hound and the people of
Afghanistan have often been commented upon, both regarding
physical characteristics and temperament. The Afghan Hound is a
breed of dignified bearing, amiable until roused, and the similarity between
its character and temperament and that of the dour, brave Afghans,
Pathans and Afridis has often been made. The breed was greatly valued by
these peoples. The women took charge of the bitches when they were bred
and kept them in seclusion; it was claimed that it was this that was responsible for the 'shyness' encountered in the breed when it first came into this
country, although others said it was more the result of the breed 'not understanding the civilisation in which we live'!

The history of the breed

The breed seems to have been little known to early artists, which is strange
when one considers that there is so much early work depicting the Afghan's
close relation, the Saluki. Miss Clara Bowring, as the guest of the Maharaja
of Jaipur, saw a collection of his early Chinese sculptures and thought that
one piece bore a marked resemblance to the Afghan Hound. A book
entitled *Letters Written in a Mahratta Camp During the Year 1809* has a colour
plate entitled 'A Meenah of Jajurh', showing a native soldier, one of a race
of well-built men, with a reasonably small Afghan Hound. The colour of
the hound is Van Dyck brown and there is a fawn trace running up the
brisket. The dog has a typical ringed tail and topknot with heavily coated
legs and feet.

The Afghan Hound is claimed by the Afghans to be the breed Noah
took into the Ark, which means that in their opinion it has been in

Afghanistan practically for ever. Nearer the present day, it is said that in some caves of the Balkh region of north-west Afghanistan there are rock carvings and wall paintings dating from *c.* 2200 BC that represent a type of Afghan Hound. One of the early names for this breed was Barakzai, which means son of Barak. Barukhzy, another name used for the breed, was the family name of the sirdars who ruled the country and, as the best dogs were owned by them, this was the name most widely used. The dogs were chiefly found in the neighbourhood of Cabul (Kabul) and Balkh, the latter being the ancient Bactria, which fell to the Medes in the seventh century BC and was later conquered by Cyrus who, incidentally, also ruled over Syria and Arabia where Salukis were domiciled from the earliest times.

The breed was referred to by classical authors, including Aristotle and Arrian, but then there is little mention of the breed for several centuries. It is possible that, because of the Afghan's somewhat startling appearance, coupled with its remarkable courage and character, which is somewhat removed from that of most canines, it was confused with some of the mythical beasts, especially the 'tigers' which were said to have had long coats and to have mated with dogs.

The nomenclature for the breed is complex for it includes not only Barakzai and Barukhzy Hounds, but also Kabul Greyhound, Kurram Valley or Kurrum Hound and Baluch Hound. Each of these names has links with Afghanistan. The Kurram Valley lay on one of the principal trade routes east of Kabul and Ghazni; the dogs of this region resembled the more sparsely coated lowland types. The breed was also found in the south of the country on the plains of Baluchistan; hence the name, Baluch Hound. We must, however, always keep clearly in our minds that the term 'Tazi', used now by some with reference to the Afghan Hound of the past, was used also for the Sloughi, Saluki and, indeed, Arab horses; it is a Persian word to denote that something is of Arab origin. In Kazakhstan the Tazi is considered the country's indigenous breed.

There was, in the sixteenth century, mention of some particularly good dogs 'imported' from the Hazarah district and it is likely that these were, indeed, what we now know as Afghan Hounds.

Croxton Smith was strongly convinced that Afghan Hounds were a modified form of Saluki, his reasoning being that the Salukis had reached Afghanistan by way of Persia in the remote ages. Dogs of Greyhound type arrived on the tide of the Celtic migration and Celts, as he rightly pointed out, followed an easterly as well as a westerly course, causing them to overflow into Persia and beyond. There are others who are equally adamant in their claims that the Afghan is a distinct breed of the oldest form of Greyhound type.

In 1815, the Hon. Mountstuart Elphinstone wrote an *Account of the Kingdom of Cabul and Its Dependencis* and in it is contained a passage which reads thus: 'The dogs of Afghanistan deserve to be mentioned. Their Greyhounds are excellent; they are bred in great numbers, particularly among the pastoral tribes, who are so much attached to hunting.' Following this there is little reference to the breed until Charles Hamilton Smith writes in *Dogs* (1839–40) of a 'powerful Persian breed' west of the Indus.

It is possible that the heavier coat type developed as a natural protection as the breed moved east and into the mountains of Afghanistan. Another theory is that the thicker coat type was the earlier of the two coat patterns but with the passage of time it became less well known than the other breeds which developed from it. We find, in H. D. Richardson's *Dogs: Their Origin and Varieties* (1847), a passage indicating his belief in the latter theory.

> The original Greyhound was unquestionably a long-haired dog, and the modern smooth-coated and thin animal, now known by that name, is comparatively of recent date. Of this we have sufficient evidence in the ancient monuments of Egypt, where, as well as in Persia and India, rough Greyhounds of great power and size still exist.

It seems that records of pedigrees were kept in Afghanistan, at least in the mid-nineteenth century, for A. W. Hughes writes in his *The Country of Balochistan* that 'Shepherd dogs and Greyhounds are greatly prized, and their pedigree is as carefully attended to by the Balochis as is that of valuable dogs in Britain.'

By 1894 Comte Henri de Bylandt's *Les Races de Chiens* appeared and in it are several illustrations of the Afghan Hound. Bylandt, though, was as much confused by the various similar breeds as other writers had been, frequently giving the double heading of 'Afghan Greyhound. Persian Greyhound'.

A report of the breed in Chaman

An account of the breed at Chaman on the north-west frontier of India was published in Hutchinson's *Dog Encyclopaedia* in 1933. It was written by an 'eye witness', using the nom de plume of 'Mali':

> Chaman, you must know, is one of our principal posts on the North-West Frontier. A former Commander-in-Chief decreed that a post should be established at Chaman to be fed by a light railway from Quetta. Two mud forts guard the railway station, one on each side; each fort is manned by one

16

company of Indian infantry, and one squadron of native mounted levies and *by dogs.*

What strikes the newcomer entering either of the forts at any hour of the day is the large, extraordinary-looking creatures sprawling all over the place, fast asleep. In size and shape they somewhat resemble a large Greyhound, but such slight resemblance is dispelled by the tufts with which all are adorned: some having tufted ears, others tufted feet, and others, again, possessing tufted tails.

They are known as Baluchi Hounds, and they get their daily food ration from the commissariat babu; he is the only permanent resident of the fort. They will have no truck with any stranger, white or black.

When 'Retreat' sounds, the pack awakes, yawns, pulls itself together, and solemnly marches out to take up positions close to the newly arrived night guard. *They appear to be under no leadership,* yet as the patrols are told off a couple of dogs attach themselves to each patrol, and they remain with their respective patrols till 'reveille' next morning. Between a deep ditch and wall of the fort is a narrow path. Throughout the night, this path is patrolled by successive couples of dogs. Immediately one couple has completed the circuit of the walls and arrives back at the main gate, another couple starts out.

When it is remembered that these extraordinary hounds have never had any training whatsoever, that their duties are absolutely self-imposed – for no human being has the slightest control over them – the perfection of their organisation and the smoothness with which they carry out their tasks make mere man gasp!

... I have a deep respect for those 'hounds of Chaman' – I always shall have.

The Afghan comes to the UK

It is highly important first of all to mention that the native chiefs were very reluctant to part with their valuable dogs and would-be importers found it difficult to obtain what they considered suitable specimens for breeding and exhibition purposes. The Afghans, Pathans and Afridis were highly jealous of their breed and in many instances they resorted to sterilization.

The first Afghan to be exhibited on these shores was not Mr J. A. Barff's Zardin in 1907, as some early writers claimed. There were others before him, one of which was Shahzada, who was first named 'Gazelle'.

'Gazelle' won joint second prize (with an Elkhound) at Crufts Show in 1895 in the foreign dog class and in December of that year came third, under the name of 'Shahzada', at the Chow-Chow and St Hubert Schipperke Club's show, being beaten, out of interest, by two Dingos! In 1896 he won two seconds and a first and in 1897 he beat another Afghan

Figure 12   Shahzada, originally named 'Gazelle'.

for the very first time. This was 'Dilkoosh' who was entered in the Kennel Club Stud Book as an 'Afghan Barukhzy Hound'. At the Kennel Club Show that same year Shahzada picked up a second prize and in 1898 won a first at the Kennel Club Show at Crystal Palace. Mrs Whitbread presented Shahzada's body to the British Museum in 1901. Mrs Whitbread also presented to the museum the body of another Afghan in 1903 but, strangely, it is not entered in the Museum register and, despite rumours to the contrary, Zardin was never presented to the Natural History Museum.

Towards the close of the last century Major T. Mackenzie, an authority on the breed at that time, and Captain Cary Barnard brought several Afghans into the country and these, one of which was Khulum, attracted a good deal of attention. Mackenzie and Barnard also imported Afghan Bob from Peshawar in 1902. He was frequently exhibited though he was far removed from what we would today consider to be a typical specimen of the breed. Shahzada, now in the British Museum at Tring, was, however, said to be particularly typical. The famous and much used drawing of Shahzada was first produced in Charles Henry Lane's *All about Dogs,* published in 1900. It is interesting to note that, though these two hounds were considered to resemble closely the 'Persian', 'Shami' (Syrian) or 'Tazi' (Arabian) type, they varied in outline and some characteristics, the Afghan being more shaggy in appearance and the distribution of the feathering being quite different. The Barukhzy or Afghan Hound was much feathered under the body as well as on the thighs, shoulders, chest, legs and feet – the latter being considered an essential point. Furthermore, the tail was sparsely feathered and 'carried like a sabre', whereas the tail of the 'Persian' type was curled and conspicuously feathered.

The Hon. Florence Amherst, so closely involved both with the Saluki and the Afghan Hound, mentions the 'Ahk-Tazeet' or 'Kirghiz Greyhound', which was similar to the 'Shami' type but larger, again with feathered legs and tail, and the tail was to have a 'complete little circle at the tip when carried naturally'. These hounds were invariably white or pale cream and 'any markings' were 'considered a blemish'. This mention of a curl at the end of the tail in this strain is extremely interesting for when one studies the majority of the early Afghan (or Barukhzy) Hounds there is no evidence of a ring at the end of the tail. I know that as yet we have not discussed today's breed types, but readers already familiar with the breed will be only too well aware that the ring tail is lacking in many of today's specimens. I venture to suggest that this may be because the breed came, originally, from

Figure 13 The Afghan Hound as drawn by Arthur Wardle and published in Theo Marples' *Show Dogs* early last century. Compare this with Wardle's drawing of the 'Persian Gazelle Hound' on page 171.

an admixture of bloodstock. Incidentally, photographs of the Kirgiz Greyhound, taken around the turn of the twentieth century, show a much closer resemblance, in other respects, to the Saluki than the Afghan.

Another who involved himself with Afghans in the early stages of the breed in this country was Mr W. K. Taunton. He had various breeds that were considered something of a rarity at the time and was possibly the first person ever to exhibit an 'Afghan Sheepdog'. This he did at two shows in 1884 and again in 1888, winning prizes with his Khelat who was sometimes incorrectly referred to as an Afghan Hound, despite the fact that he had a docked tail and more closely resembled an old-fashioned Old English Sheepdog rather than an Afghan. Another Afghan Sheepdog, Kushki, was exhibited at the Kennel Club show in 1885. Mr Taunton also had true-bred Afghan Hounds, one of which, Motee, was exhibited at Bristol in 1886 and won first prize in the Foreign Dog class. She beat her kennel mate, Empress of China, who, believe it or not, was classified as a Chinese Edible Dog! Motee and Mr Taunton's Roostam both ended up in the ownership of Mr T. R. Tuffnell and together they produced a famous fawn hound, Rajah II. Rajah II was considered quite a typical Afghan of his time and

Figure 14 Zardin, on whom the Afghan Hound Breed Standard was based

won equal third in the Foreign Dog class at Crystal Palace in 1889. Interestingly, he seemingly carried a slightly better coat than Shahzada. Mukmul was another winner during 1887, as was Moroo, a fawn bitch, both owned by Major Mackenzie. And so you see, those early writers who claimed that Zardin was the first Afghan to be shown had clearly done insufficient homework!

Zardin had an enormous influence on the breed, for it was on him that the official breed standard was based. Imported by Captain John Barff in 1907, he came to Britain from Seistan. Almost immediately following his period of quarantine he was entered in the Foreign Dog class under Mr R. Temple and won, beating Afghan Bob into second place. Zardin always attracted attention and was said never to have been beaten at a British show. With a dark mask and saddle, a typically ringed tail that was not carried above the level of the back, good top-knot and large feet, he had been exhibited at Quetta before beginning his new show career in Britain. Eventually Zardin changed hands again and became the property of a firm of animal dealers, Messrs Shackleton & Co. of Leadenhall Market. Zardin sired at least two litters, one of which was from a bitch also belonging to Mr Shackleton. Unfortunately, only two puppies survived out of this litter

Figure 15   Miss E. Denyer with some of her Afghan Hounds *(Country Life)*

21

Figure 16   Mrs M. Amps' Afghan Hound, Ch. Sirdar of Ghazni.

and one, Moti, had eventually to be put to sleep owing to a problematic skin condidon. All Mr Shackleton's dogs died under somewhat mysterious circumstances and it is unlikely that any of Zardin's offspring continued his blood-line.

At the end of World War I Major Bell-Murray set up a kennel of Afghans in Scotland. In 1920 he imported three stud dogs, Rajah, Khym and Ooty, and four bitches, Begum, Ranee, Kanee and Pushim. Miss Jean C. Manson, governess to the Bell-Murray family and, incidentally, the first Afghan breeder to take an affix, was another of the principal Afghan Hound breeders of the early 1920s and eventually took over the entire management of the Bell-Murray kennel. Another important breeder was Miss D. Evelyn Denyer, who became Mrs Barton. She later went abroad with her husband and her dogs were acquired by Captain T. S. Waterlow Fox (of Wyke). There then came a stream of imports, including the famous

Champion (Ch) Sirdar of Ghazni obtained from the kennels of ex-King Amanullah in the hills at Paghman, it being thought that the breed was of greater purity in the hills than in the plains. He resembled Zardin in many ways other than size for he was quite a small dog. He had a characteristic coat of a 'rich red' and his action was described as being 'as perfect as one could desire to see in any dog'. Sirdar was imported by Mrs Mary Amps in 1925 and in 1928 he won his first Challenge Certificate (CC), going on to win a total of eight CCs in seven years. He was outstandingly successful as a stud and sired six champions, three of each sex. Two of his champion sons went on to produce champion offspring of their own and another, Omar of Geufron, sired no fewer than three champions out of a litter of five puppies. Major Amps had been attached to the British Legation in Kabul and the Amps' involvement wih the breed began when he sent to his wife a 'honey-fawn' Afghan Hound named Khan who was intended as a guard and companion, Mrs Amps having remained in India. Khan of Ghazni, reputed to have slain three leopards in his native mountains, was also brought over to Britain.

The breed's first champion was actually made up in 1927. This was Ch Buckmall, bred and registered by Major Bell-Murray, owned by Miss Manson. Buckmall was whelped on 21 March 1923 (Ooty X Pushim) and was said to have been a very intelligent dog. At Crufts Show in 1929 the breed saw its very first bitch champion, this being Shadi, again bred by Major Bell-Murray but registered by Miss Manson. She was whelped on 27 July 1924 and was by Baluch out of Oolu; her first two CCs had come in 1927 at the Scottish Kennel Club and the Royal Veterinary College Show.

Controversy

The first breed standard was drawn up in 1925 and was based on Zardin and the description of him which had been published in the *Indian Kennel Gazette* in 1906. In a book of this nature I regret that it is not possible to detail the various changes in the standard made over the years but the controversy which arose between the Bell-Murray and the Amps hounds cannot go without mention for, indeed, it is still a subject of controversy today. In 1926 Mrs Amps claimed adamantly and publicly that she was importing, both into India and England, Afghans of a similar type to Zardin, upon which the original standard was based. In Afghanistan she had never seen an Afghan without what she considered to be the essential characteristic covering on thighs, legs, shoulders and underneath the body, although she agreed that bitches sometimes carried a little less coat than

the dogs. She believed that the Afghans living on the plains near the Indian
frontier, where the weather was usually hot, sometimes crossed a Saluki
with an Afghan so as to develop a less profuse coat. Although the crosses
she described were often seen, she was firmly convinced that those
members of the breed around Kabul and in the hill country were the best
strains, and that these had abundant coats so that they could withstand the
low temperatures of the winters in that region. Mrs Amps was concerned
that the true Afghan should never be confused with the Saluki for, as she
was at pains to point out, the two were totally distinct breeds.

Mrs Amps' comments were published in *Our Dogs* on 30 July 1926 and it
did not take long for Major Bell-Murray to have his response printed. His
letter is interesting and can be found in full in Miss Margaret Niblock's
excellent book on the breed (pp. 55 et seq.), published in 1980. He tells
readers how he lived on the frontiers of India from 1904 until 1920 and
how he was very interested in eastern hounds, owning many different kinds,
mostly what he described as Arabian Greyhounds, which by then were
already known in the west as Salukis. He pointed out that Zardin did not
even come from Afghanistan but from Chagai in the Mekram (Persia). He
himself, fascinated by a large illustration he had of Zardin, had sent trusted
agents to seek out the breed and in 1912 they had brought him what he
considered to be a perfect specimen. This was Begum, 'a pure white with
fine head, stately carriage and perfect feet and with the coat of that
wonderful texture so different from the coat of all other dogs, something of
the type of woolly silk'. Out of the many hounds he was offered in the eight
years from 1912 to 1920, he chose only nine that he considered true to type.
It was these that were the foundation stock of Miss Manson's kennels.
Major Bell-Murray went on to ask that Mrs Amps compare her own
hounds with Zardin and, if she did, she would note that not only were they
smaller but that the head was different and, above all, the coat entirely
different. He found it strange that Mrs Amps, after only a relatively short
stay in the country, had managed to find so many hounds readily available
around Kabul, whilst he had wasted so many years in his search for the true
type. He had visited India in 1925 with a view to obtaining further stock
for Miss Manson but, though he had seen Mrs Amps' hounds, he had come
home without any. It was his 'reasonable conclusion' that intense cold
tended to produce a coat far more abundant than was to be found on
animals in a more temperate climate. His experience was that, although in
this country Afghan Hounds did not produce the same profusion of coat,
the texture remained the same.

The argument went on. Mrs Amps did not agree with Major Bell-Murray
that the loss of coat was due to climate change and said that her own dogs,
with one exception due to illness, carried better coats than they had ever

done. She went on to describe the two dogs she was showing at the time, both having been bred in Afghanistan for the sole purpose of work. These were Khan of Ghazni and Sirdar of Ghazni, of which she considered Khan, who came from the north, 'on the heavy side'. Sirdar she considered to be 'almost a perfect type, but small'. Apart from one exception she claimed she had never seen a dog over 28 inches at the shoulder.

There was uproar. There were Bell-Murray followers who felt that a select panel of judges should be trained by him and there were Ghazni followers who actually formed their own club, this being the Afghan Hound Association, and brought in a new breed standard. John Barff, owner of the late Zardin, joined in the arguments and said that the hounds imported by Mrs Amps were unquestionably the true Afghan Hounds, 'which fact nobody with any knowledge of the breed will deny'. He protested strongly against there being any change to the breed standard which, when all was said and done, had been based on his own import. He asserted, however, that it was 'as difficult to take a good specimen out of Afghanistan as it [was] to bring a mare out of Arabia'. Saluki Hounds, he said, were available in plenty, but not Afghan Hounds. In the event, the standard lasted until 1931, the breed and its followers remaining firmly divided, which did nothing for the breed's popularity in the 1920s and 1930s.

The Afghan used in sport

The Afghan Hound was used in Afghanistan by the sirdars and shikaris for coursing hare, fox and small mountain deer, and sometimes to hunt wolf and jackal. But he is justly famous for his chase of the snow leopard, an elusive member of the cat family, weighing 35–55 kg (77–121 lbs). Indeed his hill-climbing power is essential in coursing and so he must have well-developed quarters, muscular thighs and second thighs and strong hocks. Other essential features, beside the eye, which in any Sight Hound is an all-important feature of its make-up, are a deep brisket and good feet with very hard pads capable of coping with rough terrain. Despite being a Sight Hound the Afghan also uses his nose in the chase and is quite able to track a spoor until the final sprint.

Seemingly it was not an uncommon occurrence for an Afghan Hound to take a snow leopard alone and the early stock which came into this country was directly from stock bred for leopard hunting, some imported specimens reputedly having killed such prey themselves.

The larger dogs were not so good at coursing as the medium-sized ones and so were kept primarily as guards and watchdogs. The *Encyclopaedia of Rural Sports* (1839–40) gives an indication that Afghan Hounds may have been used to fight other dogs, for readers are told that the Afghans 'encourage the combat of rams, dogs and camels'. Other Afghans were trained to herd goats and occasionally the Afghan sheep. The Afghan Sheepdog, mentioned earlier, was the breed most commonly used for herding. In its native country the Afghan was kept for sport in considerable numbers and was aided by trained hawks.

Early in the twentieth century, Mrs Amps wrote a fascinating account that had been passed down to her of Afghan Hounds working in their homeland:

> We used to ride out over the Chardeh Plain in the early mornings with a couple of mounted orderlies to whip-in. To see the whole pack streaming along with the galloping horses in the early morning sunlight with the keen air blowing from the snows of the distant Hindu Kush was a sight and experience never to be forgotten and I fear never to be enjoyed again. England is too small and too domesticated!
>
> In Afghanistan the hounds never show the slightest tendency to chase the innumerable sheep, cattle, camels and donkeys scattered over the countryside. They are pretty thoroughly trained from puppyhood what to hunt and what to leave alone. One of the oldest forms of hunting, which is often portrayed in old Persian and Moghul manuscripts, is still carried on in the remoter parts of Afghanistan. The quarry, a small, very swift deer called Ahu Dashti, is hunted by Afghan hounds with the aid of hawks . . . The young birds and Afghan puppies are kept together, the young hounds being fed on the flesh of deer whenever possible. The food of the young hawks is placed each day between the horns of a stuffed deer; later a string is attached to the head and it is drawn across the floor, the young bird flapping after it. As soon as they are able to fly they are released and called to this lure. As the training progresses they are flown at a young kid, and when they seize it the animal is killed and they are fed on the flesh. When fully-grown the hounds are loosed after a fawn and the hawks flown at it. The training completed, hawks and hounds are taken to the hills.

THREE

THE AFGHAN TODAY

Temperament and adaptability

I believe temperament to be one of the most important factors when selecting a breed of dog as a companion, either for the home or for the show-ring. It is true there are many other factors that must of necessity be given careful consideration, but even if everything else is right temperament is what one has to live with and in some breeds this is more difficult than in others.

I cannot think of a breed in which the temperament is all bad, indeed I doubt if such would ever have been allowed to come into existence in the first instance. However, there are some difficult aspects of temperament in some of the breeds which should not be glossed over if one is to judge whether or not one can cope adequately with the more difficult side of a dog's character. There is no point in looking at any breed of dog with blinkers on, for that can sometimes have the disastrous effect of turning what was designed as a long-term relationship into a short-term one. Rescue societies are not the places where dogs are meant to end up and I often feel that if a little more forethought were given in the initial selection of breeds of dog, and individuals within those breeds, substantially fewer dogs would end up as rescue cases.

When considering temperament it is always helpful to look back at a breed's origin and to consider its home environment and how it had to live and survive in that environment. The Afghan Hound was prized for hunting ability and he did not necessarily play any part in family life in his country of origin. But he does, indeed, like to have his comforts and there is no more lovely sight than that of a well-groomed Afghan settled comfortably on the best sofa exuding out of every pore the words of the breed standard, 'dignified and aloof'. If you try to move him you may be unlucky and see another side of his character, that stubbornness which says, I'm here and that's where I want to be, move me if you dare!'

Many people have said that the Afghan appears to be a bit dumb, but nothing could be farther from the truth. He may appear so sometimes, but that is purely by design so that you think he hasn't understood what you

27

want him to do. He's very probably understood perfectly well but has just decided not to do it. To do the work he was bred for he had to have well-developed mental and physical powers and his owner or prospective purchaser should never be misled by his elegant good looks. Although there are individual exceptions, as a breed he is capable of showing an aggressive side of his nature which, after all, is what he would need to hunt the snow leopard and other quarry. He has a composed mental attitude, although one must never allow oneself to be misled by it. In order to perform his function in life he had to be capable of thinking for himself and making decisions without instructions from others, and so it is that to this day he still makes up his own mind a lot of the time, despite what his owners tell him.

Afghans are generally patient with other animals smaller than themselves and many a time has one of my own given up the comfort of my sofa so that its warm softness might be enjoyed by a visiting cat. With small dogs they seem to have endless patience. One of my Lhasa Apsos was un-doubtedly top dog in his little pack (which included a couple of Afghans) and had a rather nasty habit of nipping at the heels of the 'Affies' if he thought they might do him any sort of injustice. They were perfectly capable of keeping him in his place and sometimes appeared to attack him quite viciously, but this was all simply an act and never did they ever cause him the slightest injury.

It is often said that Afghans are good with children but, as with all breeds, so much depends on the children themselves and, more importantly, on their parents. However tolerant an Afghan might be of a child's attentions the two should always be supervised for an Afghan has a very punishing jaw and, if roused, is perfectly capable of using it. Never lose sight of the fact that the breed standard calls for 'a certain keen fierceness' and the temperament of the breed's ancestors was described in 1908 by the Rev. H. W. Bush thus, 'They are nasty savage beasts, especially in the neighbourhood of their own villages, and bite black and white men indiscriminately . . .'

The effect of an Afghan's punishing jaws can frequently be seen in the backs of estate cars. They can become roused by the passing of another dog, and display the possessive side of their instinct, venting their anger on what-ever inanimate object is nearest. The damage they do is rarely intentional but can be considerable, given the construction of their jaws and teeth, and this is always worth remembering. If Afghans dislike something or pick up their owner's dislike of another person they can show this in a variety of ways, some of which can cause one to smile. For instance, they can express their disdain for someone by using their aloof expression and that uncanny way they have of looking at and through one. However close one is to one's Afghan it is sometimes very difficult to know exactly what is going on in

Figure 17
Afghan, Ch. Copper
'N' Purple Rain at
Altside (Imp)

that mind encased in that oh so splendid skull, behind those all-seeing eyes which give away so little.

The Afghan temperament can also sometimes express itself in a certain degree of nervousness which may take the form of quick snaps. Undoubtedly this aspect of the temperament was sometimes seen in Afghanistan and so we cannot expect that it will not rear its ugly head from time to time, any trait being difficult to breed out entirely. Naturally, it is unwise to breed from any Afghan showing such a trait. Owing to the fact that the trait seems likely to be the result of a single dominant gene, it re-appears in a high proportion of offspring from affected parents. Nervousness can, with patience, in most cases be overcome, though it takes long weeks of understanding encouragement and training by devoted, sensible owners.

Afghans are, however, loyal to their owners and are happy to protect them to the very best of their ability. Different Afghans display their loyalty in different ways and it has to be said that not all of them shower their owners with licks and kisses. Nonetheless, it is always reassuring to know that one's Afghan seems to have an innate desire to be at one with his owner and appears to understand our feelings better than we understand his. His quiet reassurance that he is there and glad to be with you is very rewarding and something never to be taken for granted.

The Afghan, like most of the Sight Hounds, is a slow maturing breed;

puppyhood is long and can be quite boisterous. They are amazingly fleet of foot and the unique construction of their hindquarters makes it easy for them to race around the sitting room at full speed without doing damage to a single item of furniture, nor even the most delicate ornament. Puppies learn quickly and it does not do to carry out any action in front of them you do not require them to copy or investigate further. I well recall seeing my mother planting something in my garden with one of my young Afghans by her side. Until that day he had never dug, but from then on he did so for the rest of his life!

Another thing worth bearing in mind is that the Afghan is strangely intolerant of pain. He can make even a wet foot sometimes appear to be a dire emergency and he is not averse to almost screaming, seemingly with pain, to try to attract attention. On the other hand, one must always remember that genuine emergencies can sometimes occur and it is good to know that the Afghan usually accepts treatment without fuss and seems aware of the fact that he is receiving help.

The Afghan's speed and gymnastic ability

If already an owner, you will probably be well aware of your Afghan's ability to move at high speed. Many Afghan owners train their dogs well enough for them to be let off the lead, in public parks, for example, but other owners have tried and failed. The Afghan can take off at great speed in some random direction, and before you know it he is out of sight. Maybe he does know exactly where he left you but sometimes I rather think he doesn't. A friend of mine once lost her Afghan for four hours in the snow in a large park; having been hunted high and low he was found in exactly the same spot from which he had gone missing. In this instance he found his way back, but just think what might have befallen him had he not. If you do decide to try to train your Afghan off the lead, that training must begin early and be done in an enclosed area, with no exits out of which any fleet-footed dog can escape unnoticed. But if you do lose your Afghan (hopefully only temporarily!), don't forget to look in the nearest and least obvious places before you search the neighbourhood for miles around. Occasionally they are to be found just a few feet away, quietly investigating the neighbour's cabbage patch, for example, when, because of their fleetness of foot, you are sure they must already be miles away.

Afghans are quite capable of squeezing through the tiniest gap in the fencing, so make sure your garden is entirely escape-proof and that any even slightly loose fencing is well secured. The shape of their foreface is ideal for widening gaps unnoticed by human eye! Some Afghans are diggers, others jumpers, and unless you are very unfortunate you will have either one or the other, but not both. Never should you underestimate your Afghan's powers of cunning or his gymnastic capabilities, so secure boundary fencing is an absolute must.

Grooming

It is all too easy when an Afghan is a puppy to think that the coat doesn't require much attention, but he needs to be accustomed to the process as early as possible. The short coat on a puppy makes it possible for you to groom him without him lying over on his side. With his long legs, all parts of his body are accessible, albeit some spots being less easy to reach than others. However, as his coat length increases you will soon find that grooming sessions are much easier if your dog has already learned to co-operate, so try to teach him from the word go. Afghans are undoubtedly strong-willed dogs and if you don't begin serious grooming until your dog is reaching maturity you will be asking for trouble; an uncooperative Afghan's coat is not an easy one to manage!

Even whilst he is a very young puppy get him used to the feel of a soft brush on his coat to help him to become used to the feel of grooming equipment. When he is at ease with the brush you can train him to lie over on his side, either on a grooming table or, if you prefer, on the floor, though

Figure 18
An Afghan puppy looks quite different from an adult

the former will be much easier on your back. The coat should never be groomed out when completely dry or you will find that ends can be broken and too much coat taken out. It is possible to use water or, alternatively, one of the many excellent grooming aids on the market, although if exhibiting your dog you must be sure to select one that does not contravene Kennel Club regulations. There are many differing techniques and aids but you cannot go far wrong with a good quality pure bristle brush and a wide-toothed comb, possibly using one of the stiffer wire brushes with protected ends for finishing off. Don't try to use the latter as you would your bristle brush or, again, you will take out too much coat. If there are knots in the coat, and hard as you might try to avoid them knots will always appear, often simply overnight, first tease out the tangle with your fingers, always working from the skin outward. When the knot has been separated you should be able to brush it out gently without too much loss of coat.

When you bath your Afghan, stand him in the bath on a non-slip surface. Use a good shower attachment and be sure to rinse out every bit of shampoo before a conditioning rinse is applied. The water should always be comfortably warm. If you plan to show your Afghan, which means bathing him probably more frequently than a pet, you will need to invest in a canine hair-drier. There are various styles, none of which is cheap, but such a machine will help you dry your dog's coat more quickly and more thoroughly than a normal human-type drier, and should give you many years of reliable service. You will also be able to get a much better finish on the coat, largely because both of your hands will be free for grooming. If your dog's coat has a slight tendency to wave this will be reduced somewhat by drying at a fairly rapid speed, provided that the coat is being groomed whilst drying is in progress. There were times when it was not an uncommon occurrence for people to allow their dogs' coats to dry naturally in hot weather but unless you perfected this technique many years ago I believe it would be hard to compete successfully with the spectacular show-coats found in the ring today. Once the dog is out of the bath, and before you use the hair-drier, towel dry the coat but always pat, never rub, for rubbing creates knots.

Never allow your Afghan to become badly matted but should this happen use scissors as an aid to removing those knots which cannot be teased out with the fingers. You will find that if you cut outward from the skin (i.e. in the direction of the growth of the coat) you will divide the knot in two, making it more manageable. It goes without saying that such use of the scissors is not acceptable on a show Afghan on which the coat must be allowed to develop naturally, as stated in the Kennel Club's Breed Standard. This brings me to the subject of the saddle which, to the uninitiated, is the short hair running along the back of an Afghan and is, sadly, found less and less frequently, despite its inclusion in the breed standard. If your Afghan is going to develop a saddle, which happens of its own accord in due course of time, you will find that the long coat in the region of the saddle dies off, looks somewhat fluffy and comes out quite easily when rubbed between thumb and forefinger. If it doesn't come out easily it either isn't yet ready or it may be that your dog will never develop a saddle. Such a change in coat pattern usually occurs as the dog reaches maturity and changes from his puppy to his adult coat.

Protecting your Afghan's show-coat

Something used by many Afghan owners, be their dogs show ones or pets, is a snood. This is a loosely elasticated piece of material which can be slipped over the foreface so that it rests comfortably around the head, holding the top-knot and ears inside and thus preventing soiling of the coat, especially when eating and drinking. Snoods can be easily hand-made, usually using what I believe is called 'sewing elastic' (regrettably I am no needle-woman), but you will often find that they can be inexpensively purchased on breed club and specialist stands at shows. Another useful part of an Afghan's wardrobe is a mackintosh and, if you haven't seen one before, I do mean one designed especially for dogs. These can be obtained from trade stands at most championship dog shows, as well as a few other outlets, and are an invaluable aid to keeping your dog dry in wet weather. Do be sure that you choose the right size (remembering that the size that is right for one Afghan may not be correct for another), and, especially if you have a male, be sure the fit is correct underneath the body. It has been known for Afghan males to 'misfire', resulting in an unpleasantly wet tummy or inside leg. Avoid allowing your dog out in his mackintosh near sharp objects. One of mine tore his to shreds on some rose bushes! It is also often possible to buy 'boots' and 'hat' (a colour to match the rest of the outfit looks the least incongruous), but an outing in these accessories needs to be carefully supervised if one wishes to avoid losing the odd 'boot' or two along the way.

Kennel Club Breed Standard © The Kennel Club

GENERAL APPEARANCE: Gives the impression of strength and dignity, combining speed and power. Head held proudly.

CHARACTERISTICS: Eastern or Oriental expression is typical of the breed. The Afghan looks at and through one.

TEMPERAMENT: Dignified and aloof, with a certain keen fierceness.

HEAD AND SKULL: Skull long, not too narrow with prominent occiput. Foreface long with punishing jaws and slight stop. Skull well balanced and mounted by a long 'top-knot'. Nose preferably black, liver permissible in light-coloured dogs.

EYES: Dark for preference, but golden colour not debarred. Nearly triangular, slanting slightly upwards from inner corner to outer.

EARS: Set low and well back, carried close to head. Covered with long silky hair.

MOUTH: Jaws strong, with a perfect, regular and complete scissor bite, i.e. the upper teeth closely overlapping the lower teeth and set square to the jaws. Level bite tolerated.

NECK: Long, strong and with proud carriage of head.

FOREQUARTERS: Shoulders long and sloping, set well back, well muscled and strong without being loaded. Forelegs straight and well boned, elbows close to ribcage, turning neither in nor out.

BODY: Back level, moderate length, well muscled, back falling slightly away to stern. Loin straight, broad and rather short. Hipbones rather prominent and wide apart. A fair spring of ribs and good depth of chest.

HINDQUARTERS: Powerful, well bent and well-turned stifles. Great length between hip and hock, with comparatively short distance between hock and foot. Dew claws may be removed.

FEET: Forefeet strong and very large both in length and breadth, and covered with long, thick hair, toes arched. Pasterns long and springy, pads well down on ground. Hindfeet long, but not quite as broad as forefeet; covered with long thick hair.

TAIL: Not too short. Set on low with a ring at end. Raised when in action. Sparsely feathered.

GAIT/MOVEMENT: Smooth and springy with a style of high order.

COAT: Long and very fine texture on ribs, fore and hindquarters and flanks. In mature dogs from shoulder backwards and along the saddle, hair short and close. Hair long from forehead backwards, with a distinct silky 'top-knot'. On foreface hair short. Ears and legs well coated. Pasterns can be bare. Coat must develop naturally.

COLOUR: All colours acceptable.

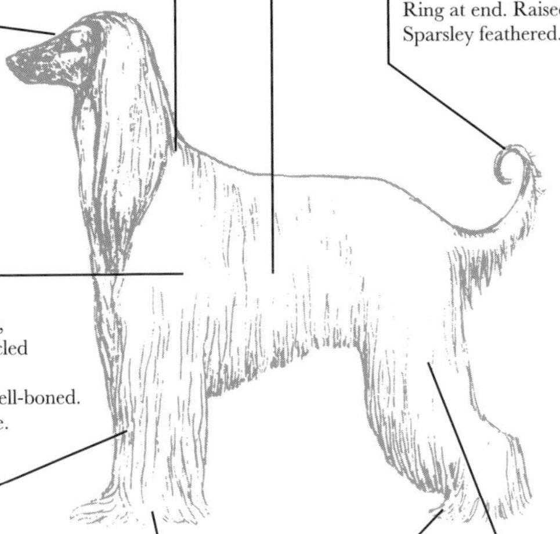

HEAD AND SKULL:
Long, not too narrow.
Prominent occiput.
Punishing jaws, slight stop.
Well-balanced.
Long 'top-knot'.
Nose preferably black;
liver permissible in light dogs.

Eyes: Preferably dark; golden
not debarred. Nearly triangular,
slanting slightly upwards to outer
corner.

Ears: Set low and well back.
Close to head. Long, silky hair.

Mouth: Strong jaws. Scissor bite.
Level bite tolerated.

NECK: Long, strong. Proud head
carriage.

BODY: Back level, moderate length,
well-muscled. Falling away slightly to stern.
Loin straight, broad, rather short.
Hipbones rather prominent and wide apart.
Fair spring of rib. Good depth of chest.

TAIL: Not too short. Set on low.
Ring at end. Raised in action.
Sparsley feathered.

FOREQUARTERS:
Shoulders long, sloping,
well set back, well-muscled
and strong, not loaded.
Forelegs straight and well-boned.
Elbows close to rib cage.

COAT: Long, fine texture on ribs,
quarters and flanks. Saddle hair short
and close when mature.
Hair long from forehead back.
Silky 'top-knot'. Short on foreface.
Well-coated ears and legs.
Pasterns can be bare.
Coat must develop naturally.

HINDQUARTERS:
Powerful, well-bent and
well-turned stifles.
Great length from
hip to hock; short
distance hock to foot.

FEET: Forefeet strong, large,
covered with long thick hair.
Toes arched.
Pasterns long and springy,
pads well down
Hindfeet long, not quite so
broad as forefeet, covered
with long thick hair.

Figure 19 The Afghan Hound breed standard in brief.

SIZE: Ideal height: dogs 68–74 cm (27–29 inches); bitches 63–69 cm (25–27 inches).

FAULTS: Any departure from the foregoing points should be considered a fault and the seriousness with which the fault should be regarded should be in exact proportion to its degree and its effect upon the health and welfare of the dog.

NOTE: Male animals should have two apparently normal testicles fully descended into the scrotum.

Judging the breed

Be careful that not too many sins are covered by a glamorous coat! The Afghan should have a smooth, springing stride which would have allowed it to hunt efficiently in its original environment. An upright shoulder or too short an upper arm will not allow sufficient freedom of movement, nor, indeed, will too narrow a chest. The rib cage must allow sufficient capacity for heart and lungs, something I feel is rapidly being lost in this lovely breed. The typical expression looks 'at and through' one and this can only be found if the eye shape is correct, triangular and slightly slanting. An incorrectly shaped eye usually means that the skull shape is also incorrect. A level top-line is required but hipbones should be prominent. Despite the fact they are seen less frequently in the ring today, the breed standard does require a saddle and thus it should never be penalized, quite the reverse. Please also bear in mind that pasterns can, indeed, be bare. A typical Afghan Hound is a strong and dignified animal; please, judges, allow him to stay that way.

The sport of Afghan racing

Popular with both the pet Afghan owner and, perhaps surprisingly, also some show-dog owners, is Afghan racing. The sight of keyed-up Afghans waiting their turn on the track is a joy to behold. Some hounds take to the race track more readily than others but most enjoy it, and those who have it in their blood to be the successful ones clearly adore their day out.

Even in 1911 the National Coursing Club permitted an Afghan Hound, Baz, to be registered in the Greyhound Stud Book. Baz was mated to a Greyhound by the name of Explosion and by all accounts the puppies, though unregistered, were fast and staying racers. There is also a report of Afghans racing in 1929.

A number of Greyhound tracks are opened up for the use of Afghans at weekends and though betting is not allowed the atmosphere around the track is fired with the enthusiasm of both dogs and owners. Thankfully it is still very much a 'fun' sport, the original fears, primarily by exhibitors, that breeders would tend to breed for speed rather than characteristics has been quickly allayed.

A star system was developed according to speed and, for the two lowest grades, the dogs are slipped rather than trapped so that their owners may have full control over them at the beginning of the race. An electric hare is used. It is surprising how quickly a novice racing Afghan comes to terms with being incarcerated in a Greyhound trap for a few seconds before the race begins. There are, though, some very funny sights to be seen on the track at weekends, such as the occasional Afghan who decides that the shortest route is across the very centre of the track or the one who is winning by a length and stops short of the finishing line to see where his chums have got to, only to be overtaken, much to the disappointment of his owner. All Afghans are muzzled when they run so that they do no harm to one another if they become over-excited. Not once in the years my own dogs participated in the sport can I recall a serious accident.

The ageing Afghan Hound

By the age of about ten an Afghan may start to suffer the geriatric complaints of most other older dogs (these are discussed in a later chapter dealing with the breeds generally). Dimmed eyesight seems to occur quite frequently in the older Afghan as does a loss of voice. With age, the bark often becomes rather gruff and howling soon becomes almost inaudible, whilst the dog may also have a retching cough. This is caused by deterioration of the mechanism of the larynx and veterinary attention should be sought from the onset of any symptoms. Treatment, however, is often to no avail, but in many cases the dog suffers no ill effects and remains otherwise in general good health. Any similar symptoms in a younger dog will most probably be for completely different reasons and are likely to need urgent veterinary treatment.

Kennel Club registrations for 1908–1934 and at five-yearly intervals from 1950–2000

1908	2	1917	–	1926	52
1909	–	1918	–	1927	59
1910	2	1919	–	1928	64
1911	1	1920	–	1929	41
1912	1	1921	11	1930	52
1913	–	1922	2	1931	55
1914	1	1923	7	1932	43
1915	–	1924	21	1933	48
1916	–	1925	65	1934	83
1950	278	1970	2,853	1990	429
1955	280	1975	3,867	1995	303
1960	273	1980	1,906	2000	310
1965	576	1985	643		

Breed clubs

The first of the twelve breed clubs was the Afghan Hound Club of which Miss Denyer became Secretary when the Club was formed in 1925. The President was Captain Waterlow Fox and Miss Clara Bowring was Treasurer. The Bell-Murrays, Miss Manson and Will Hally were also instrumental in founding the Club and together they set up a breed standard. Championship status was granted to the breed by the Kennel Club in November 1925 and CCs were first awarded at Crufts Show in 1926. Mr A. Croxton Smith had the honour of judging this event and the two Afghans which had the equal honour of being awarded these first CCs were Taj Mahip of Kaf (dog) owned by Mrs V. Barton and Ranee (bitch) owned by Miss Manson.

There are presently twelve breed clubs for the Afghan Hound, these being as follows:

> Afghan Hound Association
> Afghan Hound Club of Scotland
> Afghan Hound Club of Wales
> Afghan Hound Society of Northern Ireland
> Birmingham Afghan Hound Club
> East of England Afghan Hound Club
> Midland Afghan Hound Club

North Eastern Afghan Hound Society
Northern Afghan Hound Society
Southern Afghan Hound Club
Western Afghan Hound Club
Yorkshire Afghan Hound Society

Names, addresses and telephone numbers of the Honorary Secretaries of these clubs can be obtained from the Kennel Club.

FOUR

THE BORZOI

There is not a more elegant and graceful dog than the Borzoi
or Russian Wolfhound. Combining symmetry with strength,
the wearer of a lovely silky coat, he is essentially a spectacular
animal, attracting attention and admiration
wherever he is seen.

ROBERT LEIGHTON (1922)

The breed in Russia

A book dedicated to Czar Alexis and entitled *Rules for Borzoi Hunting* was published in Russia in 1650. This gave what was considered to be an excellent description of the breed, although it made no mention of colour or marking, little importance being attached to these aspects in the seventeenth century. Because it was a working dog interest was focused on the construction of the dog, the strength, speed and agility required for it to perform its task. Crosses were made and were seemingly accepted, provided that, in the opinion of the owner, the introduction of new blood would help the dog to work more efficiently. It seems that in these early days the word 'Borzoi' was actually synonymous with 'Sight Hound' and therefore the treatise incorporated several different types of coursing hound which fell within the physical description given.

The word 'Borzoi' actually means light, swift and agile and in Russia was therefore used somewhat loosely, in much the same way as, in Britain, we used the word Greyhound to encompass many slightly differing breeds. Levrier would be the French equivalent and Windhund the German. The Russians themselves referred to the Asiatic Borzoi, Polish Borzoi and Crimean or Tartar Borzoi, though this seemed to resemble a Saluki more closely than the Borzoi we know today. There is no doubt that behind the Russian Borzois of today there was the Caucasian Borzoi, which was somewhat barrel chested, the Courland Borzoi, which had a curly coat, and the Crimean dogs, which were altogether bigger in bone. The breed, too, can hardly fail to carry some Irish Wolfhound blood for, writing in 1813, Dr Clarke, in his *Travels in Russia,* says, 'We saw several dogs of a gigantic breed,

40

resembling the Irish wolf-dog, especially towards Karakuban.' Orme, in 1814, also noticed a great similarity between the 'Irish greyhound' and the 'Russian fan-tailed greyhound'.

It may have been fortunate for the breed that, owing to distances and difficulties of travel, many breeders were compelled to inbreed, thus fixing a type; indeed the breed might otherwise have died out. Thanks to the close inbreeding, the crosses made later did no harm. Because of the breed's importance there was undoubtedly much forethought and consideration prior to making the later crosses. In the main dogs of Greyhound type were used and there was, overall, less of the indiscriminate breeding which was happening in the nineteenth century in Western Europe.

The Russians believed that the Borzoi was first known to the Arabs, thence being adopted by the Mongols and finally reaching Russia after the Tartar invasion.

The year 1724 was a highly important year in the breed's history, for it was then that a dog show was held in Moscow and Borzois were exhibited. This led to a change of thinking and crosses were no longer considered desirable. Breeders now needed to breed to type so that their dogs would have success at shows. Crosses were looked upon with disfavour and, at last, colour and markings were taken into consideration. The general feeling was that clear patches of colour with a distinct outline indicated Greyhound blood; other colours were said to come from 'breed impurity', such as markings of black and yellow or black and tan on the same dog. All true-bred Russian Borzois were white with spots or markings, small in area, giving a misty appearance, and they were definitely not to have distinct edges to them. Pure white dogs were most highly prized and exceedingly difficult to obtain for it was believed that their owners must have been persons of high rank.

As with other foreign breeds, early history is difficult to obtain but Buffon's *Natural History* of 1798 contains two illustrations of what are clearly Borzois and there was mention of a breed like this in a book dated 1812, the author of which had been to Russia and described the Russian people, including their huntsmen in gaily coloured costumes and large boots. These men, he said, took with them the 'Fan-tailed Greyhound', a breed of Greyhound of exceptional beauty, when they went wolf-catching. He told his readers that the court spent much on keeping and training these dogs, constantly attempting to improve them for the arduous and dangerous work in which they were employed.

It is clear that originally the Borzoi was owned only by noblemen in Russia but the social status of the Borzoi was altered with the abolition of serfdom in 1861. The liberation of the serfs caused the majority of large estates, on which Borzois had been used for hunting wolves and other

Figure 20   The Russian Greyhound as depicted in J. G. Wood's *Illustrated Natural History*, 1861. Compare this with the Scotch Greyhound on page 81 and Persian Greyhound on page 172.

game, to close. As a result the breed degenerated somewhat for a temporary period but, thankfully, in 1873 the Society for the Development of Hunting Dogs and Proper Conduct for Hunting was founded in Moscow. The Society not only aimed to improve conformation and hunting abilities but it also arranged dog shows.

A supporter of the Society was Archduke Nicolai Nikolajawitsch who, in 1887, founded the Perchino kennel which was to become world-famous amongst Borzoi enthusiasts. His kennel was founded on what he considered to be the best Sight Hound blood then available. The Archduke was immensely fond of hunting and his kennel manager kept an informative and detailed description of the kennel, including its routine and hunting programmes.

The kennel started with sixty Borzois of varying ages. The dogs were accommodated in stone houses, each containing boxes for twelve hounds.

Each house had three paddocks and all buildings which housed bitches or puppies were heated. Throughout the year there was no heating in the kennel areas of the males. As far as possible the dogs were grouped together in colours and it was the Archduke's aim to breed about fifty puppies each year. In addition to the kennels described above a further pack of about thirty hounds of high quality was kept to be shown to visitors.

The reduction in breeding of Borzois, especially during the years between 1861 and 1873, gave rise to fears that pure blood-lines might be lost, and so it was that the Russian Imperial Society for the Encouragement of Sport selected from seven of the remaining hunts at that time what it considered to be excellent specimens for breeding purposes. In addition a more detailed standard was drawn up and undoubtedly, from that date, there was more uniformity in the Borzois which came to Britain from Russia.

On the panel of this Society was Artem Boldareff, who owned the Woronova Hunt and whose wife had handled a single Borzoi at a hunt since the age of nine. When she visited England many years ago she told the distressing story of how, so that her hounds might avoid the hands of the Revolutionaries, she watched from a window as, each with a kennelman, they were led out trustingly and gaily to the woods to be shot.

The Borzoi used in sport

When on a wolf hunt the Archduke Nicolai Nikolajawitsch took about thirty-five 'couples', each couple consisting not of two but of three hounds, namely two dogs and a bitch. The couples were grouped together in colours. The field was a large patch of forest running parallel to open fields and in the region of forty people on horseback would go ahead of the hunters to surround the territory to be hunted. Nets were laid when necessary to prevent quarry from escaping. Initially a pack of Foxhounds was sent in to flush out the quarry, the Borzois being restrained on long leads by riders galloping after the wolves. The hounds were then slipped and pursued the quarry until they were alongside and then bumped its flanks, with a third dog harassing from behind. When the wolf eventually lost its balance the dogs caught it by the ears or throat and held on until the hunters arrived to bind up its legs, forcing a wooden wedge between its teeth.

Each wolf hunt lasted around an hour and any young, healthy wolves caught were again released into the forest. On other occasions the Borzois might be released after the wolves in packs of forty or fifty; this method is shown in the Russian film version of Tolstoy's *War and Peace*.

The hunting season fell into summer coursing of hare and fox between

June and early August and summer training for Borzois in August. This involved fifteen miles of walking and trotting with horses, followed in early September by training on captive wolves. The wolf coursing season followed in September and October. Occasionally sledges were used in the hunt from October, the wolves being fed to keep them in the hunting areas.

The figure given for wolf kills on the Perchino reserve between 1887 and 1913 was 681. This, at first glance, looks high but averages twenty-six wolves per year. During the same period 743 foxes, 4,630 brown hares and 4,026 white hares were killed and the highest proportion of kills overall were made by Borzois.

The Perchino kennels were clearly well run and the Archduke was known to buy not only from other breeders in Russia but also to import stock from England and France so as to improve his own. That which was imported always went back to dogs of Russian origin. His aim was to breed both for beauty and speed and he kept up a keen interest in the dog shows held in Moscow so that he could compare dogs and ultimately improve his own breeding programme. At its peak the Perchino kennel comprised 130 Borzois and fifteen Greyhounds and a staff of about eighty people was employed.

As the years progressed it became a national custom of the people of Russia to keep a Borzoi and at the Czar's kennel at one time fourteen men were employed there to train the dogs for wolf coursing. Other kennels kept hundreds of Borzois under the supervision of highly trained staff in whose charge they were both by day and by night. The kennelling was extensive and in lavish style. Two hundred coursing hounds and over 450 Greyhounds were said to have been kept by Czar Peter II, and Prince Somzonov of Smolensk, who called himself Russia's Prime Huntsman, had no fewer than 1,000 hounds.

The Borzoi was primarily used as a coursing hound rather than as a hunting breed and its principal quarry was the wolf, though he was also used to course smaller game such as foxes and hares. There is mention of a Russian hunting dog in the mid-thirteenth century although it refers to a dog which hunted hares rather than wolves. By the late nineteenth century eleven different types of hunting hounds were listed in a Russian encyclopaedia, all of which bore some resemblance to the modern Borzoi, despite certain differences in coat and conformation.

When training young dogs, live young wolves were taken to the kennels, having been retained in enclosures for use in training. The dogs were taught to race up to a wolf and to catch hold of it close to the ears in such a way that the wolf would fall over. The dogs were then taught to pin the wolf to the ground until the huntsmen approached to tie it securely.

When wolves were reported to be present in an area the most usual way of dealing with them was for hunters to go out on horseback, each with a leash of three Borzois held in the left hand. The three were to be as well matched as possible in size, speed and colour. Equality in speed was especially important, for if one dog arrived at the prey in advance of the others he would be unable to deal with the wolf alone. The huntsmen were stationed by the chief huntsman at separate points, located roughly every 100 to 200 yards around the wood, according to the ground and the proximity of the next cover. A pack of hounds described as 'commoner and less aristocratic', was sent in to draw the quarry and when the wolves broke cover the dogs leashed by the nearest huntsman were slipped, and chased and seized their prey by the neck. They held the wolf until the hunter arrived on horseback, dismounted and used his knife to kill the quarry.

There were, however, various slightly differing methods of hunting the wolf and in 1904 Herbert Compton tells us that the Borzois were generally slipped in couples and that if one was a noted 'flier' 'a single hound may be allowed to show itself off'. I believe in the more commonly held theory that the dogs would have been equally matched because one dog would find it difficult to cope alone. Without exception I have found that in all accounts the dogs are said to have held on securely until the huntsmen arrived. The Borzoi was quite capable of giving the wolf the *coup de grâce* if the huntsmen were delayed. Most hounds rarely seemed even to get scratched in their encounters. The wolf was often taken alive to be utilized in training young hounds for the 'sport'; in these cases it was conveyed in a cage on wheels.

In 1931, Edward Ash gave extracts from an article by Mr F. C. Low who had visited the south of Russia as the guest of Mr Kalmoutsky, a well-known sportsman who owned twenty square miles of land and large kennels. Ash tells us that in the kennels visited by Low 300 benches were arranged on two sides and that there was a room at each end for a 'man'. This was said to be the finest pack of Wolfhounds in the world, numbering twenty-two couples. No expense had been spared, as much as £300 having been paid for one dog alone and the total value of the kennel was reputed to be around £5,000. Mr Low described how the hound had never to lose its hold on the wolf for in such a case the wolf would turn and bite through the dog's leg. It took three hounds to hold the best wolf powerless at which time the men would dismount from their horses and muzzle the wolf, the wolf having been bowled over by the hounds. The dogs held on to him 'like grim death' so that a man could get astride the wolf and 'gather him up by the ears'.

The breed was considered a savage one and had the reputation of being a terrible fighter in the kennel. Now, despite the fact that wolf coursing on such a grand scale no longer takes place, the Borzoi still contributes in his own way to the economy of Russia. He is capable of catching foxes without mauling them, thereby not spoiling their fur as would happen if a gun was used. Catching foxes by using Borzois is apparently easier than trapping. Borzois continue also to be used for hare coursing.

Coat type and colour

There were two principal coat types and these, to a large extent, went hand in hand with a certain construction. The shorter-haired Borzoi was generally thought to be the most ancient variety and was frequently of a pale colour, either lemon and white or brindle and white. That generally said to be the more dominant was usually dark in colour, finer and more rangy and with more stamina than the larger variety. The belief was that the darker of the two had been crossed with the Crimean Hound which was thought to carry Saluki blood and was usually black with yellow eyes. Such dogs, of Borzoi type, can be seen chasing boars and stags on hunting frescoes in the Sophia Cathedral in Kiev dating back to the eleventh century.

At one time black coats were disliked by the Russian nobility because they stood out against the snow and disclosed their presence to the quarry. For this reason, one grand duke actually made a ruling that dark-coloured

Figure 21   The Duchess of Newcastle's Borzoi, Ch. Ivan Turgeneff

dogs be disqualified from hunting, though some said it was because not only did he have a personal preference for lighter-coloured dogs but the darker hounds owned by a rival were superior hunters to his own. Whatever the real reason, it is undoubtedly true that a pale-coloured dog would be more suitable for use in hunting in the snow. On the other hand, poachers certainly had a preference for dark-coloured dogs because they could not be seen at night.

In 1904 Herbert Compton told his readers in *The Twentieth Century Dog (Sporting)*, 'Contrary to popular belief, it is the smooth coated borzoi which is most common in England.' He had been told by the Duchess of Newcastle that the rough Borzoi (Goustopsovy) was rarer than the smooth (Psovy), even in Russia, and that both types of coat could be produced in the same litter. The import, Kaissack, carried the 'real' rough coat, which was almost unknown in England. Actually, his coat was never again as good as when he first arrived in England. Another import, Korotai, also had a heavy coat, but his was coarser and therefore less good in 'mixture'. Certainly, of the early dogs these two carried the heaviest coats and those Borzois bred in England with heavy coats were sired by one of them or by their descendants. Another that arrived in England with a heavy coat was Sverkay, although, like Kaissack's, it did not remain in such splendour whilst living here.

The breed in Britain

Queen Victoria was made a present of 'dogs of astonishing size', known as 'Greyhounds of Siberia'. Indeed, the breed went under the guise of various different names including Siberian, Corcassian, Orloff, Circassian Orloff and Russian Wolfhounds.

Little interest was initially taken in the breed in England and it was rarely used in sport for it had little chance of taking over from the Greyhound for general coursing purposes. However, occasionally specimens of the breed were presented to royalty and prominent persons in Britain from the Russian Royal House. The first record of a Borzoi being exhibited in Great Britain was that of Sultan, classified as a Russian Wolf Hound and owned by the Duchess of Manchester. In May 1863 he was exhibit number 103, entered in the Foreign Hounds class, at the first Great International Show of Sporting and Other Dogs at the Agricultural Hall, Islington. Sultan was priced at £1,000 and had been bred by Prince Charles of Prussia. The Borzoi became much loved by the aristocracy of Britain and the Duchess of Manchester exhibited a Borzoi named Katae, bred by the Czar, at the fourth Birmingham Show in 1863 and held, incidentally, at The Old

Wharf, Broad Street. Described as a 'Fan-tailed Greyhound', apparently her 'great beauty and gracefulness caused many to admire her' but I gather she did not win, for it was reported that all the winners in the Large Foreign class were St Bernards.

The Czar sent to King Edward VII, then Prince of Wales, two Borzois, Molodetz and Owdalzk, and others, two of which, named Alex and Ajax, were also sent to the Princess of Wales, later, of course, to become Queen Alexandra. The Queen became exceedingly attached to her Borzois and exhibited them with much success winning hundreds of prizes and several champion certificates; Ajax became a Champion. From the Czar's kennels she later had a bitch named Gatchina who was dam of several winners. The Queen's interest was instrumental in the start of the breed's popularity in this country.

At the Grand National Exhibition of Sporting and Other Dogs held at Crystal Palace in 1871 several exhibits bred out of Dorgoi and Labedka, presented to Lady Emily Peel by the Emperor of Russia, were shown. Soon afterwards good specimens were imported by the Rev. J. C. Macdona, and

Figure 22 'Sokol' (by Ash), exhibited at Crufts, was one of the Grand Duke Nicholas's team and was sold after the show.

Figure 23 Ch Ouslad (by Ash), imported from Russia by the Duchess of Newcastle in 1891.

Lady Emily Peel's Sandringham and Czar 'excited general admiration'. The breed at this time was known primarily as the Siberian Wolfhound and other early breeders of repute were Lady Charles Innes Kerr, Colonel Wellesley and Mrs Alfred Morrison. It was not long before the breed also became fashionable in the USA and some 'excellent examples' were apparently shown at Madison Square Gardens.

The year 1888 saw the crowning of the first British Borzoi champion, Killrut, owned by Colonel Wellesley, also the owner of Daman who was said to have had one of the best heads seen in the breed. Shortly after this, the Duchess of Newcastle became interested in the breed and in 1891 purchased an entire kennel of Borzois which had recently been imported from Russia. One of these was Ouslad, a white dog who went on to become a champion and an important sire. Other imports were Perchino and his brother Argos, who was black and tan and had won the silver medal in Moscow in 1892. Argos became the breed's first international champion for he gained his title both in England and in America. The Duchess of Newcastle's mother also had a bitch, which had been given to her by a Spanish noble, and the Duchess also bought Ivan II, a winner at the Paris

Show of 1889. Interest in the breed had now undoubtedly been stirred and in 1892 the Czar and the Grand Duke Nicholas sent a team of Borzois to Cruft's. Numerous people reportedly went to the show just to see them and were said to have gone 'mad over the breed'. At the close of the show the entire team of dogs was put up for auction and one, by the name of Oudar, made the highest price of the day at £200. Oudar's height was recorded as 30½ inches and his weight as 105 lbs. He was bought by the Duchess of Newcastle whose 'of Notts' Borzois at one time reached over a hundred. Sadly an outbreak of distemper caused the loss of over fifty of her hounds.

The first Borzoi specialist show was held in Southport in 1897. The Duchess of Newcastle was to judge, but, disappointingly, 'only 200 visitors passed through the turnstile'; the glamour had begun to wear off and the public were not sufficiently interested in attending a show where they could see only one breed of dog. (The Duchess continued to judge the breed until her last appointment in 1948 at Brighton Championship Show.)

There was much confusion over the death of the breed's first champion,

Figure 24
The Duchess of Newcastle with Podar and Vodky of Notts (c. 1933)
(Sport General)

Killrut. In 1899 he was reported dead but 'some long time after' a litter of puppies was registered and his name given as the sire. There was uncertainty as to whether the death of the dog had been falsely reported or whether the name of the sire on the registration document was made by 'some inexperienced person'. Unlike today, artificial insemination was not an option.

The Borzoi apparently became quickly anglicised, for it was earlier felt that it might not be able to adapt itself well to its new environment having come from such 'outlandish climes'. It was considered a 'docile creature' in its English domicile, although it had not lost its habit of chasing anything it might consider quarry, making it necessary to exercise great care when taking it on walks.

The twentieth century

There were only fifteen entries of the breed at the Kennel Club's Show in 1900 but the entries rose to sixty-one, fifty-three and seventy-two in the following three years, most probably owing to the continued royal interest in the breed. 'To possess a borzoi was to be in the first flight of fashion,' it was said. A Borzoi at the heel of its owner invested the latter with a certain 'distinguished air', which, it was said among the fancy, no other breed could do. Herbert Compton tells us that at a fashionable seaside parade, 'in reference to a very meagre specimen that was rather dejectedly following a somewhat seedy-looking individual', he overheard the following comment, 'Look! that's one of the Queen's dogs!' There were, though, people who felt that the breed had achieved popularity on its own merits and didn't need the added attention drawn to it by the royal household.

As the breed moved further into the twentieth century many dogs appeared which became very well known. Those named as being most typical of the breed in 1904 were Champions Velsk, Tsaritsa, Kieff, Statesman, Zenietra, Volno, Vikhra and Selwood Olga. Ch Velsk, sired by Korotai and with Ch Vikhra as his dam, was owned by the Duchess of Newcastle and whelped in December 1895. In his time he was the most heavily coated dog on the show-bench and also the strongest boned. He stood 31 inches and weighed 114 lbs. He was white with silver-grey markings and had an 'absolutely perfect expression'. His owner did, however, deign to say that she would have preferred him to be a little shorter in back and to have had a 'trifle more arch', but otherwise she could find no fault with him. By 1904 he had won eleven championships and no fewer than seventy-six first prizes. Velsk sired 'an immense number' of winning progeny, amongst them being Champions Tatania, Velsk, Votrio, Knois

Figure 25   Borzois bred by Queen Alexandra at Sandringham

and Theodora. Another of his claims to fame was that he was the sire of four Borzois exhibited by the Queen in 1903.

Perhaps the most famous dogs from Mrs Borman's kennel were Ch Kieff and Ch Miss Piostri. Ch Kieff stood 33 inches at the shoulder and had a girth of 35 inches; his head measurement was 12½ inches. Ch Miss Piostri stood at 31 inches with a girth of 34½ inches and a head length of 11½ inches. Another well-known dog, bred by the Duchess of Newcastle out of her Ch Sunbeam, was Ivan Turgeneff; her bitch Ch Revival of Notts was also held in high regard. Mrs Aitcheson's Ch Strawberry King and Mrs Vlasto's Reptile of Addlestone are also worthy of mention.

There is no doubt that the first dogs introduced to this country were heavy, large and strong and were much better than those depicted earlier by Buffon. Later, however, there was much desire to improve the head which sometimes occasioned the breeding of dogs with attractive heads but of less sound construction. This caused very great damage to the breed for judges tended to put up the dogs with the outstanding heads even though they may have lacked other breed attributes. As is the age-old story, the dogs that won were the ones used frequently at stud. This hindered the progress of the breed and, together with its lack of constitution, prompted doubts as to whether it would be kept in this country in any substantial number. But breeders were, thankfully, aware of the problem and there was eventually a return to sound bodies and legs and to 'powerful constitutions'. By the 1930s, however, the breed had in no way returned to the powerful build of the first dogs introduced to the country, but it was more graceful than ever before and its popularity was once again increasing. The height was raised in the breed standard from 27 inches to

29 inches and upwards for dogs and from 26 inches to 27 inches upwards for bitches. However, the average height of the breed already exceeded these heights, and those standing 29 inches had little or no chance of success under the majority of English judges, 32 inches being considered more the norm. The tallest dog that had been recorded by 1904 was Caspian who measured 34 inches. Bitches were rather smaller than the dogs but those up to 29 and 30 inches were by no means uncommon. They were not to be too heavy for it was difficult to breed a typey hound free from coarseness. In Russia the dogs were judged from the point of view of their working ability, whilst the bitches were judged according to the stock they were likely to produce, although breed type had to be kept in view at all times. After the First World War breed prices were high but they had come down again by the late 1920s.

Descriptions given of the 'ideal' Borzoi

Two prominent people in the breed, the Duchess of Newcastle and Miss Helen Arnold, were asked to give a description of the ideal hound. Their 'ideals', described shortly after the turn of this century, make interesting reading:

> A perfect borzoi should show substance combined with quality. A long head, rather Roman-nosed; dark, almond-shaped eyes, soft and expressive, set half-way between occiput and point of nose; small ears, set on high, but not prick; a strong neck, which should appear rather short in proportion to the size of the hound; well set-back shoulders, sloping to the points; well sprung ribs (but not round, like a barrel); deep chest, arched loin, stern set low. Very strong muscular quarters, so that, standing behind, they appear the widest part of the hound; hocks well bent and let down; stern long and carried low; long, silky coat, white, and should curl slightly on neck; legs straight and well feathered; the bone and muscle on legs should not appear round, but flat. Feet rather long, with not too much bridge to the toes. Height from 29 to 32½ inches. (Duchess of Newcastle)

> My ideal only exists in fancy at present, but some day I hope to exhibit him to the public. He shall be about 33 inches high, with a lovely, long, curly, silky coat, waving up round his ears with quite a Queen Elizabeth ruffle, to set off a head 13½ inches long, with a skull 16½ inches in circumference, flat on top, and oval to the sides. The skin on his head will be so thin and the hair so fine that his veins will be perceptible all down his aristocratic 'Wellington' nose. His eyes will be very dark and penetrating; his ears small, thin, and always alert when exercising, but tightly folded back when at ease.

When he is fully furnished his chest will measure 3 inches more in circumference than his height; his ribs will not resemble a 'weather-board', but he will be 'fish-sided'. There will be room for his heart to beat and his lungs to expand, so that I may not lose this dream of years (when I get him!) by sudden failure of the heart's action. He will cover as much ground as his height, and will be wider behind than in front, owing to his sloping, muscular hindquarters. He will have a strong but not too short neck, and a sloping shoulder; his stifle well bent, his hind legs brought up nicely under him, owing to a good roach of back, which roach will be a harmonious curve, not a camel's hump of a thing. His long tail and his hind and forequarters will all be well feathered with long, silky hair; the bone of his fore legs will be flat, gradually tapering down to his hare feet, which must be this shape in case some day duty calls him to his proper work, which is, in winter, on the snow; and I should like him to meet his Russian brothers on equal terms. His temper will be generous and kind, and he will be equally happy in house or kennel; always willing to share his bed and food with his companions, as all mine do now. I hope his colour will be white, with deep auburn markings, shading off to black in the face, or a beautiful steel-grey. If I get all the other points I shall not mind if he is fawn, lemon, or orange-marked, though I believe Russians prefer a peculiar red-grey brindle if they cannot get a whole white, and for breeding many keep a whole-coloured bitch in the kennel, as such a one generally breeds good puppies, and is healthy and strong, thereby proving the old adage, 'The darker the colour, the stronger the dog.' (Helen Arnold)

Constructive comments and criticism ninety years ago

Light eyes were said to be becoming too common and breeders thought too much about obtaining height, in the process developing flat sides and insufficient depth of chest. All too frequently one heard of dogs dropping down dead after galloping. The Duchess of Newcastle felt that if a dog stood 30 inches at shoulder it should have a girth of at least 35 inches for she wished to stress to breeders the importance of 'not going for leggy, weedy animals'. Mr Hood-Wright was not satisfied with type, thinking that breeders were losing sight of the original use of the dog and were sacrificing type for coat and size. He felt also that too much attention was paid to length of head and insufficient attention to breadth causing them to lose 'brain power and intelligence'.

The silky coat, so prized by Russians, was also thought to be lost and according to Miss Arnold in *The Twentieth Century Dog (Sporting),* 'Many think the silky curly coat wrong in a borzoi, but it is amongst the chief points in a Russian hound, as it clings closer to the body, and keeps out the weather (silk is warmer than wool).' The Borzoi's arch was to give his back a rounded appearance but many had a 'spikey look'. Mrs J. M'lntyre said that there were many different 'types' of Borzoi and that not only did no two judges judge alike but that not one in ten was consistent in his judging throughout the classes.

There was criticism from some that the Club's book did not set down a scale of values. Miss Helen Arnold and Major Borman offered their own views. Miss Arnold suggested this, 'Head, including eyes, ears and expression, 20; neck, shoulders, and fore legs, 20; body between shoulders and hips, 20; hindquarters and hind legs, 20; coat, tail, and general type, 20; total – 100.' The Major's suggestion was more in keeping with the way in which points were set down for other breeds: 'Head and expression, 20; legs and feet, 20; loin, 15; coat, 10; eyes, 5; ears, 5; tail, 5; girth and general symmetry of outline, 20; total – 100.'

Indeed there was much to be said about the breed and people were forthright with their comments, though that given below is from an unnamed lady-fancier:

> If – but that is a big 'if' – you can get them over distemper, they are very ornamental, affectionate, and – jealous. For all intents and purposes they are pet dogs in England; they never knock over furniture or ornaments in a drawing room; but otherwise they are stupid, and not always good-tempered under punishment which is frequently necessary from their in-bred habit of chasing everything. But they are so graceful and so insinuating that one forgives them much. One thing greatly in their favour is that they have no 'doggy' smell which especially fits them for the house.

The following is the standard for the breed as published in 1892 and makes an interesting comparison with the current standard as quoted in the next chapter.

HEAD: Long and lean. The skull flat and narrow; stop not perceptible, and muzzle long and tapering. The head from the forehead to the tip of the nose should be so fine that the shape and direction of the bones and principal veins can be clearly seen, and, in profile, should appear rather Roman-nosed. Bitches should be even narrower in the head than the dogs. Eyes dark, expressive, almond-shaped, and not too far apart. Ears like those of a Greyhound – small, thin, and placed well back on the head, with the tips, when thrown back, almost touching behind the occiput.

NECK: The head should be carried somewhat low, with the neck continuing the line of the back.

SHOULDERS: Clean, and sloping well back.

CHEST: Deep, and somewhat narrow.

BACK: Rather boney, and free from any cavity in the spinal column, the arch in the back being more marked in the dog than the bitch.

LOINS: Broad and very powerful, with plenty of muscular development.

THIGHS: Long and well developed, with good second thigh.

RIBS: Slightly sprung at the angle of the ribs – deep, reaching to the elbow, and even lower.

FORELEGS: Lean and straight. Seen from the front they should be narrow from side to side, broad at the shoulders and narrowing gradually down to the foot, the bone appearing flat, and not round, as in the Foxhound.

HINDLEGS: The least thing under the body when standing still, not straight, and the stifle slightly bent.

MUSCLES: Well distributed and highly developed.

PASTERNS: Strong.

FEET: Like those of a Deerhound — rather long. The toes close together and well arched.

COAT: Long, silky (not woolly), either flat, wavy or curly. On the head, ears and front legs it should be short and smooth. On the neck the frill should be profuse and rather curly. On the chest and rest of body, the tail and hindquarters, it should be long. The forelegs should be well feathered.

TAIL: Long, well feathered, and not gaily carried.

HEIGHT: At shoulder of dogs, from 28 inches upwards; of bitches, from 26 inches upwards.

FAULTS: Head short or thick; too much stop; parti-coloured nose; eyes too wide apart; heavy ears; heavy shoulders; wide chest 'barrel' ribbed; dew claws; elbows turned out; wide behind.

Recommendations for starting up a kennel in the 1920s

For a favoured few, for whom money was no object, champions could be bought and it was recognised by all that the best way of starting up a kennel was to buy a really good bitch. One that was strong, healthy and of good pedigree could usually be purchased from £15 upwards. A good bitch, once purchased, was to be mated to the best dog available whose 'blood nicks' with her own and it was strongly recommended that it would be a waste of both time and money to use a 'fourth-rate stud dog' for in doing so one would be certain to meet with disappointment.

Those with little or no experience of dogs might have preferred to begin with a puppy and it was advised that they should place themselves in the hands of a breeder with a reputation at stake. 'Even a "cast off" from a good strain that has been bred for certain points for years is more likely to turn out a better dog than a pup whose dam has been mated "haphazard",' said Robert Leighton in *The Complete Book of the Dog*. It was considered wise to select the puppy with the longest head, biggest bone, smallest ears and longest tail. If all these attributes were not to be found in one dog one was advised to seek as many as possible! Coat in a young pup was considered a secondary matter and the purchaser was advised to be guided by the coat of the sire and dam.

Measurements of youngsters were given as a guide; 19 inches at shoulder was about right for a three-month-old, 25 inches at six months and 27–29 inches at nine months. Growth was then slow although some continued to gain height until they were eighteen months old. Girth of chest increased and muscle developed up to the age of two and at the age of three or four it could be considered to be in its prime.

Prices for a really good eight- or ten-week-old pup in the 1920s ranged from £5 to £10 and anyone paying less would probably only be obtaining something of inferior quality. Having obtained a puppy there were three principal considerations in correct rearing: diet was to be varied; unlimited exercise was said to be a necessity, so it should never be chained; and internal parasites had to be kept in check. Newly-weaned puppies required food at least five times per day and this could consist of 'porridge, bread and milk, raw meat minced fine, and any table scraps, with plenty of new milk'. Well-boiled paunch was apparently also greatly appreciated and, 'being easily digested , could be given freely! I must point out to present-day new owners of puppies that they really must take the advice of their puppy's breeder with regard to diet and that they should not make any attempt to follow the recommendations given seventy years ago!

Neither an adult nor a puppy was to be chained up but housed in a kennel with a railed-in run; a loose box could be used as an alternative for those kept outside. The Borzoi was considered as hardy as the majority of large breeds, despite his delicate appearance. He could cope with cold provided that he was given a sturdy, dry kennel, plenty of straw, sensible food and plenty of exercise.

Hunting for furs

Despite the fact that we connect the breed's history with hunting the wolf for its food and skin, certainly around the 1950s commercial hunting for other furs was also carried out. Indeed the fur industry in Russia constituted a substantial proportion of the country's economy and a survey carried out in the south of Russia in 1950 showed that more than 50 per cent of the foxes killed for their furs had been hunted by Borzois. Borzois can be trained to catch and kill fur animals without causing damage to the skins and are invaluable where hunters find trapping impractical because of the difficulty of finding the traps again in snowy weather.

A single Borzoi can catch a fox by the neck, throttle it, then compress the chest to be certain of its dispatch. Working in pairs both Borzois simultaneously catch the fox by the throat and by the chest and in doing so avoid damage to the skin. In the latter half of the twentieth century the Borzoi has been taught to bark when the prey has been caught. Hunting is now usually carried out on foot rather than on horseback. The Borzoi in Russia hunts on all types of terrain and the long-legged Borzoi has an obvious advantage over the game in snow. Occasionally there have been reports of the Borzoi being carried on the saddle of a camel so that it can see the prey from a greater distance, and there have been other reports of Golden eagles being used with the Borzoi. In the latter cases the Borzoi is used to chase the prey to open ground for the eagle to catch it.

Russian opinions

Despite the fact that the British Borzoi is very similar to the breed in Russia, many Russians consider the British Borzoi to be degenerate. For them the prime consideration is whether or not a dog is suitable for hunting. The Russian State Kennels have been responsible for supposedly breeding the best Russian stock. Russian standards are high and they have clear and decisive theories regarding conformation. It is believed in Russia that over-long backs and very low stifles which are over bent can lead to hip dysplasia. Pigmentation is important to the Russians; toe-nails must be black, and there are rules about the colour of the iris of the eye. The Borzois in Russia are clearly working dogs in hard form and some in the show-ring bear the scars of their toils.

FIVE

THE BORZOI TODAY

Temperament and adaptability

Borzois possess a strong character and perhaps one of the most obvious things about the personality of the majority is their outwardly expressed likes and dislikes. They enjoy affection from humans and respond well to kindness and personal attention. Never forget their origins. Even now, when tracing pedigrees back, frequently one finds that a Borzoi used for hunting is not so many generations back, and thus the instinct for hunting is not entirely lost, despite the fact that the breed is considered now to be a very tolerant one. Ill temper in the breed is much rarer than it was in earlier years (which is just as well when one considers the size of the breed) and quarrels, even between dogs, seem to be a rare occurrence.

As with all Sight Hounds it should never be forgotten that a Borzoi will hunt if given the opportunity and has a tendency to follow anything which moves – and that applies not only to wild rabbits but often also to the neighbour's much-loved cat!

Given care and attention, the Borzoi is a breed that gives its owner high rewards. Surprisingly perhaps, it is able to adapt to its environment and is generally happy to fit in with the general life-style, even though that may be a humdrum life of domesticity. It is not a breed that needs a great deal of maintenance but nor can it be left to fend entirely for itself.

It is exceedingly fast in its reactions and for this reason it is sometimes difficult for owners to avert unfortunate situations should they be about to occur. It is, indeed, possessed of an ultra-rapid nervous reaction that must not be confused with nervousness. One does come across the occasional nervous Borzoi but then that can be said of all breeds. Many Borzois are friendly with strangers but it has to be said that there are others who view strangers with a certain suspicion.

Almost without exception they reserve their greatest affections for their owners, to whom they are devoted and constant companions. In common with other large Sight Hounds they have a charming and graceful way of thieving the occasional item but should one feel the need to chastise them this should be done with restraint for, being a sensitive and intelligent breed, they quickly learn what is and is not expected of them and a severe reprimand should not be necessary.

When introducing the Borzoi to children it is advisable to make that introduction whilst the dog is still young and, naturally, the success of the relationship depends to a very great extent upon the adult members of the family adopting a sensible attitude with both canines and humans. Usually the Borzoi is gentle with children and can be very tolerant but owing to its size it is always wise to exercise caution, especially in the early days of the relationship.

A Borzoi's very size and appearance can make it suitable as a deterrent to intruders and often it can appear to be more savage than it actually is, but it is certainly not a breed that is to be considered as 'guard dog' and is not a very vocal animal.

The Borzoi likes to be clean and is easy to house-train provided that one is sensible about this and allows the dog out at regular intervals, especially during the early months. An 'accident' by a Borzoi, or any other of the large breeds, is little short of a lake!

Coat care

The Borzoi's coat is not at all difficult to keep in good condition for, being a fine and silky coat of not too extreme a length, dirt tends not to stick to it. Naturally a clean, dry bed is essential but, given this, and provided that the general atmosphere is relatively clean, the Borzoi can quite easily be kept clean and spruce. Straw in the bedding of a white dog should be avoided, though, for it can tend to stain the coat.

Coats do, however, differ and as with so many breeds the texture varies to a greater or lesser extent according to the colour pattern. In an orange and white Borzoi the white often has a slightly creamy tinge and needs somewhat less attention than the white found on a dog with black markings, this usually being somewhat less resistant to dirt.

Most exhibitors bath their Borzois prior to a show but those kept as pets need be bathed only rarely. After a bath they should, of course, be kept warm and a little exercise is beneficial in restoring general body warmth.

Grooming with brush and comb is not difficult, nor indeed too time-consuming, but special attention must be paid to the frills on the legs and to tail furnishings. In general Borzois enjoy their grooming sessions but they can be a touch sensitive on their legs and you will need to exert your authority from the outset so that your hound is not allowed to get the better of you and make grooming sessions a trial rather than a pleasure. For newcomers to the breed it may be worth noting that the coat on the neck, back and the top of the ribs is frequently brushed forward in order to enhance the overall appearance, especially in a dog which has a straighter coat.

The coat of the Borzoi is remarkably tolerant to rain and mud. Dry cleaning powders, though they may at first glance appear an 'easy option', are not to be recommended for they are totally unsuitable for any breed required to have a silky coat. In emergency, though, a powder might be used on a set of dirty feet, for it can be washed out with relative ease soon afterwards.

Unfortunately Borzois do moult, at which time it is especially important to groom the coat out regularly to avoid too many hairs around the home.

Advice about housing

A very high proportion of Borzois live as house dogs, possibly because they are generally well mannered and clean. Despite their size, they seem to take up very little space and are often quite content to have a bed tucked away in a corner somewhere. As always, it is for you, the owner, to teach your dog what he is and is not allowed to do around the home and where he may and may not go. It is advisable for the bed, which must be raised slightly from the ground, to be well padded to avoid the bed sores that can some-times occur if this breed is bedded on very hard surfaces. A fairly

Figure 26   Borzoi, Ingledene Impressario, in relaxed mood

standard-sized bed for this breed is about 2½–3 feet × 3–3½ feet.

When the dog is kennelled outside, provided that the kennel is well lined, thoroughly dry and free from draughts, heating is not essential. Indeed, the Borzoi tolerates the cold extremely well and, if anything, has a tendency to become lethargic in hot weather. For this reason it is important that plenty of shade is available for dogs kennelled with outside runs. Take care that too much heat is not allowed to build up inside the kennel on a hot day; it is alarming how hot a kennel can become, especially a wooden one, when the midday sun is on it. This is something which needs bearing in mind when siting a kennel.

The Borzoi is a breed which rarely soils its kennel, and should therefore never be closed in for too long a period or he may feel uncomfortable, owing to his desire to be clean in what he considers to be his home. As with most dogs it is probably fair to say that a Borzoi is happiest when kennelled with another dog but they usually learn to live alone if obliged to do so.

Exercise

A fully mature Borzoi in the peak of condition is well able to enjoy as much as a ten-mile outing and the breed runs well beside horses. Thankfully, although they can cope easily with a large amount of exercise, such extremes are not necessary, although a certain amount of exercise is, of course, a must. They are capable of jumping but rarely commence this activity without encouragement. Digging seems to be more popular with them. This being the case, if your Borzoi does turn out to be a digger, it is perhaps wise to allow him his own certain digging patch (from which he must have no chance of escape) to prevent him from setting to his industrious work in various different areas!

Kennel Club Breed Standard © The Kennel Club

GENERAL APPEARANCE: Well balanced, graceful, aristocratic, dignified and elegant.

CHARACTERISTICS: A coursing hound which must be courageous, powerful and of great speed.

TEMPERAMENT: Sensitive, alert and aloof.

HEAD AND SKULL: Head long, lean and in proportion to dog's size and substance. In bitches head finer than in dogs. Well filled-in below eyes.

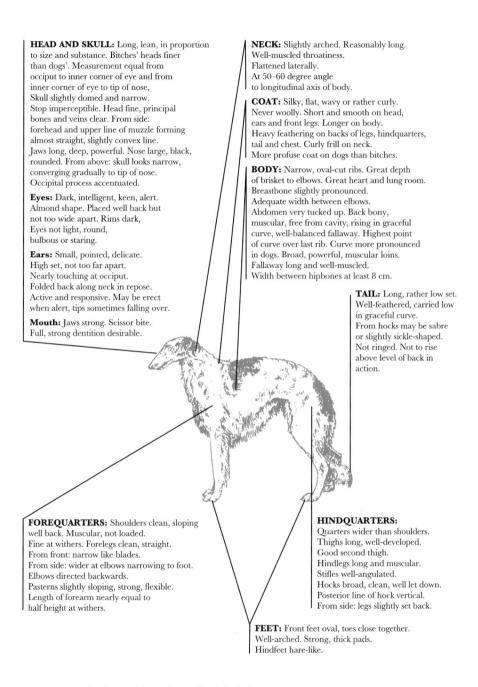

HEAD AND SKULL: Long, lean, in proportion to size and substance. Bitches' heads finer than dogs'. Measurement equal from occiput to inner corner of eye and from inner corner of eye to tip of nose, Skull slightly domed and narrow. Stop imperceptible. Head fine, principal bones and veins clear. From side: forehead and upper line of muzzle forming almost straight, slightly convex line. Jaws long, deep, powerful. Nose large, black, rounded. From above: skull looks narrow, converging gradually to tip of nose. Occipital process accentuated.

Eyes: Dark, intelligent, keen, alert. Almond shape. Placed well back but not too wide apart. Rims dark, Eyes not light, round, bulbous or staring.

Ears: Small, pointed, delicate. High set, not too far apart. Nearly touching at occiput. Folded back along neck in repose. Active and responsive. May be erect when alert, tips sometimes falling over.

Mouth: Jaws strong. Scissor bite. Full, strong dentition desirable.

NECK: Slightly arched. Reasonably long. Well-muscled throatiness. Flattened laterally. At 50–60 degree angle to longitudinal axis of body.

COAT: Silky, flat, wavy or rather curly. Never woolly. Short and smooth on head, ears and front legs. Longer on body. Heavy feathering on backs of legs, hindquarters, tail and chest. Curly frill on neck. More profuse coat on dogs than bitches.

BODY: Narrow, oval-cut ribs. Great depth of brisket to elbows. Great heart and lung room. Breastbone slightly pronounced. Adequate width between elbows. Abdomen very tucked up. Back bony, muscular, free from cavity, rising in graceful curve, well-balanced fallaway. Highest point of curve over last rib. Curve more pronounced in dogs. Broad, powerful, muscular loins. Fallaway long and well-muscled. Width between hipbones at least 8 cm.

TAIL: Long, rather low set. Well-feathered, carried low in graceful curve. From hocks may be sabre or slightly sickle-shaped. Not ringed. Not to rise above level of back in action.

FOREQUARTERS: Shoulders clean, sloping well back. Muscular, not loaded. Fine at withers. Forelegs clean, straight. From front: narrow like blades. From side: wider at elbows narrowing to foot. Elbows directed backwards. Pasterns slightly sloping, strong, flexible. Length of forearm nearly equal to half height at withers.

HINDQUARTERS: Quarters wider than shoulders. Thighs long, well-developed. Good second thigh. Hindlegs long and muscular. Stifles well-angulated. Hocks broad, clean, well let down. Posterior line of hock vertical. From side: legs slightly set back.

FEET: Front feet oval, toes close together. Well-arched. Strong, thick pads. Hindfeet hare-like.

Figure 27   The Borzoi breed standard in brief.

Measurement equal from occiput to inner corner of eye and from inner corner of eye to tip of nose. Skull very slightly domed and narrow, stop imperceptible. Head fine so that bones and principal veins can be clearly seen. Viewed from side, forehead and upper line of muzzle form an almost straight, slightly convex line. Jaws long, deep and powerful; nose large and black, nicely rounded, neither cornered nor sharp. Viewed from above skull should look narrow, converging very gradually to tip of nose. Occipital process very accentuated.

EYES: Dark and intelligent, keen and alert expression. Almond-shaped, set obliquely and placed well back but not too wide apart. Eye rims dark. Eyes not light, round, bulbous or staring.

EARS: Small, pointed and delicate. Set high but not too far apart. Nearly touching at occiput; when in repose folded back along neck. Should be active and responsive, may be erect when alert, tips sometimes falling over.

MOUTH: Jaws strong with a perfect, regular and complete scissor bite, i.e. upper teeth closely overlapping the lower teeth and set squarely to the jaws. Full, strong dentition desirable.

NECK: Slightly arched; reasonably long and well-muscled. Free from throatiness, flattened laterally, set at an angle of 50–60 degrees to the longitudinal axis of body.

FOREQUARTERS: Shoulders clean, sloping well back. Muscular but not loaded. Fine at withers but not accentuated. Forelegs clean and straight. Seen from front, narrow like blades; from side, wider at elbows narrowing down to foot. Elbows directed backwards, neither turning in nor out. Pasterns slightly sloping, strong and flexible. Length of forearm nearly equal to half total height at withers.

BODY: Chest, ribs of narrow oval cut, great depth of brisket reaching to elbows, giving great heart and lung room, especially in mature dogs. Breastbone slightly pronounced with adequate width between elbows and abdomen very tucked up. Back rather bony, muscular and free from any cavity, rising in a graceful curve with well-balanced fallaway. Highest point of curve is situated over last rib. Curve is more pronounced in dogs than in bitches. Loins broad and very powerful with plenty of muscular development. Fallaway long and well muscled. Width between hipbones at least 8 cm. (3 ins.)

HINDQUARTERS: Quarters wider than shoulders, ensuring stability of stance. Thighs long, well developed with good second thigh; hindlegs long and muscular; stifles well angulated, hocks broad, clean and well let down.

Posterior line of hock vertical. Seen from side, legs slightly set back.

FEET: Front feet oval, toes close together, well arched over strong, thick pads, turning neither in nor out. Hind feet harelike, i.e. longer and less arched.

TAIL: Long, rather low set, when measured between thighs reaches up to top of nearest hip bone. Well feathered, carried low in a graceful curve. From level of hocks may be sabre or slightly sickle-shaped but not ringed. In action not rising above level of back.

GAIT/MOVEMENT: Front, straight with long reach, pasterns springy. Hind, straight with powerful driving hocks. Moving wider than front. Viewed from side, appearance in action should be that of effortless power.

COAT: Silky, flat, wavy or rather curly (but never woolly). Short and smooth on head, ears and front of legs; much longer on body with heavy feathering on backs of legs and hindquarters, tail and chest. Neck carries a large curly frill. More profuse in dogs than bitches.

COLOUR: Any colour acceptable.

SIZE: Minimum height at withers: dogs 74 cm (29 inches); bitches 68 cm (27 inches).

FAULTS: Any departure from the foregoing points should be considered a fault and the seriousness with which the fault should be regarded should be in exact proportion to its degree and its effect upon the health and welfare of the dog.

NOTE: Male animals should have two apparently normal testicles fully descended into the scrotum.

Judging the breed

Whilst seeking a graceful, aristocratic hound, a judge must also bear in mind that the breed should also be able to catch and hold a wolf. Indeed the Borzoi should be fairly narrow, but too narrow a front which would not allow a dog to move sufficiently well to perform the work for which it was originally intended is not at all desirable. Look for a well-balanced dog with an arch to the loins and a broad, sloping croup, wide, powerful quarters and well let down hocks.

Figure 28
Graham Hill and his
Borzoi, Ch. Dimland
Music Maker

Concerning construction

The slight changes made to the general conformation of the breed over the years are not detrimental to the health of the Borzoi provided that sufficient lung and heart room is available. One of the most outstanding features of the breed is the great depth of rib and brisket and it is important that the chest must not be narrowed too greatly, for coupled with an extremely narrow chest are forelegs which are positioned too close together to balance the dog sufficiently well. In this breed the forelegs need to support two-thirds of the body weight and it is essential, therefore, that they are correctly positioned to aid static balance. Another feature which needs to be borne in mind at all times is that if the bone structure is too light there is an increased risk of fracture.

Too low a head carriage destroys the appearance of alertness and dignity and a shallow, snipey muzzle would simply not be serviceable in the dog's original environment.

Imports in the twentieth century

Mr Khrushchev presented Sir Rudi and Lady Sternberg with a Borzoi dog named Boran in 1964. The gift came about because the Sternbergs had given a Sheepdog demonstration at a Moscow agricultural show and had subsequently given the dog to Mr Khrushchev; he in return gave them Boran as a token of his gratitude. Boran had won working and show medals in Russia and was seemingly a wonderful character, despite the fact that during the six years he lived in England prior to his death it was said that not once did he respond to any word spoken in English. Boran is behind a number of English-bred dogs, especially those of Miss Murray (Fortrouge) and Mr J. Bennett-Heard whose wife, Jackie, had strongly believed in retaining Russian blood. Boran produced five champion offspring out of three litters. He died in 1970 at the age of nine, this being a fairly average life span for the breed.

Despite many difficulties encountered in doing so, in 1972 Mrs Bennett-Heard imported Keroj of Keepers from Russia and in 1990 Derek Pye also imported a dog.

Lure coursing and racing

Borzois have never been coursed or raced seriously in Britain, although Mr and Mrs Edgar Sayer, breeders of Borzois and Greyhounds, did hold trials on their own track. Occasionally the Borzoi is now raced on the track at race meetings for other breeds. During recent years an increasing number of highly enthusiastic Borzoi owners have participated in lure coursing, events for Sight Hounds being held regularly in a variety of locations.

Breed clubs

In 1992 the Borzoi Club celebrated its centenary year. The Club's in-augural meeting took place at the Albemarle Hotel in Piccadilly on 29 March 1892 and in the Chair was none other than the Duchess of Newcastle. Nine people at that time wished to become members of the Club, the majority of whom had addresses in central London, which may now seem somewhat strange for a hound breed, but it is highly likely that all were people of some means with other country residences. Indeed, the annual subscription was two guineas, no mean sum more than a hundred years ago. The first Treasurer of the Club was Mr Krehl.

At first the Borzoi Club used the Russian breed standard, this having been drawn up in 1889 by the Russian Imperial Society for the Encouragement of Sport. The Russians set an evaluation of points in the following order: hindquarters, forequarters, ribs, back, general symmetry, muzzle, eyes and ears (i.e. head features together) and, lastly, tail. It can be appreciated from this that the Russians were still seeking specimens of the breed which could achieve functional success in the field. By 1893 the Club had drawn up its own, very descriptive, standard of points, based on the Russian standard but with a notable change to the height clause, dogs from 26 inches and bitches from 24 inches. A scale of points was also given but this was virtually a reversal of the Russian scale for general appearance and outline rated lowest, whilst the head topped the list.

A northern branch of the Club was started in 1930 but this failed owing largely to the ill health of the organiser. In the 1930s the Borzoi Owners' and Breeders' Association was set up and though it survived the war years and held what was apparently a very satisfactory show at Cheltenham in 1947, this too had to be closed down, owing largely to lack of support as well as ill health.

During the war years, by the way, it is interesting to note that the Borzoi Club's very splendid trophies were stored in the cellars of Clumber, home of the Duchess of Newcastle. Two of the trophies, given to the Club in 1896, are in sterling silver and are 28 inches high plus the plinth; each weighs 6½ lbs. Another, the Bleriot Challenge Bowl, first awarded in 1913 is also in sterling silver and weighs 4½ lbs. The Club now boasts some fifty or so cups and trophies of which it is justly proud. Following the war, a most successful show was held at the Jubilee Hall in London when all were interested to discover what stock had survived through those difficult years.

The Club maintained northern and Scottish representatives to see to the interests of members in their areas but over the years there were various swings in the membership figures up and down the country and, as a result, a social section was formed so that the Club could spread its activities where needed most. The first major event held under this new arrangement concerned gastric torsion and took place at the Royal Veterinary College in London where there were over a hundred participants. To this day the Club holds a variety of events including a Judges' Development Programme and Health Scheme.

Borzoi owners in the north eventually succeeded in forming a club and in 1975 the Northern Borzoi Association was founded. As the northern areas were, in consequence, to be covered, the Borzoi Club no longer provided representatives in the area.

There are just two breed clubs for the Borzoi, these being the Borzoi Club and the Northern Borzoi Association. The names, addresses and telephone numbers of the Honorary Secretaries of these clubs can be obtained from the Kennel Club.

Kennel Club registrations for 1908–1934 and at five-yearly intervals from 1950–2000

1908	129	1917	27	1926	201
1909	130	1918	8	1927	298
1910	101	1919	18	1928	269
1911	107	1920	57	1929	246
1912	83	1921	54	1930	270
1913	64	1922	88	1931	246
1914	73	1923	117	1932	242
1915	41	1924	171	1933	310
1916	31	1925	248	1934	249
1950	177	1970	293	1990	264
1955	70	1975	319	1995	138
1960	119	1980	310	2000	156
1965	137	1985	180		

Six

The Deerhound

U ndoubtedly the Deerhound as we know it today owes its origin to the Greyhound and, more specifically, to the various rough-coated Greyhounds which have developed through the centuries. It has frequently been confused with the Irish Wolfhound but good specimens of each are remarkably different, the head of the Deerhound being much closer to that of a Greyhound and the breed in general being of a much lighter frame. Robert Leighton described him in the following manner, and I hope the reader will not mind my using his description for I believe it would be presumptuous to attempt to improve upon it:

> The Deerhound is one of the most decorative of dogs, impressively stately and picturesque wherever he is seen, whether it be amid the surroundings of the baronial hall, or out in the open, gracefully bounding over the purple of his native hills. Grace and majesty are in his every movement and attitude, and even to the most prosaic mind there is about him the inseparable glamour of feudal romance and poetry. (Robert Leighton, *The Complete Book of the Dog* 1922)

The Deerhound in history

Clearly the breed is one of great antiquity but the much reported statement that the lords took with them their 'Deirhoundis' in Hector Boethius' Pitscottie's *History*, first published in 1575 is, regrettably, untrue. Boethius did indeed mention three varieties of Scottish dogs of 'marvellous nature', one of which was 'hardy and swift', but the former statement was an unfortunate error made by Hugh Dalziel and copied by numerous writers thereafter. The reason for Dalziel's error involved confusion with another book written by Robert Linsay of Pitscottie 153 years later and subsequently reprinted in 1814 with certain amendments. It was at this point that the word 'Deirhoundis' was substituted for the word 'Hounds'. This change, coupled with the fact that Linsay was 'of Pitscottie', presumably caused Dalziel to be misled.

Figure 29   White Hairy Greyhound – Aldrovandus 1637

Having said that, it is highly likely that Deerhounds were kept in Scotland in the middle of the sixteenth century, for in the later edition of Pitscottie's *History of Scotland*, printed in 1577, there is a large dog (which Edward Ash calculated to be 33 inches at shoulder), seemingly of Greyhound type. Whether it is smooth- or rough-coated is difficult to say, although there is some unevenness of coat on the tail. Again in 1583 we find a rough-haired Greyhound depicted in a book of animals and Sir John Nicol gave an account of Queen Elizabeth's amusements at Cowdrey Park in 1595 in which we read, 'Then rode her Grace to Cowdrey to dinner, and about six of the clock in the evening, sawe sixteen bucks pulled down with grey-hounds in a laund.' By 1637 Aldrovandus shows us a dog of clearly Deerhound type which he calls a 'White-Hairy Greyhound'. Un-fortunately, though, he makes no statement in his work that the 'White-Hairy Greyhound' is Scottish, despite having referred to the Scottish dogs mentioned by Boethius. I have very recently discovered a drawing of a 'Deerhound' by Abraham Hondius and dated 1682.

In 1769 we find the first clear written evidence of a Deerhound described by Pennant, when he visited Gordon Castle, as 'the true Highland Greyhound'. His portrayal was of a large dog covered with long hair and used by the Scottish chiefs in 'stag chases'. He also said that the breed had become very scarce.

By 1790, in Ralph Beilby's *A General History of Quadrupeds*, we are told that the 'Scottish Highland Greyhound, or Wolfdog' was formerly used by Scottish chieftains in their grand hunting parties. One had been seen some years previously and was 'a large, powerful, fierce-looking Dog; its ears were pendulous, and its eyes half hid in the hair; its body was strong and muscular, and covered with harsh, wirey, reddish hair, mixed with white'. A year later in the *Encyclopaedia Britannica* we hear once again that the 'Highland gre-hound' had become very scarce, it was 'of very great size, strong, deep chested, and covered with long rough hair' and again we are told that it was used by the chieftains in their 'hunting matches', but we learn too that it had 'sagacious nostrils as the bloodhound, and was as fierce'. One cannot help but feel that the Highland Greyhound was slightly removed from the Deerhound we know today.

Before we move on to be enlightened a stage further by Messrs William Scrope and John Meyrick, let us dwell for a moment on Scott's Maida.

Sir Walter Scott's famous Maida

Maida was undoubtedly the favourite of Sir Walter Scott's many dogs and despite the fact that he has been referred to by various names, he was more or less what we would today describe (at least in phenotype) as a Deerhound, though he was the offspring of a Glengarry dam and a Pyrenean sire, the latter possibly being responsible for the admixture of white in his coat and possibly having some bearing on the white which is found in some coats even to this day. By the early twentieth century it was said that many of the best 'modern' Deerhounds were descended from Maida who 'was a magnificent animal, partaking of the appearance of his Deerhound dam, but having height and power from his sire'. Washington Irving described him as 'a giant in iron grey'. We do not know the age to which Maida lived for we first learn, in 1817, that he was already an old dog.

In the following extract Irving, bearing a letter from Thomas Campbell, had halted his carriage near Abbotsford and had sent down his card, asking if Scott would receive him:

> The noise of my chase had disturbed the quiet establishment. Out sallied the warder of the establishment, a black greyhound, and leaping on one of the blocks of stone, began furious barking. This alarm brought out the whole garrison of dogs, all open mouthed and vociferous. In a little while, the lord of the castle himself made his appearance. I knew him at once, by the like-

Figure 30 Deerhounds visiting Sir Walter Scott's home, Abbotsford, in 1992

ness that had been published of him. He came limping up the gravel walk, aiding himself by a stout walking staff, but moving rapidly and with vigour. By his side jogged along a large iron-grey staghound, of most grave demeanour, who took no part in the clamour of the canine rabble, but seemed to consider himself bound, for the dignity of the house, to give me a courteous reception.

Upon receiving the requested invitation, which, incidentally, lasted a few days, Irving goes on to tell us much about the dogs inside the establishment:

Maida deported himself with a gravity becoming of his age and size, and seemed to consider himself called upon to preserve a great degree of dignity and decorum in our society. As he jogged along a little distance ahead of us, the young dogs would gambol about him, leap on his neck, worry at his ears, and endeavour to tease him into a gambol. The old dog would keep on a long time with imperturbable solemnity, now and then seeming to rebuke the wantonness of his young companions. At length he would make a sudden turn, seize one of them, and tumble him in the dust, then giving us a glance as much as to say, 'You see gentlemen, I can't help giving way to this nonsense', and would resume his gravity, and jog on as before.

Maida's mannerisms amused Scott and he was said by Irving to comment,

I make no doubt when Maida is alone with these young dogs he throws gravity aside, and plays the boy as much as any of them; but he is ashamed

73

to do so in our company and seems to say – 'Ha' done with your nonsense, youngsters: what will the laird and that other gentleman think of me if I give way to such foolery?'

The comments made by Irving and Scott ring such true bells in the ears of those of us who have owned the breed ourselves. They talk of the sharp, petulant barking from the smaller dogs and tell how, when sufficiently roused, Maida would join in the chorus with a 'deep-mouthed bow-wow . . . but a transient outbreak', following which he would look up dubiously at his master's face to assess his response. Scott likened Maida's barks of this kind with the great gun of Constantinople, 'it takes so long to get it ready, that the smaller guns can fire off a dozen times first; but when it does go off, it plays the very devil'.

In May 1818 Lockhart describes Scott, in his room in Castle Street, Edinburgh:

> While he talked, his hands were hardly ever idle – sometimes he folded letter-covers – sometimes he twisted paper into matches, performing both tasks with great mechanical expertness and nicety; and when there was no loose paper fit so to be dealt with, he snapped his fingers and the noble Maida aroused himself from his lair on the hearthrug, and laid his head across his master's knees to be caressed and fondled.

Despite his progressing age, we know Maida remained active for in a letter to his son, Walter, dated October 1819 Scott writes:

> Sir William Rae and his lady came to us on Saturday. On Sunday Maida walked with us, and in jumping the paling at the Greentongue Park contrived to hang himself up by the hind-leg. He howled at first, but seeing us making toward him he stopped crying, and waved his tail by way of signal, it was supposed, for assistance. He sustained no material injury, though his leg was strangely twisted in the bars, and he was nearly hanging by it. He showed great gratitude, in his way, to his deliverers.

But three months later, at the beginning of 1820, Scott is parted from Maida, he being at Castle Street and his faithful companion at Abbotsford. The winter was exceptionally severe that year and Scott, concerned about Maida in cold weather, wrote thus to William Laidlaw:

> Dear Willie – I have yours with the news of the inundation, which, it seems, has done no damage. I hope Mai will be taken care of. He should have a bed in the kitchen, and always be called indoors after it is dark, for all the kind are savage at night. Please cause Swanson to knock him up a box, and

fill it with straw from time to time. I enclose a cheque for £50 to pay accounts, etc.

Yours W.S.

A little more than two years later, Scott writes to his younger son, Charles, to say that 'Maida died quietly in his straw last week', adding that he is 'buried below his monument', this being a stone figure of Maida carved by Scott's mason and placed at the gate of Abbotsford a year before Maida died. On the epitaph was engraved a couplet, the work of Lockhart, in what Scott described as 'Teviotdale Latin':

Maidae marmorea dormis sub imagine Maida,
　　Ad januam domini sit tibi terra levis.

Meaning, in Scott's own words:

Beneath the sculptured form which late you wore,
　　Sleep soundly, Maida, at your master's door.

Unfortunately there was an error in the Latin, the stone having been engraved before Scott could get it corrected. To make matters worse it was copied and printed in the *Kelso Mail* with a further error, these being repeated in the Edinburgh and London papers. Scott may have been vexed by what he called a 'contemptible rumpus' but, as he wrote subsequently

Figure 31　Deerhounds by Maida's grave at Abbotsford

75

to Lockhart, 'So Maida died, but lives.' And so he did, for in Scott's *Woodstock* we read much of Bevis and there can be no doubt that Bevis was none other than Scott's favourite of all, Maida.

The next references of significance are to be found in Scrope's remarkable work *The Art of Deerstalking*, published in 1839. He was as much confounded by the interaction and change of nomenclature as any other writer and was at pains to distinguish between the various breeds, especially the Irish Wolfhound and the Scottish Deerhound. The desperately low numbers of the breed at the time are graphically described by Scrope thus, 'In Wales some of this breed may still exist, although no evidence of the fact has reached us. In Scotland (from a perfect knowledge of every specimen of the breed) we know that very few, perhaps not above a dozen, pure deerhounds are to be met with.' In attempting to give an accurate idea of the size and 'proportions' of the Deerhound he takes into account the fact that degeneracy must have taken place 'arising from diminution in number, neglect in crossing, selection and feeding' and deduces that 'at a remoter period' they averaged 30 inches in height, 34 inches in girth and weighed 100 lbs.

Despite the fact that he felt certain the breed had degenerated he still believed that no other member of the canine race had such a combination of qualities: speed, strength, size, endurance, courage, perseverance, sagacity, docility, elegance and dignity. It was Scrope's opinion that previous attempts to improve the breed by crossing with other breeds had utterly failed. He felt that attempts to cross with the Bull-dog had added courage but in doing so speed, strength and weight had been lost, as had 'that roughness which is necessary for the protection of the feet in a rocky mountainous country'. In crosses made with the Bloodhound the only quality gained was that of smell whilst speed and size were diminished. Crosses with the Pyrenean Wolf-dog, in his opinion, fared no better, for although there was some increase in weight this was to no avail as speed and courage were both lost. In Scrope's opinion the finest specimens of the breed at that time were four belonging to Captain McNeill, the younger, of Colonsay. These were the two famous dogs, Buskar and Bran, and two bitches, Runa and Cavak. He described two as being of a pale yellow and the others a sandy red; they also varied in the length and quality of their hair. Common to all was the fact that the tips of their ears, their eyes and muzzles were black and that they were each of a uniform colour. He felt that this was 'a never failing accompaniment of purity of breed'. He thought them to be quite as swift as a well-bred Greyhound, describing them as 'much more sagacious' and, in disposition, 'more playful and attached, but much bolder and fiercer when roused'.

The measurements of Buskar taken in 1836 were: height at shoulder, 28

Figure 32   Deer Stalking from William Scrope's *Art of Deerstalking* 1839

inches; girth of chest, 32 inches; weight in running condition, 85 lbs.

There was a striking difference in size between dogs and bitches and Scrope considered this difference to be more remarkable than in any other species of canine. For the sake of comparison I give measurements of a full-grown stag described by Scrope and, as he says, when one compares the great difference in size it is not surprising that few dogs, if any, are capable of bringing down a stag single-handed.

Height at shoulder	3 ft 11¼ ins
Girth at shoulder	4 ft 7¾ ins
Height from top of head to the fore foot	5 ft 6 ins
Length of antler	2 ft 6 ins
Extreme height from the top of antlers to the ground	7 ft 10 ins
Weight as he fell	310 lbs

A wiry elasticity of the hair was thought by Highlanders to be a criterion of breeding and this was one of Buskar's attributes. He was pale yellow in colour and was thought, from his shape and coat texture, to be 'remarkably pure in his breeding'.

Scrope commented on the decided difference in coat texture dependent upon the colour of the coat. The grey coats and, incidentally, it was believed that dark grey was at one time the prevailing colour in the Highlands, were softer and more woolly than the yellow or reddish colours. The greys were also thought to be generally less lively with a tendency to 'cat hams' and less development of muscle on the back and loins.

In 1861 we are told by John Meyrick that the Highland Deerhound was gradually dying out as a breed but he does not agree with Scrope that crossing the Scotch Greyhound with the Foxhound had provided a substitute. Meyrick was of the opinion that the Deerhound 'Colley' cross was 'in many forests of the north preferred to any other breed'.

Meyrick goes on to describe the Queen's Deerhound which was said to be 'thoroughbred' and he did not know of any other 'really pure-bred Deerhound' in the country. He felt that if such animals did indeed exist they were very rare and recommended that any claims as to the purity of the breed should always be looked upon with suspicion. The Queen's specimen was 'nearly 31 inches in height, and measured 36 round the chest; his colour was a dark grey, running into a dusky fawn, with a black muzzle, and slightly pendulous ears; his coat harsh and shaggy, especially on the jaws and neck'. Meyrick felt that although many dogs were called Deerhounds by their owners, these were in fact either the Scotch Greyhound, which did have some true Deerhound blood, or else they were a cross between this and the Bloodhound or some other breed.

The 'Scotch Greyhound', as described by Meyrick, resembled the Deerhound both in colour and in shape but was smaller, being generally below 26 inches in height with the bitch somewhat smaller than the dog. Even in proportion to his size, it was less strongly made. It seems, however, that the Scotch Greyhound was often 'passed off for and sold as the Highland Deerhound'.

Meyrick also itemises the 'Welsh Rough Greyhound' as an individual breed but tells his readers that 'it does not differ in shape or colour from the Scotch breed, of which he seems to be only a variety'.

The Deerhound used in sport

By law, the red deer belonged to the kings of Scotland and in the reign of Queen Mary drives, often lasting several days, were made to round up the herds into different neighbourhoods for the pleasure of the court. However, under the Stuarts, organised coursing by the courtiers ceased and it was left in the hands of the retainers who used it as a means to replenish the larders of their chiefs.

The breed was used not only for coursing stags in open country but also to overtake a wounded stag and hold it at bay; thus it needed both strength and speed. But with the coming of the rifle stags were less likely to cover a great deal of ground after they had been shot and so the Deerhound was

Figure 33 'On the Look-out' by Sir Edwin Landseer, 1827.

not required to the same extent as formerly and so, once again, lost the patronage of many of the owners of deer forests. The breed was in peril of dying out completely. Edward Ash feels that it was probably due largely to Scrope's book with its excellent illustrations that interest in reviving the use of Deerhounds came about, for by 1842 it was once again commonly kept in Scotland and 'could claim to be a national breed'. Personally I suspect that the breed must have been at least partially revived before the publication of Scrope's infamous work, for three years was an extremely short space of time in which to enjoy such a remarkable turn-around in popularity and I wonder, too, how great that turn-around really was, for other writers still regarded the Deerhound as decidedly rare, at least in its purest form. It is interesting to note that in 1907 Robert Leighton described Scrope's book as 'neglected'.

The tenacity of Deerhounds at work is illustrated by two of Scrope's half-bred dogs, Percy and Douglas, who, between them, kept a stag at bay from Saturday night until Monday morning. Bran, who was pure-bred, pulled down alone two unwounded stags, one with ten and the other eleven tines.

At that time the Menzies of Chesthill, Loch Tay, had a notable pure strain and the Deerhounds owned by the McNeills of Colonsay were also well known. Certain confusion, however, arose between the rough-haired Greyhound of Yorkshire and the Scottish Deerhound. Indeed Dr John Walsh stated that they were two different breeds but were 'identical',

Figure 34   'Near the Finish' by Sir Edwin Landseer, 1820.

although they could be 'readily distinguished by the way they ran and the way they played'!

The breed comes into fashion

Queen Victoria had Deerhounds in her kennels both at Windsor and at Sandringham where they were under the care of Mr Cole, and some dogs were known later as the 'Mr Cole Breed'. In the Highlands it reached its greatest popularity when Queen Victoria and Prince Albert were in residence at Balmoral where Solomon, Hector and Bran were amongst the Balmoral hounds. It was Bran who was used for Landseer's model in his picture 'High Life'; by repute he was an especially fine dog, standing over 30 inches at shoulder. Keildar was used for hunting deer in Windsor Park and at that famous show at Islington in 1869 four of Her Majesty's Deerhounds were shown.

Going still further back through those old show records it is interesting to note that Deerhounds were one of the very few breeds classified separately, albeit with only one class, at the first Manchester Dog Show at Belle Vue Zoological Gardens in 1861. Moving on to the Islington Show of 1863 Deerhounds were said to be one of the breeds in which there were 'fair entries', one, Oscar, being awarded a first prize. At the fourth Birmingham Show of that same year the Duke of Beaufort took several prizes with the various breeds of dogs exhibited by him at the show, some of which were

Figure 35 Scotch Greyhound as depicted in J. G. Wood's *Illustrated Natural History*, 1861. Compare with the Russian Greyhound on page 42 and Persian Greyhound on page 172.

Deerhounds. Indeed classes for the breed seemed to be scheduled with some consistency throughout the 1860s and 1870s.

The breed had been reduced in size, many standing no more than 26 inches at the shoulder, although there were occasionally some larger specimens such as Lord Breadalbane's King of the Forest, measuring 33 inches at withers. It was at this point that concerted efforts were made to bring the breed back to its former excellence and this was done by the introduction of completely new blood from other breeds. A dog named Spey, whelped in 1868, had Bloodhound in his pedigree and Captain Graham made an interesting purchase from Mr Cole's widow on 15 February 1870. This was Keildar who, as mentioned earlier, was used to stalk deer at Windsor. He stood 30¼ inches at the shoulder, and was brindle fawn in colour with a soft but not woolly coat. One of his grandsires was a 'black Russian Wolfhound' and elsewhere in his pedigree he went back to a purebred Deerhound male named Tank who was bought by Mr Cole from

Tankerville Castle in about 1858 (see pedigree page 83). Captain Graham had started his kennel of Deerhounds upon return from India in an endeavour to 'rebuild' the Irish Wolfhound.

Size seems always to have been a topic of conversation in the breed. Dr John Henry Walsh who, incidentally, wrote under the pseudonym of 'Stonehenge', used as his representative dog in 1852, Buskar, who measured 28 inches at shoulder. In 1872 the following list of measurements was given:

Dogs	Inches	Bitches	Inches
Charlie	27½	Brae	27
Arran	29¾	Luffra	26
Colin	28	Hilda	26
Morna	30	Meg	26
Torrum	30	Bertha	26
Bruce	28	Juno	26
Oscar	28	Hylda	29
Young Torrum	30¼	Brenda	28
Bismarck	28		
Oscar	28		
Warrior	28		
Young Warrior	28		
Roswell	28		
Aitkin	28		

Opposite is the pedigree of Mr Dadley's Hector who was whelped in 1873. Described as a 'fine, big dog of the McNeill strain', he stood 31 inches at shoulder.

Deerhounds in the mid-nineteenth century were very varied, some with good hard coats, others with woolly ones, resembling that of a sheep. Whilst some were well built and full of quality, others were very coarse. Edward Ash describes Ch Old Torrom, born in 1866 and descended from King of the Forest, as having 'a bad coat and bad limbs, and a very coarse head and big ears', earlier described as 'all over of the coarsest'. And yet he was a champion!

In the 1880s Captain Graham drew up a list of the most notable Deerhounds over the previous century and in the list he included Sir St George Gore's Gruim (notable 1843–4), Black Bran (notable 1850–51), King of the Forest, Mr Beasley's Alder (notable 1863–7) who was bred by Sir John McNeill of Colonsay, Mr Donald Cameron's Torrum (notable 1869) and his two sons Monzie and Young Torrum. Mr Dadley's Hector was also included, he being probably the best-bred dog living in the early 1880s.

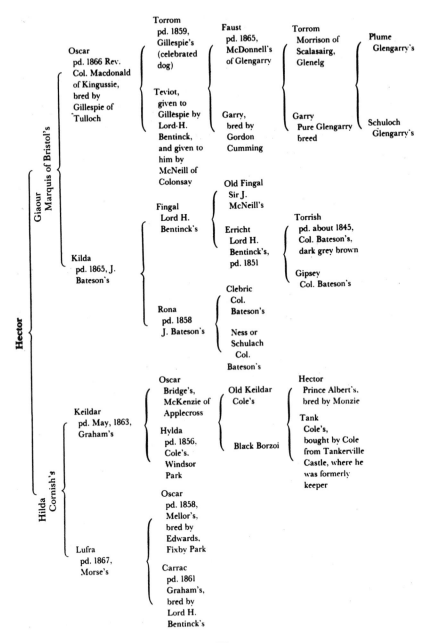

Figure 36 The pedigree of Mr Dadley's Hector.

Of the above, Torrum seems to have been the most successful stud dog and was a 'grand specimen of his race, strong framed, with plenty of hair of a blue brindle colour'. Described as 'one of the most elegant and aristo-cratic looking Deerhounds ever seen' was Captain Graham's own dog, Keildar, trained for deerstalking in Windsor Park. He stood 30 inches high, weighed 95 lbs and had a girth of 33 ½ inches; he was bluish fawn in colour, slightly brindled and his ears were blue. In terms of 'perfection', other than Hector, Keildar's nearest competitor was probably Mr Hood Wright's Bevis; standing 29 inches at shoulder he was 'a darkish red brown brindle'.

E. Watson Bell, writing in 1892, felt that the judges of his day had 'fads'. In his opinion, the head was to be 'broad at ears where set on'. He stressed that it was not to be thick and coarse 'but should show a distinct line from ear to ear, flat at top, then taper gradually to the eyes, and then distinctly to the nose'. Bell's comments about the eye are fascinating:

> The eye should as near as possible resemble the eye of the terrier. This is a description given me in account of the true breed by an experienced old breeder in the North; but this is now almost lost, owing to the fact that the Deerhound was at one time crossed with the bulldog and bloodhound. Naturally, the small eye was of great use to this dog, as it enabled him to see a greater distance than does the bold round eye which he now possesses. Regarding the colour of the eye, some say a light coloured dog should have a light eye; others, again, affirm that the colour of the eye should be black, or nearly so. From our stand-point they should possess dark eyes. *(The Scottish Deerhound)*

He also considered the ear to be very important, as indeed it is, saying that:

> A coarse, flat ear on a dog, built on the finest-made lines, takes from him entirely his beauty and aristocratic bearing, and at once indicates that a 'cross' has been introduced at one time. The ear should lie flat on the sides of his head, folded back, well set on, and small. Some of the dogs of the present day have hair all over their ears, with a long fringe, and yet are looked upon as fine specimens of the breed.

He goes on to explain how the breed at that time was labouring under a decided mixture of strains and that breeders were 'so mixed up' that they had many 'different types of animals' appearing before them so that 'dark ears, with hair long and fringy, or not' was still a matter of opinion. In his opinion he believed that whilst the black, smooth-eared dog certainly had a very striking appearance, it took away from the 'general shaggy, rough, Highland tyke-like look' which he thought the Deerhound should possess. Bell went on to make many constructive comments but it is, sadly, not possible to include them all here. I do, however, feel that some description of the actual construction of the breed cannot be omitted:

> The shoulder blades should be close together, and shoulders sloping; for if the tops of the shoulders are wide apart and the stifle straight, the hound cannot give a proper bound but only a short jump. When, however, the shoulder blades are close together and the stifle well bent, then the hound can give a bound and spring twice his own length. . . . Feet well set up and toes close together and by no means flat, though some hounds are weaker here than others, and if made to jump, or run after a horse or carriage on hard roads too much, they have a great tendency to become flat-footed. . . . The body should be long, not cobby; slightly arched, showing elasticity, grace and freedom. The hips should be broad, showing great strength, with thighs of good muscular development, long and well-defined. Herein lies the chief moving power of the deerhound for the spring and bound. Stifles well bent, long thighs, and broad hips. When all are put into action he is so constructed as to give a greater length of spring than any other dog of his size.

His comments about coat might be helpful to owners of the breed today and so I shall include them for it would be a pity to leave out more than necessary of Bell's wisdom. As many readers will know only too well, seaching for an original copy of his book is like searching for gold-dust!

> The coat or hair of the deerhound should be hard and rough, wiry and straight, not going into a curl. I have had and seen hounds with soft coats mixed with hard, and this is in many cases caused by the undercoat not being allowed to come up and choke the coat proper; and if this wool is taken away or kept down, the hard or original coat will reappear.
>
> The deerhound in olden times was not housed in the same way as he is at present, and had more of his natural exercise. This alone kept his coat in perfect order, which in almost all cases was crisp and hard. For example, take a herd of Highland cattle; keep them out all winter, in all weathers, and their coat will no doubt get thin, but finer, freer, and more wiry than those stalled in a byre. There the coat gets choked up by the undercoating, and after the cattle are turned out into the fields this again falls off.

The favourite colour of breeders for the show-bench was 'dark-blue' or 'grey-brindle' although formerly the light fawn colour was much more desirable, the dark dogs being despised. The reason lighter ones were originally preferred was said to be that they could be more easily seen on the hillside (although I would have thought that they might also be more easily seen by the quarry). Other colours being bred just before the turn of the twentieth century were blue-brindle, fawn, brindle, red-brindle, red, fawn, sandy-coloured and 'almost black and white'. White was not considered a proper colour for the breed, some authorities saying that it denoted a cross although fine specimens of the breed could also be found in this colour. Indeed white markings on the hound were considered a sure sign of impure blood although a little white on toes and chest was 'passable'. Bell felt that although some specimens of the breed were said to have been 33–36 inches in height, no authenticated records of these could be found and in his opinion 'they could not have been deerhounds at all'.

The very varied opinions held by breeders and judges of the day caused many exhibitors to keep a large kennel of hounds of varying 'types', each hound being shown only under the judges which would appreciate his qualities. The very fact that there was such a variety of preferences could not have been good for the breed and many thought that great harm was being done. Apparently breeders of Deerhounds 'fluctuated greatly' and at that time there were very few who had bred and exhibited the breed for more than twenty or twenty-five years.

In the light of the foregoing comments, it perhaps comes as no surprise that the Deerhound Club was formed in 1892. With its formation the use of outside crosses came to an end and a standard of points was drawn up. There were feelings at the time, however, that the curtailment of outside crosses was not to the breed's advantage for it had not yet fully recovered.

The breed only just managed to hold its own in the years which followed and dogs were sold from renowned kennels at prices ranging from as little as one guinea to six guineas. Mr Hood Wright was also the breeder of Ch Selwood Morven who was at his peak of winning in 1897, later becoming the property of Mr Harry Rawson. Morven stood 32⅜ inches at the shoulder and had a girth of chest of 34½ inches; he was a 'dark heather brindle'. In 1898 Selwood Callach was considered to be one of the best dogs living but from photographs it appears that his hindquarters could have been somewhat improved.

The following 'Description of the Deerhound' was drawn up by Messrs Hickman and Hood Wright; amended and approved at a meeting of the Deerhound Club on 26 November 1892 it was finally endorsed at a Club meeting held in Shrewsbury in June 1901:

HEAD: The head should be broadest at the ears, tapering slightly to the eyes, with the muzzle tapering more decidedly to the nose. The muzzle should be pointed, but the teeth and lips level. The head should be long, the skull flat, rather than round, with a very slight rise over the eyes, but with nothing approaching a stop. The skull should be coated with moderately long hair, which is softer than the rest of the coat. The nose should be black (though in some blue-fawns the colour is blue) and slightly aquiline. In the lighter coloured dogs a black muzzle is preferred. There should be a good moustache of rather silky hair, and a fair beard.

EARS: The ears should be set on high, and, in repose, folded back like the Greyhound's, though raised above the head in excitement without losing the fold, and even in some cases semi-erect. A prick ear is bad. A big thick ear hanging flat to the head, or heavily coated with long hair, is the worst of faults. The ear should be soft, glossy, and like a mouse's coat to touch, and the smaller it is the better. It should have no long coat or fringe, but there is often a silky, silvery coat on the body of the ear and the lip. Whatever the colour, the ears should be black or dark-coloured.

NECK AND SHOULDERS: The neck should be long – that is of the length that befits the Greyhound character of the dog. An over-long neck is not necessary nor desirable, for the dog is not required to stoop to his work like a Greyhound, and it must be remembered that the mane, which every good specimen should have, detracts from the apparent length of the neck. Moreover, a Deerhound requires a very strong neck to hold a stag. The nape of the neck should be very prominent where the head is set on, and the throat should be clean cut at the angle and prominent. The shoulders should be well-sloped, the blades well back and not too much width between them. Loaded and straight shoulders are very bad faults.

STERN: Should be tolerably long, tapering, and reaching to within 1½ inches of the ground, and about 1½ inches below the hocks. When the dog is still, dropped perfectly straight down, or curved. When in motion it should be curved when excited, and in no case to be lifted out of the line of the back. It should be well-covered with hair, on the inside, thick and wiry, underside longer, and towards the end a slight fringe not objectionable. A curl or ring tail very undesirable.

EYES: The eyes should be dark; generally they are dark brown or hazel. A very light eye is not liked. The eye is moderately full, with a soft look in repose, but a keen far-away look when the dog is roused. The rims of the eye-lids should be black.

BODY: The body and general formation is that of a Greyhound of larger size and bone. Chest deep rather than broad, but not too narrow and flat-sided. The loin well-arched and drooping to the tail. A straight back is not desirable, this formation being unsuitable for going uphill, and very unsightly.

LEGS AND FEET: The legs should be broad and flat, a good broad forearm and elbow being desirable. Forelegs, of course, as straight as possible. Feet close and compact, with well-arched toes. The hindquarters drooping, and as broad and powerful as possible, the hips being set wide apart. The hindlegs should be well bent at the stifle, with great length from the hip to the hock, which should be broad and flat. Cow hocks, weak pasterns, straight stifles, and splay feet are very bad faults.

COAT: The hair on the body, neck and quarters should be harsh and wiry, and about three or four inches long, that on the head, breast and belly being much softer. There should be a slight hairy fringe on the inside of the fore and hindlegs, but nothing approaching the 'feather' of a Collie. The Deerhound should be a shaggy dog, but not overcoated. A woolly coat is bad. Some good strains have a slight mixture of silky coat with the hard, which is preferable to a woolly coat, but the proper coat is a thick, close-lying, ragged coat, harsh or crisp to the touch.

COLOUR: This is much a matter of fancy. But there is no manner of doubt that the dark blue-grey is the most preferred. Next comes the darker or lighter greys or brindles, the darkest being generally preferred. Yellow and sandy red or red fawn, especially with black points, i.e. ears and muzzles, are also held in equal estimation, this being the colour of the oldest known strains, the McNeill and the Chesthill Menzies. White is condemned by all the old authorities, but a white chest and white toes, occurring as they do in a great many of the darkest coloured dogs, are not so greatly objected to, but the less the better, as the Deerhound is a self-coloured dog. A white blaze on the head or a white collar should entirely disqualify. In other cases, though passable, yet an attempt should be made to get rid of white markings. The less white the better, but a slight white tip to the stern occurs in the best strains.

HEIGHT OF DOGS: From 28 to 30 inches, or even more if there be symmetry without coarseness, but which is rare.

HEIGHT OF BITCHES: From 26 inches upwards. There can be no objection to a bitch being large, unless too coarse, as even at her greatest she does not approach that of the dog, and therefore could not have been too big for work, as over-big dogs are. Besides, a big bitch is good for breeding and keeping up the size.

WEIGHT: From 85 to 105 lbs in dogs; from 65 to 80 lbs in bitches.

As the breed moved into the twentieth century prominent owners included Mrs H. Armstrong, who bred Talisman and Laird of Abbotsford, two reputedly 'beautiful' dogs. She also had two typically good bitches in Fair Maid of Perth and Bride of Lammermoor. Mrs W. C. Grew was another who had many 'admirable specimens', including Blair Athol, Ayrshire,

Kenilworth and Ferraline. Ayrshire was considered by some judges to be the most perfect specimen of the breed exhibited at that time and though perhaps a little larger than desirable was of 'excellent quality and character, having a most typical head, with lovely eyes and expression, perfect front, feet and hind-quarters'. There were other judges, though, who preferred Mr Harry Rawson's St Ronan's Ranger, sire of Ch St Ronan's Rhyme, the bitch who was, in 1906, to be awarded Best in Show (all breeds) both at Crystal Palace and the Scottish Kennel Club Shows, under different judges. She was said to be 'possibly the most flawless Deerhound of any time'. Other leading breeders of the period were Mrs Janvin Dickson, Miss A. Doxford and Mr H. McLauchlin.

In 1907 Robert Leighton published some of the notes made by Mrs H. Armstrong which read as follows:

> Though fast disappearing from the annals of hunting, the Deerhound is a great favourite to-day as a household pet and personal companion, and well worthy is he of his place; for not only is he wondrous gentle for his great size, but he is faithful, sensible, and quiet. The latter quality, indeed, may almost be considered a fault, for except for his formidable size and appearance, which strikes terror in the hearts of evildoers, he cannot be said to be a good watch, inasmuch as he will either welcome all comers as personal friends, or he will of his dignity and stateliness overlook the approach of strangers *(The New Book of the Dog)*.

Mrs Armstrong goes on to make the following comment:

> Unfortunately, today the Deerhound is a most delicate and difficult dog to rear. Perhaps this is due to the extraordinary amount of inbreeding which has been so largely resorted to in this race. In order, probably, to keep the type and character, as also the pure lineage, we have the same names occurring over and over again in the same pedigree.

Mrs Armstrong's closing paragraph still rings true of the breed today:

> In conclusion, let me add that I think 'once a Deerhound lover, always a Deerhound lover', for there is something about the breed which is particularly attractive; they are no fools, if brought up sensibly, and they are obedient, while, for all they are so large, it is astonishing what little room they occupy: they have a happy knack of curling themselves up into wonderfully small compass, and lying out of the way. They do not require a very great amount of food, and are readily and easily exercised, as, if let loose in some field or other place, they soon gallop themselves tired. They are as a rule excellent followers, either in town or country, keeping close to heel and

walking in a dignified manner; while on the approach of a strange dog, a slight raising of the head and tail is all the notice they deign to give that they have even seen a passing canine.

Shortly before the First World War, of sixty deer forests there were only six in which Deerhounds were kept for sporting purposes and in 1922 Leighton, in *The Complete Book of the Dog,* was to say, '. . . the inventions of the modern gunsmith have robbed one of the grandest of hunting dogs of his glory, relegating him to the life of a pedestrian pet, whose highest dignity is the winning of a pecuniary prize under Kennel Club rules'.

Fact or fable?

There are many stories about dogs which were thought to be Deerhounds, though it is sometimes debatable as to whether or not they were indeed true representatives of the breed. In the days of Bruce a white deer escaped the hounds on several occasions and it was said that two hounds belonging to Sir William St Clair could take the deer. These were the now famous Help and Hold. The King bet the Forest of Pentland Moor against the head of Sir William that the hounds would not take the stag before it reached the other side of March Burn. Sir William kept his head and obtained Pentland Moor, thanks to his hounds, Help and Hold. Their owner now rests in Rosslyn Chapel with, so it is said, a Deerhound at his feet but the effigy bears little resemblance to one of the breed.

The story of Bran is also now famous. He was purchased by Lord Tankerville from a poacher, and had never missed a deer. After parting with the dog the poacher went home with understandable misgivings. Much to his surprise, however, Bran came out to meet him having made his way back to his former home. There being only two ways back it is presumed that he did not take the road on which the poacher was returning but swam across the loch, which was no less than fourteen miles long.

Beth Gelert

The story of Beth Gelert as described in the following poem is perhaps one of the most loved and descriptive canine stories ever, one to trouble the hearts of any dog lover. I have included it in the Deerhound section for it is with this breed that the story is most frequently associated and, undoubtedly, the story is worthy of inclusion somewhere in this book. Written by Willam Robert Spencer and dated 11 August 1800, the poem runs thus:

90

The Deerhound

The spearmen heard the bugle sound,
And cheerly smiled the morn;
And many a brach, and many a hound,
Obeyed Llewellyn's horn.

And still he blew a louder blast,
And gave a lustier cheer;
 'Come Gelert, come, wer't never last
Llewellyn's horn to hear.

'Oh, where does faithful Gelert roam,
The flower of all his race;
So true, so brave, a lamb at home,
A lion in the chase?'

'Twas only at Llewellyn's board
The faithful Gelert fed;
He watched, he served, he cheered his lord'
And sentinel'd his bed.

In sooth, he was a peerless hound,
The gift of Royal John;
But now no Gelert could be found,
And all the chase rode on.

And now, as o'er the rocks and dells,
The gallant chidings rise,
All Snowdon's craggy chaos yells
With many-mingl'd cries.

That day Llewellyn little lov'd
The chase of hart and hare
And scant and small the booty prov'd,
For Gelert was not there.

Unpleased Llewellyn homeward hied,
When near the portal seat,
His truant Gelert he espied,
Bounding his Lord to greet.

But then he gain'd his castle door,
Aghast the chieftain stood;
The hound all o'er was smear'd with gore,
His lips, his fangs, ran blood!

Llewellyn gaz'd with fierce surprise;
Unus'd such looks to meet,
His Fav'rite check'd his joyful guise,
And crouch'd and lick'd his feet.

Onward in haste Llewellyn pass'd –
And on went Gelert too –
And still, where'er his eyes were cast,
Fresh blood-gouts shock'd his view!

O'erturned his infant's bed he found
The bloodstained covert rent;
And all around, the walls and ground,
With recent blood bespent.

He called his child – no voice replied;
He searched – with terror wild.
Blood! blood! he found on every side,
But nowhere found the child!

'Hell-hound! my child's by thee devour'd'
The frantic father cried;
And to the hilt his vengeful sword
He plung'd in Gelert's side!

His suppliant looks, as prone he fell,
No pity could impart;
But still his Gelert's dying yell
Pass'd heavy o'er his heart.

Arous'd by Gelert's dying yell,
Some slumberer wakened nigh:-
What words the parent's joy could tell
To hear his infant's cry?

Conceal'd beneath a tumbled heap
His hurried search had miss'd,
All glowing from his rosy sleep,
The cherub-boy he kiss'd.

Nor scathe had he, nor harm, nor dread,
But, the same couch beneath,
Lay a gaunt wolf, all torn and dead,
Tremendous still in death!

Ah, what was then Llewellyn's pain!
For now the truth was clear:
His gallant hound the wolf had slain
To save Llewellyn's heir.

Vain, vain, was all Llewellyn's woe:
'Best of thy kind, adieu!
The frantic blow that laid thee low,
This heart shall ever rue!'

And now a gallant tomb they raise,
With costly sculpture decked;
And marbles, storied with his praise,
Poor Gelert's bones protect.

Here never could the spearman pass,
Or forester, unmoved;
Here oft the tear-besprinkled grass
Llewellyn's sorrow prov'd.

And here he hung his horn and spear;
And there, as evening fell,
In fancy's ear he oft would hear
Poor Gelert's dying yell.

And, till great Snowdon's rocks grow old,
And cease the storm to brave,
The consecrated spot shall hold
The name of 'Gelert's Grave'.

Well, would you like to think the story true, or would you rather it were not? As my heart tears without fail each time I read it, I have a leaning toward the latter, despite the fact that there is, in Caernarvonshire, a stone under which the faithful Gelert was apparently buried. Indeed there is good reason to believe that it is nothing more than a fable. There was a guide-book called *Bedd Gelert: Its Facts, Fairies and Folklore* published in Portmadoc in 1899, for which the author, Mr D. E. Jenkins, seems to have carried out a good deal of local research. It is said that until 1793 no one had heard of a dog named Gelert but in that year an enterprising landlord of the Royal Goat Hotel at Bedd Gelert needed to attract customers. Recalling the Welsh proverb, 'I repent as much as the man who slew his greyhound,' he decided that the greyhound might well have been slain on that very spot, and might well have been called Gelert, for the translation of the place name means 'grave of Gelert'. And so he placed a gravestone and told the story of the faithful, but unfortunate, Gelert to many including Spencer. When one looks more closely into the various stories in folklore one can see strong similarities between this story and others of Europe as well as those of India.

SEVEN

THE DEERHOUND TODAY

Temperament and adaptability

The temperament of the Deerhound is such that it was not even mentioned in earlier breed standards. Many present-day Deerhound enthusiasts continue to look to the original standard, so I suppose I should not have been surprised when at a seminar a speaker erroneously advised the audience that there was no temperament clause for the breed. 'There does not need to be,' said she. Clearly the point of Kennel Club Breed Standards is that we abide by them and breed dogs true to type so that they fit the standard. Therefore, now that a temperament clause does exist, we must do our utmost to breed to meet its stipulations. Having said that, temperament is, in general, not a problem within the breed although, sadly, one does very occasionally encounter an ill-tempered Deerhound. Miss Norah Hartley, a lady who has spent her whole life with the breed, described him as 'obedient and gentle, trusting and unsuspicious' and said he 'gives companionship to people who value those qualities'.

It may seem strange that a breed which is so large can be easy to manage, but an adult Deerhound is so, primarily because it is exactly as specified by the relevant clause in the Standard, 'Gentle and friendly. Obedient and easy to train because eager to please.' A Deerhound is a true friend and when he looks up at you with those meaningful, deep eyes which have not changed through the centuries you know that he will be faithful to you through thick and through thin. I think that one of the most lovely pictures I have hanging on my wall is one by Herbert Dicksee, etched in 1894, and entitled 'Silent Sympathy'. A young girl looks down, somewhat sadly, into the glow of a fire whilst her faithful Deerhound stares up at her face as if to ask, 'Is there *anything* I can do to help?' That certain look has gone on unchanged through the years and it is easy to understand why so many enthusiasts of the breed have remained faithful to it throughout their lives. Interestingly, it is said that the Deerhound is one of only two breeds which has remained entirely unchanged over the last century.

The following paragraph, from a letter written in 1902, was quoted in the *History of the Deerhound Club:*

. . . if anyone wants a delightful and graceful companion, one who will give his heart's devotion to his owner; who will either rejoice in the gaiety of a happy mood, or, noting the serious humour of his master, will walk with his muzzle in the hand he so loves, let them, before all breeds, keep and cherish that most noble, most historic and romantic dog – the Deerhound.

A Deerhound certainly seems to miss his owners when they are not at home, judging from the jubilant welcome he gives even after very short absences. I sometimes wonder whether Deerhounds have perhaps an inability to judge length of time, or is it just that they love us so much that they don't want us out of their sight for one minute!

A Deerhound will never mean to cause you any harm but sometimes just

Figure 37
Characteristics of the Deerhound as sketched by Miss B Branfoot in the early 1930s

a quick upward movement of the head can be sufficient to do damage, possibly to one's own underjaw if one is seated in an armchair, for example. A Deerhound is built strongly enough to bring down a stag and the strength of neck, especially, needs to be felt to be believed. The breed, though, is very little trouble and can quite happily find a discreet spot away from the main activity of the sitting room and most will take their ease and relax through whatever happenings are going on in the house.

The need for reprimand is infrequent and never should they be too severely checked for they are a sensitive breed and risk losing their gaiety if treated harshly.

When exercising, again it is important to recognise that a Deerhound can have travelled a good distance from your side before you realise it and there are, unfortunately, an uncomfortably high number of stories of accidents which befall the breed when it is out running. The breed is, however, biddable, but it must be trained early. Most Deerhound owners have the odd story about how, on just that one occasion, old so-and-so did something totally out of character. I used to live surrounded by grouse moors on and around which sheep grazed almost throughout the year, and I found

Figure 38   Co-bred by the author and Carol Ann Johnson is Modhish Lilly Langtree at fourteen weeks, with her three-year-old dam, Kilbourne Lottie at Modhish

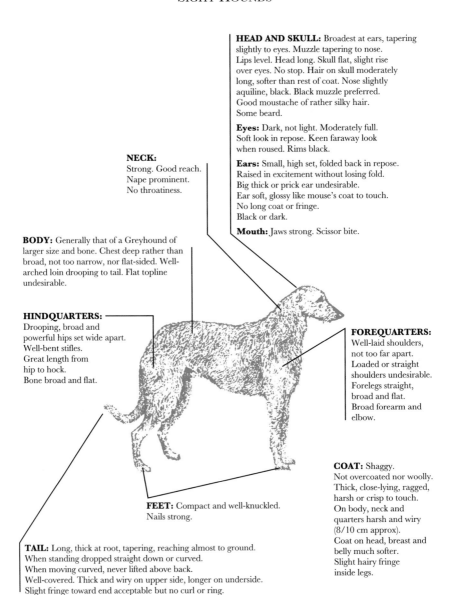

HEAD AND SKULL: Broadest at ears, tapering slightly to eyes. Muzzle tapering to nose. Lips level. Head long. Skull flat, slight rise over eyes. No stop. Hair on skull moderately long, softer than rest of coat. Nose slightly aquiline, black. Black muzzle preferred. Good moustache of rather silky hair. Some beard.

Eyes: Dark, not light. Moderately full. Soft look in repose. Keen faraway look when roused. Rims black.

Ears: Small, high set, folded back in repose. Raised in excitement without losing fold. Big thick or prick ear undesirable. Ear soft, glossy like mouse's coat to touch. No long coat or fringe. Black or dark.

Mouth: Jaws strong. Scissor bite.

NECK: Strong. Good reach. Nape prominent. No throatiness.

BODY: Generally that of a Greyhound of larger size and bone. Chest deep rather than broad, not too narrow, nor flat-sided. Well-arched loin drooping to tail. Flat topline undesirable.

HINDQUARTERS: Drooping, broad and powerful hips set wide apart. Well-bent stifles. Great length from hip to hock. Bone broad and flat.

FOREQUARTERS: Well-laid shoulders, not too far apart. Loaded or straight shoulders undesirable. Forelegs straight, broad and flat. Broad forearm and elbow.

COAT: Shaggy. Not overcoated nor woolly. Thick, close-lying, ragged, harsh or crisp to touch. On body, neck and quarters harsh and wiry (8/10 cm approx). Coat on head, breast and belly much softer. Slight hairy fringe inside legs.

FEET: Compact and well-knuckled. Nails strong.

TAIL: Long, thick at root, tapering, reaching almost to ground. When standing dropped straight down or curved. When moving curved, never lifted above back. Well-covered. Thick and wiry on upper side, longer on underside. Slight fringe toward end acceptable but no curl or ring.

Figure 39   The Deerhound breed standard in brief.

it essential for my hounds to be trained so that they could be totally trusted with sheep.

A Deerhound is not a noisy dog and it is sometimes easy to forget where they are, their having secreted themselves in some quiet corner. They will usually welcome a stranger provided that their owner equally gives a warm welcome, but their very size can act as a deterrent to any would-be intruder.

A Deerhound in good health does not need artificial heat if kennelled outside but those who are ageing or ailing, and also young puppies, greatly appreciate a heated pad or an infra-red heat lamp, positioned where it cannot cause harm.

Young puppies should not have a great deal of exercise until the period of fastest growth is over but when full-grown they will take as much exercise as their owners wish to give.

Kennel Club Breed Standard © The Kennel Club

GENERAL APPEARANCE: Resembles a rough-coated Greyhound of larger size and bone.

CHARACTERISTICS: The build suggests the unique combination of speed, power and endurance necessary to pull down a stag, but general bearing is one of gentle dignity.

TEMPERAMENT: Gentle and friendly. Obedient and easy to train because eager to please. Docile and good-tempered, never suspicious, aggressive or nervous. Carries himself with quiet dignity.

HEAD AND SKULL: Broadest at ears, tapering slightly to eyes, muzzle tapering more decidedly to nose, lips level. Head long, skull flat rather than round, with very slight rise over eyes, with no stop. Skull coated with moderately long hair, softer than rest of coat. Nose slightly aquiline and black. In lighter coloured dogs black muzzle preferred. Good moustache of rather silky hair and some beard.

EYES: Dark. Generally dark brown or hazel. Light eyes undesirable. Moderately full with a soft look in repose, but keen, far-away look when dog is roused. Rims black.

EARS: Set on high and in repose folded back. In excitement raised above head without losing the fold and in some cases semi-erect. A big thick ear hanging flat to the head or a prick ear most undesirable. Ear soft, glossy and like a mouse's coat to the touch; the smaller the better, no long coat or fringe. Ears black or dark-coloured.

MOUTH: Jaws strong, with a perfect, regular and complete scissor bite, i.e. the upper teeth closely overlapping the lower teeth and set square to jaws.

NECK: Very strong with good reach sometimes disguised by mane. Nape of neck very prominent where head is set on, no throatiness.

FOREQUARTERS: Shoulders well laid, not too far apart. Loaded and straight shoulders undesirable. Forelegs straight, broad and flat, a good broad forearm and elbow being desirable.

BODY: Body and general formation that of a Greyhound of larger size and bone. Chest deep rather than broad, not too narrow and flat-sided. Loin well arched and drooping to tail. Flat topline undesirable.

HINDQUARTERS: Drooping, broad and powerful, hips set wide apart. Hindlegs well bent at stifle with great length from hip to hock. Bone broad and flat.

FEET: Compact and well knuckled. Nails strong.

TAIL: Long, thick at root, tapering and reaching almost to ground. When standing dropped perfectly straight down or curved. Curved when moving, never lifted above line of back. Well covered with hair; on upper side thick and wiry, on under-side longer, and towards end a slight fringe is not objectionable. A curl or ring tail undesirable.

GAIT/MOVEMENT: Easy, active and true, with a long stride.

COAT: Shaggy, but not overcoated. Woolly coat unacceptable. The correct coat is thick, close-lying, ragged; harsh or crisp to the touch. Hair on body, neck and quarters harsh and wiry about 8 cm (3 inches) to 10 cm (4 inches) long; that on head, breast and belly much softer. A slight hairy fringe on inside of fore- and hindlegs.

COLOUR: Dark blue-grey, darker and lighter greys or brindles and yellows, sandy-red or red fawns with black points. A white chest, white toes and a slight white tip to stern are permissible but the less white the better, since it is a self-coloured dog. A white blaze on head or white collar unacceptable.

HEIGHT OF DOGS: Minimum desirable height at withers 76 cm (30 inches).

HEIGHT OF BITCHES: 71 cm (28 inches).

WEIGHT: About 45.5 kg (100 lbs) for dogs, about 36.5 kg (80 lbs) for bitches.

FAULTS: Any departure from the foregoing points should be considered a fault and the seriousness with which the fault should be regarded should be in exact proportion to its degree and its effect upon the health and welfare of the dog.

NOTE: Male animals should have two apparently normal testicles fully descended into the scrotum.

Judging the breed

A Deerhound should be instantly recognisable as one of its kind and should in no way bear more than a passing resemblance to its cousin, the Irish Wolfhound. The breed should have a somewhat rugged look about it and clearly an uncharacteristic ear is undesirable, as is too heavy a skull. One should seek well-laid shoulders and powerful quarters and under no circumstances should a judge be misled by the slightly curved topline, which is correct for the breed. The tail, which should be of good length, should also be low-set and one should seek moderate bone throughout. It is not always easy to find the desired gait, which should ideally be easy, active and true, as required by the standard.

Figure 40
Angela Randall with her Deerhound, Ch. Kilbourne Celtic at Hammonds

Movement

Especially in recent years the movement of the Deerhound has come in for some criticism and as the breed standard says very little about the subject, it may be prudent to elaborate slightly although, unfortunately, in a book of this nature space does not permit a complete analysis of the breed's construction.

The Deerhound's stride can be compared to that of a racehorse, being long and low. In profile one should be able to see a good free stride both fore and aft and the feet should be lifted clear of the ground. A hackney action is definitely not required and this faulty movement can be caused by a short upper arm or, alternatively, a shoulder which is too steep. If shoulder placement is incorrect the dog can often also be out at elbow and, in the Deerhound, this can be seen both from the front and from the back when the dog is stacked. Naturally, any dog which is out at elbow will show this clearly in his movement, usually 'pinning in' as a result. Unfortunately, all too frequently a Deerhound suffers from a combination of these structural faults in the forehand and there is a danger of it not always being noted as incorrect.

Sometimes a Deerhound can be well constructed but can still move badly and this is often due to the fact that there is insufficient development of muscle, something which is very important, especially in a breed as large as this. Besides a certain amount of roadwork a Deerhound must be given sufficient exercise by way of free running if it is to reach its potential in the show-ring.

Grooming

Some exhibitors bath their Deerhounds quite frequently, others only rarely, if ever. However, a certain amount of 'tidying up' is done to the coat by owners of many show specimens. Clearly the coat needs an occasional groom with a wide-toothed comb for there is some length to the coat and tangles can occur. One of the benefits of a coat which tangles is that the coat does not shed greatly. Deerhounds, incidentally, do not have a 'doggy' smell.

The texture of the coat on the ear should be like that of a mouse and, to emphasise the appearance of neatness and smallness of size of the ear, any long hairs which inconveniently grow on it are discreetly taken out by hand. Similarly, any hair detracting from the typically compact shape of the foot is removed. It is important that nails are kept in trim, especially in a breed which requires the feet to be well-knuckled. You may note that the breed standard calls for strong nails and indeed they are! Straight-edged nail clippers, of however good a quality, will hardly touch the nail and tend to leave jagged ends, apart from which extreme strength is required. Thankfully, after some years of struggling with the former, I discovered that clippers of the guillotine type seem to work much more efficiently and are strongly to be recommended. If your hound will tolerate it, an electric nail file can also be useful.

Ailments or lack of them

Although occasional problems crop up from time to time, there are no particular ailments which seem to trouble the Deerhound more than any other breed; indeed they are rarely troubled by interdigital cysts or ear infections. It is unusual for a Deerhound to become grossly overweight but it is important to remember that they should not be exercised for a good while before or after feeding. Unfortunately they can do themselves damage when running freely, especially on rough terrain, but I regret that this is one of those risks one has to take with a large, fast-moving breed.

Kennel Club registrations for 1908–1934 and at five-yearly intervals from 1950–2000

1908	85	1917	14	1926	59
1909	95	1918	3	1927	84
1910	71	1919	25	1928	97
1911	71	1920	27	1929	77
1912	73	1921	31	1930	68
1913	62	1922	41	1931	76
1914	35	1923	48	1932	48
1915	46	1924	64	1933	78
1916	14	1925	83	1934	68
1950	72	1970	146	1990	252
1955	44	1975	110	1995	257
1960	62	1980	170	2000	249
1965	88	1985	216		

The Deerhound Club

The Deerhound Club, which celebrated its centenary in 1986, is something of an institution. It still has one club and one alone, and an enormous membership despite the fact that following the First World War it was predicted that the breed might even die out altogether. One of the things which stands out when looking through records of the Club's history is the very substantial number of years that certain people have held office. The late Miss Nora Hartley (Rotherwood), for example, was Hon Secretary for no fewer than thirty-two years, after which she became Chairman and served the club faithfully until she died. The late Dr Phyllis Poyner-Wall (Melchoir), also sadly no longer with us, served many years as Hon Secretary and the late Miss Anastasia Noble (Ardkinglas) rose to President in 1980, having been Chairman of Committee for twenty eight years beforehand. Another long-serving Officer of the club was Miss Cecily Cox (Dufault) who remained so loyal to the Deerhound Club until the end of her days. The very consistency and devotion of people such as these can only augur well for a breed club. They, and others, held the breed together through the years and tried to keep it in the hands of enthusiasts, rather than those who might attempt to exploit it. The Hon Secretary is now Miss Mary Girling (Pyefleet), another very loyal devotee of the Club.

Indeed, even from the early days the Club has had many people who have given it long service, not least of these being Sir Walter Evans, who was President for twenty-five years and, incidentally, also President of the Birmingham National Show. Members of the Club owe their thanks to Sir Walter's generosity for the design and die of the Club badges.

The joint Honorary Secretaries and Treasurers in 1921 were the Misses Loughrey (Ross) who saw the Club through the war years and gave devoted service to it, Miss H. M. Loughrey remaining its President until her death. Her sister was breed note correspondent for *Our Dogs* from 1928 until 1970, no fewer than forty-two years. In 1947, when the Club resumed full activity after the war, Miss Marjorie Bell (Enterkine) was appointed Treasurer. One had to smile as Miss Hartley described how she and Miss Bell sorted through the Club's accounts at the close of each year. It seems that Miss Bell was at her most mathematical early in the day whilst she was at her best nearer to midnight! Miss Bell eventually gave up her toils as Treasurer, though not until 1963, and her place was filled by Miss Linton who was a meticulous keeper of accounts, aided to a certain extent by Mr Culley.

The Deerhound Club's newsletter is ever-popular and the Club also has a Coursing Section which holds a few meetings each year, primarily in the east of England and in Scotland where hares are plentiful.

Since 1966 the Deerhound Club has had a Breed Show each year and this, of the Club's choosing, has remained an Open Show event. It was felt by the majority that were it to have championship status the atmosphere would be lost. After all, say the Deerhound people, 'We don't want any more sets of Challenge Certificates, we have quite enough.' How refreshing it is to meet a club which still values things that other clubs have lost. One Open show a year it might be, but what a show it is! Held in a different location each year, it spans two days and musters enormous entries which include not only the dogs which have been campaigned consistently throughout the year but also some which are kept primarily as pets and just come out to the Club's annual event. The Club manages to take over a large hotel for the weekend or perhaps a number of smaller hotels, depending on the location, and at one of the formal dinners the Club's trophies are awarded. I have been to a goodly number of events held by many different clubs over the years, but never have I ever seen such a thoroughly splendid display. There is also a Club Show held, since 1982, in conjunction with the Hound Association's Championship Show and at which many special trophies are on offer. It was first mentioned in Club records in 1912 but is believed to have commenced before then. In recent years the Deerhound Club has also held a Limited Show, which is also strongly supported.

For the Club's centenary year Annette Pink put together a most interesting and comprehensive booklet entitled 'The History of the Deerhound Club' which discloses a wealth of fascinating information. We read of Deerhounds becoming mascots of several famous regiments during the First World War, one of these being Bruce of Abbotsford who led the 1st Battalion Scottish Regiment. It was typical of such a thoughtful club that subscriptions were waived for all members on foreign service whilst they were attached to an overseas force. Sadly we read also of the depression affecting entries in the early 1930s and the fact that classification had to be reduced owing to a drastic fall in entries, but the breed slowly regained strength and by the end of the decade things were much improved. However, in Deerhounds, as in all other breeds at that time, the approach of the Second World War brought with it concern as to the welfare of dogs and there was controversy as to whether owners should or should not have them put down. The Secretary of the Deerhound Club, ever mindful of the breed, wrote in *Our Dogs*:

> If war comes the Government has pointed the way to all animal lovers. Large establishments will doubtless have to make very many sorrowful decisions, but there is no reason why, besides the dearly loved companion, who will help to dispel the gloom of dark hours, a nucleus of important lines should not survive until reasons are shown for more drastic measures. We are not

at war yet; no one knows what may happen before these lines are in print, but one thing is certain, dog owners will pull their weight.

Within one week, the following message was printed.

> Hitler has let loose the dogs of war. How far these terrible beasts will affect our dogs is something only time will show. The war that was fought to end all wars took toll of many kennels, and it is a sobering thought to realise that of all those that came through that conflict only the Ross hounds remain today. On the brighter side we can take comfort from the Government's assurance that there is no reason to destroy animals at the moment.

Club members thankfully kept in touch with each other throughout those difficult years and many hounds were 'evacuated' to other breed enthusiasts living in country areas. There were about sixteen breeders who managed to retain a limited amount of breeding stock through the war and some good dogs were exported to the USA, thus preserving some of the best lines. There were reports of some hounds going back to their owners towards the end of 1944 and by the end of the war there was still an enthusiastic band of members intent on resuming their breeding and showing activities. Despite there being no championship shows for a while the Club urged members to attend as many of the smaller shows as possible so as to let the public know that the breed was far from extinct.

Indeed the success and stability of the breed today owes much to the Deerhound Club which has served the breed so faithfully for well over a hundred years.

The name, address and telephone number of the Honorary Secretary of the Deerhound Club can be obtained from the Kennel Club.

EIGHT

THE GREYHOUND

> He is a combination of art and Nature, that challenges the
> world, unequalled in speed, spirit, and perseverance, and, in
> elegance and beauty of form, as far removed from many of his
> clumsy ancestors as an English thoroughbred from a coarse
> dray-horse.
>
> HUGH DALZIEL

Early Greyhounds

The Greyhound, Mastiff and Molossian hound were the three kinds of dog
principally used by the Greeks. Socrates spoke of snares and nets having
been prohibited, from which we can deduce that the use of such methods
of capture was unsporting.

In AD 124 Arrian, the Greek historian, described a Greyhound bitch he
had bred, saying she was swift, hard-working, courageous and sound-
footed, proving a match for four hares. At home his bitch stayed by his side,
and followed him when outdoors. When she wanted her share of the food,
she would pat him with one foot, and then the other. Indeed Arrian loved
his Greyhound for he spoke of her with such affection and even suggested
that such hounds should sleep with a person, for they rejoiced in the
company of human beings.

Arrian's *Treatise on the Greyhound* was not
published in English until 1831, at which
time readers were treated to many a word
of wisdom about this glorious breed. In
describing how to judge a fast, well-bred
Greyhound he said, 'First, let them stand
long from head to stern . . . let them have
light and well-knit heads . . . Let the neck be
long, rounded and supple . . . Broad breasts
are better than narrow, and let them have
shoulder blades standing apart and not

Figure 41   Celtic Greyhound   fastened together . . . loins that are broad,

Figure 42
Celtic Greyhound on silver coin

Figure 43
Celtic Greyhound on brass coin

strong not fleshy, but solid with sinew . . . flanks pliant . . . Rounded and fine feet are the strongest.'

It is generally believed that the Celts introduced the Greyhound to Britain from Asia, although the date is not clear. However, it is also commonly accepted that the Celtic tribe known as the Belgae took with them hounds when they emigrated to Scotland and to Ireland.

It is clear that by Saxon times the Greyhound was firmly established in Britain. In AD 500, as we recall, two 'white-breasted brindled greyhounds' ran beside Prince Kilburgh in south-west Wales, as he travelled to Arthur's court. In the eighth century, Elfric, Duke of Mercia had in his kennels dogs of unmistakably Greyhound type, and there is a ninth century manuscript portraying a Saxon chieftain with his huntsman and a brace of Greyhounds. We know, too, that Edward the Confessor took great delight in following a pack of swift hounds in the pursuit of game.

The breed was mentioned in King Canute's Forest Laws, these made at Winchester in 1016. Commoners were forbidden to own Greyhounds, although freemen could keep them under certain stringent conditions. Those that lived within ten miles of the forest had to be cut at the knee, so as to prevent them from hunting. This was not necessary if they lived further away, but if they approached the forest any nearer the fee payable was twelve pence per mile. If a Greyhound was found inside the forest, its owner had to forfeit the hound and also pay ten shillings to the king.

We know that at this time the Greyhound was large and powerful enough to hunt both the wolf and wild boar and before the signing of the Magna Carta in 1215 it was evident that the breed was held in enormously high esteem, for if such a hound were destroyed it was treated as being equal to the murder of a man. Greyhounds could also be used in payment for debts owed, sometimes coupled with other prized animals, such as horses.

Records show that in 1203, in payment for a debt owing to him, King John received 500 marks, ten horses and ten leashes of Greyhounds.

Between the eleventh and fourteenth centuries, the Greyhound was undoubtedly a symbol of class regalia, and considered the dog of royalty and nobility. So much did the ruling classes wish to preserve their own hold on the breed that special officers travelled around the country, calling at hamlets and villages so that any local Greyhounds they found could be maimed. It is important to realise that at this time the countryside was incredibly dense and bridle paths and pilgrims' routes were often the only way of reaching hamlets. England's countryside teamed with game and was an essential source of food supply, not only for the ruling and upper classes, but also for common folk. As a result, in practice, the Forest Laws represented a period of class prejudice in which those who enjoyed sport with the Greyhound kept utterly under their control those who actually relied on the breed for obtaining their food.

Despite the stringent laws, the breed was not destroyed, and some people continued to retain their hounds. Proof that the breed was kept other than by royalty and nobles in the Middle Ages comes to us from Chaucer who wrote of his Monk who had swift Greyhounds that hunted hare. The Greyhound has long played an important part in British life, for the very name 'Isle of Dogs' in London was derived from the fact that it was where Edward II (1327–1377) kept his Greyhounds and Spaniels.

A particularly interesting description of a Greyhound, the first of its kind, was a written by Edmund de Langley, a son of Edward III. Langley was Master of the Hounds and Hawks to Henry IV and in around 1360 he wrote a treatise *Master of Game* as a book of instruction in Greyhound matters. This was for the pleasure of Prince Henry, who was of course later to become King Henry V.

> The Greihound should have a long hede and somedele grete, ymakyd in the manner of a luce; a good large mouth and good sessours, the one again the other, so that the nether jaws passe not above them, ne that thei above passe not him by neither.
>
> The neck should be grete and longe, and bowed as a swanne's neck.
>
> Her shuldres as a roebuck; the for leggs streght and grete ynow, and nought to hind legges; the feet straught and round as a catte, and great cleas; the boones and the joyntes of the cheyne grete and hard as the chyne of an hert; the thighs great and squarred as an hare; the houghs streight; and not crompyng as of an oxe.
>
> A catte's tayle, making a ring at eend, but not to hie.
>
> Of all manere of Greihoundes there byn both good and evel; Natheless the best hewe is rede falow, with a black moselle.

The Boke of St Albans

In 1486, the celebrated *Boke of St Albans* was written, this marking the first time in English literature that the whole subject of Greyhounds and hare hunting had been addressed. Authorship is much disputed, but the following verse is attributed to Dame Juliana Berners who was thought to have been prioress of Sopewell nunnery.

'A grehund should be heded lyke a snake and necked lyke a drake, foted lyke a kat. Syded lyke a bream. Chyned lyke a beme.' Thc following is just one of the many slightly differing versions printed over the years:

> A greyhound should be headed like a Snake,
> And necked like a Drake,

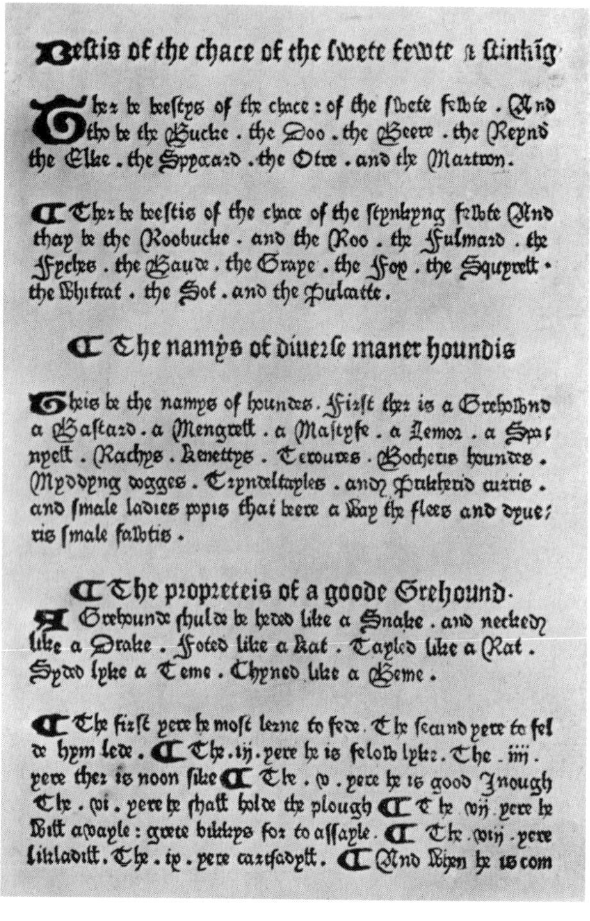
Bestis of the chace of the swete fewte & stinkyng

Ther be bestys of the chace: of the swete fewte. And tho be the Bucke. the Doo. the Beere. the Reynd the Elke. the Spycard. the Otre. and the Martron.

Ther be bestis of the chace of the stynkyng fewte And thay be the Roobucke. and the Roo. the Fulmard. the Fyches. the Baude. the Grays. the Fox. the Squyrell. the Whitrat. the Sot. and the Pulcatte.

The namys of diuerse maner houndis

Thies be the namys of houndes. First ther is a Grehownd a Bastard. a Mengrell. a Mastyfe. a Lemor. a Spanyell. Rachys. Kenettys. Teroures. Bocheris houndes. Myddyng dogges. Tryndeltaylles. and Prikherid currys. and smale ladies popis that bere a way the flees and dyuers smale fawtis.

The propreteis of a goode Grehound.

A Grehounde shulde be heded like a Snake. and necked like a Drake. Foted like a Kat. Tayled like a Rat. Syded lyke a Teme. Chyned like a Beme.

The first yere he most lerne to fede. The secund yere to feld hym lede. The.iij.yere he is felow lyke. The.iiij.yere ther is noon sike. The.v.yere he is good Inough The.vi.yere he shall holde the plough The.vij.yere he will avayle: grete bikkys for to assayle. The.viij.yere likladill. The.ix.yere cartsadyll. And when he is com

Figure 44
First page of *The Boke of St Albans* 1486

Footed like a Cat,
Tailed like a Rat,
Sided like a Team,
Chined like a Bream.

The first year he must learn to feed,
The second year to field him lead,
The third year he is fellow-like,
The fourth year there is none sike,
The fifth year he is good enough,
The sixth year he shall hold the plough,
The seventh year he will avail
Great bitches for to assail,
The eighth year lick ladle,
The ninth year cart saddle,
And when he is comen to that year

Figure 45 Dr Caius' sketch of a Greyhound as described by Dame Juliana Berners.

Have him to the tanner,
For the best hound that ever bitch had
At nine year he is full bad.

Some sixty years later, in *Country Contentments*, Gervase Markham said that
the Greyhound was 'of all dogs whatsoever the most princely, strong,
nimble and valiant'. He went on to say, 'Now after your dog comes to full
growth, as at a year and a half, or two years old, he would then have a fine
long lean head, with a sharp nose, rush grown from the eye downwards; a
full clear eye with long eyelids, a sharp ear, short and close falling, a long
neck and a little binding, with a loose handing wezand, a broad breast,
straight forelegs, side hollow, ribs straight, a square and flat back, short and
strong fillets, a broad space between the hips, a strong stearn or tayl and a
round foot and good large clefts.'

Figure 46
Greyhounds hunting
the hare in 1686

Still, though, we are given no indication of size of the breed and virtually no mention of coat, but it is highly likely that even then there were two general types, one larger and rougher, used to hunt larger game, and a smaller, finer dog, used for hares. This is borne out by Dr Johannes Caius, who in *English Dogges*, written in 1576, talks of some 'of a greater sorte', and 'some of a lesser'. He also tells his readers that 'some are smooth skinned and some are curled'.

Clearly much of the information above relates to the Deerhound we know today, though it must be appreciated that at that time all such hounds, whether they be large or smaller, smooth coated or longer-haired came under the general title of 'greyhound'.

Coursing the Greyhound

> As when the impatient Greyhound, slipped from far,
> Bounds o'er the glade to course the fearful hare
> She in her speed does all her safety lie,
> And he with double speed pursues his prey,
> Overruns her at the sitting turn; but licks
> His chaps in vain; yet blows upon the flix.
> She seeks the shelter which the neighbouring covert gives,
> And, gaining it, she doubts if yet she lives.

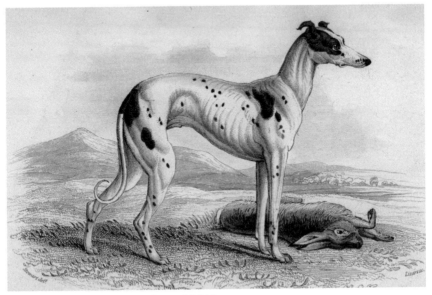

Figure 47   The British Greyhound 1840

The above verse was written by the Latin poet, Ovid, and it is through his work and that of Virgil that we can be sure that the Greyhound was used in sport around the time of the birth of Christ.

Even as far back as 4000 BC there was a competitive element in coursing, leading eventually to codes of practice. In the latter part of the sixteenth century the Duke of Norfolk stipulated that a hare was never to be coursed with more than a brace of Greyhounds, and that she could not be killed whilst 'on her seat'. The quarry also had to be given twelve score yards before the hounds were loosed so they would leap on her before she rose. In Tudor England the Greyhound was used on deer, hare and fox and certainly in hare coursing the dog that actually killed was not necessarily considered the better of the two forming the brace.

Although Queen Elizabeth I did not always hunt personally, she frequently witnessed coursing by Greyhounds from the comfort of her residence. She was a great devotee of the chase and apparently enjoyed hunting hare as much as she did deer. She was said to be as enthusiastic about her 'deer hounds' as she was about her Greyhounds. At her command, the Duke of Norfolk codified many conventions and practices, raising coursing

Figure 48 'Death of ye Hare with Fleet Hounds' 1640

Figure 49 Queen Elizabeth I hawking (from Turberville's *Booke of Falconrie*, 1611 edition).

to the status of a sport. This set of rules ensured fairness both to the quarry and to the hounds, and it was really from the mid-sixteenth century onward that coursing became such a great field sport.

Lord Orford formed the first coursing club in 1776. This was at Swaffham. Lord Orford was a tremendous enthusiast, and indeed bred the very famous Czarina who was unbeaten in forty-seven courses. Remarkably, at the age of thirteen, she whelped to Claret, who in turn was to become the sire of another famous coursing hound, Snowball.

Lord Orford set about developing a faster Greyhound and for this he experimented with several crosses, including the Bulldog, Deerhound, Lurcher and Italian Greyhound. His reason for using the Bulldog was to increase persistence and although his theories were in general considered somewhat absurd, he did indeed develop a breeding programme of which he could be proud. His dogs were considered by many to be the fastest and the most sturdy, making them the most efficient running dogs. He never parted with a Greyhound until it had had sufficient time to prove its speed, and sometimes kept as many as fifty brace of Greyhounds.

115

Figure 50   Greyhound from Wood's Natural History

When Lord Orford died, Colonel Thornton bought his best hounds and so they moved to Yorkshire and to Norfolk. However, on flat country their success fell below expectations.

The Swaffham Club was a great success and following in its footsteps were Ashdown Park (1780), Malton (1781), Newmarket (1805), Amesbury (1822) and the widely acclaimed Altcar Society in 1825. Altcar was to become to coursing what Wimbledon is to tennis, or Lord's to cricket. The eight-dog stake for the Waterloo Cup of 1836 was increased to a sixteen-dog stake the next year and by 1838 had been enlarged still further, to thirty-two. In 1857 it became a sixty-four-dog stake and remained so.

Some famous early winners

Cerito weighed around fifty-one pounds, won her first cup in 1850 and went on to win three Blue Ribands in four attempts, a remarkable feat given that a bitch is generally believed to lose pace more quickly than a dog. In all she won forty-five of her fifty-three courses.

Master McGrath was Lord Lurgan's famous black dog who successfully

116

Figure 51   Fullerton – Waterloo Cup winner

contested his fourth Cup at the Altcar Classic in 1871. After this victory, Queen Victoria desired to meet him and Master McGrath was duly presented at Court. Along with Fullerton, Master McGrath can probably be counted as the greatest coursing Greyhound of all time.

Other early greats were Bab At The Bowster, Bed of Stone and Miss Glendyne. Bab ran sixty-seven courses and Bed of Stone, a bitch, ran eighty. This remarkable lady won thirty courses out of thirty-one, in her very first season. Coomassie was probably the smallest Greyhound to win at Altcar, for when she won the Cup in 1877, she was a fawn puppy weighing only forty-two pounds.

Of course there have been many greats since Fullerton, but it is fitting that in his memory we should close this short section with a little more about him. Sired by Greentick and out of Bit of Fashion, Fullerton, bred by Edward Dent, was purchased by Colonel North as a puppy for the sum of 840 guineas, this then being a record price for a Greyhound. He was a well-built, brindle hound, weighing some sixty-five and a half pounds. He won thirty-one of his thirty-five courses, three Waterloo Cups outright, and one divided. His Purses amounted to £1,910. Fullerton's last success was in 1892. Fullerton's body, along with that of Mick the Miller, another famous winner idolised by many in the 1920s, is preserved in the British Museum.

The coursing Greyhound to this day is smaller than that found in the show ring, and interestingly the majority of winners of the Waterloo Cup have been fairly small. The numbers of coursing Greyhounds registered far exceed numbers registered with the Kennel Club for show purposes.

Track racing

From coursing developed track racing, which was in part to create a means of controlling the crowds of onlookers at coursing meetings. The artificial lure was developed and first used in England in 1876. This was at a sporting show at the Welsh Harp, Hendon where one of the attractions was two Greyhounds chasing a mechanical lure. This was a stuffed rabbit that ran on a four hundred yard-long rail; it was operated by a windlass and pulled from one end of a field to the other. The hounds were said to have followed the artificial hare 'like so many kittens after cork' and that it was amusing to watch the Greyhounds striving to overtake the phantom hare. Unfortunately it did not prove popular at this early stage, but it is enormously fascinating that the winner of this race was Charming Nell, who was bred by Mr Edward Dent, the breeder of Fullerton.

Soon, though, the American entertainment industry recognised the potential of the sport of track racing. Racing in Florida was a novelty at first but was to become an entertaining spectacle that gripped its audience. Other states followed and dog racing became all the rage in the United States.

In the early years of the twentieth century track racing become popular in Britain too, when a lure was developed that could be run around a track. In 1926 the first track racing stadium was created at Belle Vue in Manchester. It proved difficult to obtain the hounds to take part in the new sport, for coursing owners were not prepared to co-operate. They thought their true coursing hounds would not be sufficiently stupid to chase a 'tin-rabbit'! As a result the Greyhound Racing Association had to actually buy the dogs so that enough dogs would be available to run the first event.

How wrong the coursing fraternity proved to be! On the first night the crowd was 1,700, of which only half of them had paid an admission fee, but only a couple of meetings later 16,000 people paid for admission at Belle Vue's turnstiles. Greyhound racing had come to stay.

In April of 1927 Liverpool had opened a track, with White City at Shepherd's Bush, London, opening in June. Two other tracks opened in Harringay and Wembley also that year. But track racing was soon to become a victim of its own success, for competition became fierce in this sport in which betting played such an integral part. To counter this, in 1928 the National Greyhound Racing Society and the National Greyhound Racing Club were formed to protect the interests of those engaged in, or otherwise interested in Greyhound racing.

118

The early Greyhound in the show ring

In 1903 we read that Greyhound classes at shows varied greatly in the number of dogs exhibited. Generally they were not well filled and it was the exception rather than the rule to find any coursing dog of merit entered on the show-bench. However, there were exceptions, Maney Starlight being one, a bitch who was a good courser and a show-bench winner. Major Harding Cox's brindle bitch, Ch True Token, was another hound successful in the coursing field and in the ring. She weighed sixty-one pounds and had wonderful symmetry. It appears that some took exception to her flat ribs, but her owner explained that this was due to her great turn of speed, for she had tremendous depth through the brisket, wonderful staying power and lovely flush shoulders. Although she was seldom shown, she easily gained her Championship title, but sadly she left no progeny.

Writing in 1907, Robert Leighton said 'It appears like descending from the sublime to the ridiculous to mention the Greyhound as a show dog, after the many brilliant performances that have been recorded of him in the leash, but there are many dogs elegant in outline to be seen in the judging ring.' Mr George Roper's fawn and white Roasting Hot was one of the most

Figure 52   Greyhound 'Lauderdale' 1881

prominent winners of the day, added to which he was also good in the field. Indeed at that time there were indeed a few hounds that could both run well and win prizes at shows. This could be said of several Greyhounds in the kennels of Major Harding Cox, Miss Maud May and Mrs A. Dewé.

Major Harding Cox, or Mr as he was then, considered that on the show-bench there was a tendency to pay too much attention to size, and yet amongst running Greyhounds there was often too great a lack of bone and depth of brisket. Staying power was frequently regrettably sacrificed to points of speed. Harding Cox wrote so eloquently when he said, 'I love the Greyhound for its great beauty of balance, its striking symmetry, its exemplification of a perfect piece of living speed machinery, and its high-bred quality; and lastly, for the exhilarating sport it affords in the coursing field.'

Miss Maude May thought much had been done to improve the Greyhound, but she wondered whether or not the breed's staying power of fifty years prior had been retained. She saw the Greyhound as the most courageous and graceful of all dogs and, when kindly treated, the most affectionate of companions.

Writing in 1904, Mrs A. Dewé, who had then been breeding them with some success for twenty-one years, was not satisfied with many then on the show-bench. She felt that the Greyhound that was fancied in the show ring would have been useless for the purpose for which it was originally intended, namely coursing. She did, however, consider many excellent dogs were indeed shown, and that they had improved over the last year or two. Her biggest complaint was that there were in the ring several with poor quarters, wheel backs, flat sides with no heart room, and no muscle at the shoulder. Their long necks would have been absolutely no use to them in the field.

I quote another eloquent writer, Theo Marples, former Editor of *Our Dogs* who wrote a few decades on, 'The loins should be slightly arched, very broad and thick, like two big Atlantic cables traversing the dog's back, and merging into broad and big hindquarters, the muscles of which should resemble two big round loaves of bread stuck on the dog . . . Colour is an altogether immaterial point; a good Greyhound, like a good horse, cannot be a bad colour. The tail should be long and strong, since it is to the dog what the rudder is to the ship.'

In the late 1920s and 1930s several Greyhounds were exported to the USA, so that various US kennels were founded on British stock prior to the Second World War. In Britain, the Canlanga and Parcancady kennels that had been well-established prior to the war were two of a handful of dominant kennels that put together breeding programmes after the war had finished, when food had become more readily available.

The breed standard drawn up by the South West Greyhound Club in 1938 was based on Ch Lady of Lelant who had won the Challenge

Certificate at Crufts in 1938 and Best in Show at Paignton the following year. In its early days the current Greyhound Club used the same breed standard.

A Greyhound kept in India

In 1904 Herbert Compton gave a most interesting account of a Greyhound he had kept in India as part of a 'scratch pack' for jackal coursing. This hound, 'Chris' was a gaunt brindle and white, bred from parents that had been taken to India from England. As he pointed out, the cost of the freight of a dog to India was £5, so Chris's parents must presumably have been worth more than their passage money!

Compton's intention in buying Chris was to add speed to his pack, although he thought he would not be up to the task of tackling a jackal. He therefore also bought a Rampur Hound, a much heavier animal, and altogether stronger and more savage. As it turned out, Chris soon proved himself far the better of the two. Chris assisted in killing numerous jackals, doing the major part of the work himself. Compton even witnessed him detecting something from the verandah and setting off to hunt on his own account, killing a jackal on his own.

Amongst Chris's many plucky feats was a 'battle royal' with a huge jungle cat which he described as being like a leopard in miniature. Chris followed the cat into a small cave or hole where he had no room to turn and fought in the dark. The Rampur Hound stood respectfully at the entrance, encouraging him. No Bull Terrier could have tackled the cat more valiantly than Chris, and his owner had never known a more remarkable deed carried out by a non-fighting dog. The cat was one of many that Chris killed; indeed his proboscis was so chronically swollen that his muzzle often looked more like a Great Dane's than a Greyhound's, from the effects of maulings by fangs and claws.

This remarkable Greyhound's devotion was equal to his enterprise. He would follow his master out snipe-shooting, and even though he hated wetting his feet, would go into the water after a wounded duck. But not all his toils were completely successful. On one occasion he made a clumsy attempt to climb a tree after a squirrel, but got stuck half way up. At this point he set to work howling to be helped!

Chris was never averse to a bit of mousing and killed the odd scorpion, something he did, like other dogs in India, by cracking them with his teeth, his lips tucked back as neatly as possible. There were no wolves in the area, but his master thought that had there been any, judging from the way he manfully overcame the big dog-jackals, he would certainly have had a go at them. Lastly, it is perhaps worth mentioning that Chris developed a keen sense of smell and would frequently put up game or his master whilst out shooting. These he tracked to cover by scent alone.

What's in a name?

The name 'Greyhound' has been spelled in many different ways over time. 'Grehouunde', 'griehounde', 'grayhounde', 'graihiound', 'grewhound' and 'grewnd', are all names by which the breed has been known.

There are various differing theories as to the derivation of this hound's name, one that it was drawn from the ancient English word *grech* or *greg*, meaning 'dog'. Others believe the name, including the word 'grey', albeit spelled in different ways, refers to the colour of the breed in its early days. Having said that, there is no reason to believe that grey has at any time been the prevailing colour.

Another possibility is that the name actually implies that the breed is a Gallic hound, which originated in Gaul. The word *'grew'* however, was also used for 'Greek', which might indicate that the breed had a connection with Greece.

The Greyhound in the Americas

The Greyhound found its way to the Americas with the Spanish in the sixteenth century, and also with early British colonists. On America's Great Plains they were used to protect crops from devastation by rabbits, and they were also highly useful in protecting livestock from coyotes. They were versatile in the different types of game they hunted, but were most highly renowned for their expertise with hare and rabbit.

The Greyhound was one of the first six hound breeds to be registered with the American Kennel Club, but it was actually the only Sight Hound amongst them. To this day, the breed is kept as a sporting hound as well as a companion, and since the 1920s it has been used for track racing. Perhaps it is understandable that America's infamous Greyhound buses carry the breed's name, clearly a name that conjures up immediate images of efficiency, speed and endurance.

NINE

THE GREYHOUND TODAY

Temperament

An affectionate, gentle and faithful breed with an even temper and quiet disposition, the Greyhound makes a wonderful companion dog. The Greyhound can also be fun to live with for it has a quiet sense of humour too. It is a highly expressive breed and delightfully relaxed in its demeanour. Sensitive and intelligent, the Greyhound is a quick learner. It is also a pack dog and is quite happy to accept a human into its pack, but sensible management is of course necessary so that the Greyhound fully realises that the human is the pack leader. However, owners must never overlook the fact that the Greyhound has an enormous amount of stamina and that the fastest of the breed can run at over forty-five miles an hour, so those who choose to own this breed need sufficient time, and space to allow their hound to live a happy, fulfilled life.

It is also essential to remember that Greyhounds have the ability to chase and to catch virtually anything that moves, and this can include cats. If brought up to accept smaller animals from puppyhood, many a Greyhound can live alongside family pets in total harmony, but a stray cat venturing into the garden is likely to be prey, so please be warned! Those who take on a retired racing Greyhound should also realise that it is unlikely to have been trained to accept cats and other family pets, though can indeed be trained to tolerate them.

Grooming

Grooming the Greyhound is not enormously time-consuming, but none-theless, coat care is an integral part of good canine management. To keep the coat looking its shiny best a natural bristle brush or a hound glove will be needed; either or both of these can be used for regular daily care. Daily brushing will remove any dead hair and will stimulate the Greyhound's natural oils to give a shine to the coat. Regular grooming sessions are enjoyable for the hound, and provide an opportunity to build up a close rapport between dog and owner.

Frequency of bathing depends on personal preference and whether or not the Greyhound is a show specimen. Many owners consider bathing essential to maintain a healthy coat and skin. Bathing should commence at an early age, so that the bathing routine has become thoroughly familiar by the time he is fully grown.

Brush the hound thoroughly before wetting the coat, and be sure there is a non-slip surface to stand on. A shower or hose attachment is essential for thoroughly wetting and rinsing the coat, and of course it is important to check the water temperature, before it touches the dog. When applying the shampoo this should be worked into a good lather, working the shampoo all the way down to the skin, but leaving the head until last and taking care not to allow the shampoo to drip into the eyes. Rinse off very thoroughly because any shampoo left in the coat can irritate the skin. Apart from protecting the eyes, do not allow water to get into the ear canal. After a bath a Greyhound should be kept in a comfortably warm environment until the coat is thoroughly dry, or an artificial drying aid can be used if preferred.

It is important to keep ears and teeth clean, and nails in trim. Owners should start to trim a Greyhound's nails early in life, so that he becomes accustomed to the procedure, for many hounds tend to be rather sensitive about a pedicure! Hounds that have plenty of road work will need their nails trimming less frequently, but they must be regularly checked. Some owners like to use an electric nail file, either to use instead of clippers, or just to put a neat finishing touch.

Exercise

Given the nature of the breed, the Greyhound clearly needs plenty of exercise. Indeed this is a high maintenance breed to keep in optimum physical shape. Controlled walking on a hard surface is essential, but so is the opportunity to have a good free run in a large garden or enclosed field.

No dog should suddenly be given a large amount of exercise, but this should be built up slowly and as with any large breed, exercise during the growth stage should be very carefully controlled.

Kennel Club Breed Standard © The Kennel Club

GENERAL APPEARANCE: Strongly built, upstanding, of generous proportions, muscular power and symmetrical formation, with long head and neck, clean well laid shoulders, deep chest, capacious body, arched loin, powerful quarters, sound legs and feet, and a suppleness of limb, which emphasise in a marked degree its distinctive type and quality.

CHARACTERISTICS: Possessing remarkable stamina and endurance.

TEMPERAMENT: Intelligent, gentle, affectionate and even-tempered.

HEAD AND SKULL: Long, moderate width, flat skull, slight stop. Jaws powerful and well chiselled.

EYES: Bright, intelligent, oval and obliquely set. Preferably dark.

EARS: Small, rose-shape, of fine texture.

MOUTH: Jaws strong with a perfect, regular and complete scissor bite, i.e. the upper teeth closely overlapping lower teeth and set square to the jaws.

NECK: Long and muscular, elegantly arched, well set into shoulders.

FOREQUARTERS: Shoulders oblique, well set back, muscular without being loaded, narrow and cleanly defined at top. Forelegs, long and straight, bone of good substance and quality. Elbows free and well set under shoulders. Pasterns of moderate length, slightly sprung. Elbows, pasterns and toes inclining neither in nor out.

BODY: Chest deep and capacious, providing adequate heart room. Ribs deep, well sprung and carried well back. Flanks well cut up. Back rather long, broad and square. Loins powerful, slightly arched.

HINDQUARTERS: Thighs and second thighs wide and muscular, showing great propelling power. Stifles well bent. Hocks well let down, inclining neither in nor out. Body and hindquarters, features of ample proportions and well coupled, enabling adequate ground to be covered when standing.

FEET: Moderate length, with compact, well knuckled toes and strong pads.

TAIL: Long, set on rather low, strong at root, tapering to point, carried low, slightly curved.

GAIT/MOVEMENT: Straight, low-reaching, free stride enabling the ground to be covered at great speed. Hindlegs coming well under body giving great propulsion.

COAT: Fine and close.

COLOUR: Black, white, red, blue, fawn, fallow, brindle or any of these colours broken with white.

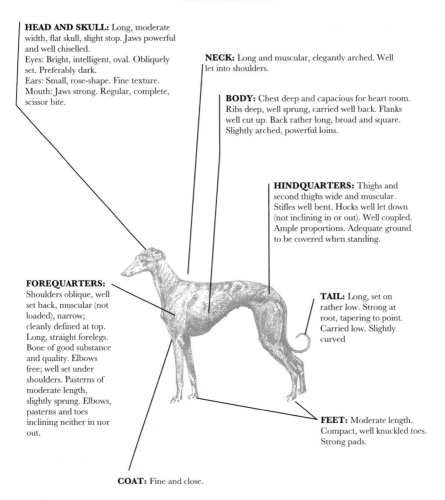

HEAD AND SKULL: Long, moderate width, flat skull, slight stop. Jaws powerful and well chiselled.
Eyes: Bright, intelligent, oval. Obliquely set. Preferably dark.
Ears: Small, rose-shape. Fine texture.
Mouth: Jaws strong. Regular, complete, scissor bite.

NECK: Long and muscular, elegantly arched. Well let into shoulders.

BODY: Chest deep and capacious for heart room. Ribs deep, well sprung, carried well back. Flanks well cut up. Back rather long, broad and square. Slightly arched, powerful loins.

HINDQUARTERS: Thighs and second thighs wide and muscular. Stifles well bent. Hocks well let down (not inclining in or out). Well coupled. Ample proportions. Adequate ground to be covered when standing.

FOREQUARTERS: Shoulders oblique, well set back, muscular (not loaded), narrow; cleanly defined at top. Long, straight forelegs. Bone of good substance and quality. Elbows free; well set under shoulders. Pasterns of moderate length, slightly sprung. Elbows, pasterns and toes inclining neither in nor out.

TAIL: Long, set on rather low. Strong at root, tapering to point. Carried low. Slightly curved

FEET: Moderate length. Compact, well knuckled toes. Strong pads.

COAT: Fine and close.

Figure 53   The Greyhound breed standard in brief.

SIZE: Ideal height: dogs: 71–76 cms (28–30 ins); bitches: 69–71 cms (27–28 ins).

FAULTS: Any departure from the foregoing points should be considered a fault and the seriousness with which the fault should be regarded should be in exact proportion to its degree and its effect upon the health and welfare of the dog.

NOTE: Male animals should have two apparently normal testicles fully descended into the scrotum.

Judging the breed

There is absolutely do doubt that the show Greyhound is quite different from the Greyhound bred for the track, the latter usually being considerably smaller. However, a few racing and coursing Greyhounds do find their way into the show ring and there is increasing interest in the Special Coursing classes which are scheduled for Greyhounds and breed shows, the Hound Show and Crufts.

The Greyhound is one of the more strongly built of the Sight Hound breeds, though of course the Irish Wolfhound is much more massive. Although a bitch should be smaller than a male, she should not be fine or delicate in any way.

A show Greyhound is required to have suppleness of limb, which means that it should not be overly muscled but elastic and supple, displaying the distinctive quality for this rather regal hound. It is of vital importance that this, a running breed, has a deep, capacious chest, so as to provide adequate

Figure 54   Knut Fr Blutecher and his Greyhound bitch English, Int., Nord. Ch. Showline Silent Step

heart and lung room, and the ribs should be well-sprung and carried well back.

There are not many Greyhounds in UK show rings, so it is not always easy to gain hands-on experience if not closely involved with the breed. However there are many stunning hounds out there and any judge worth his salt, when he sees one, will know its good qualities and appreciate them to the full.

Major wins in the UK

Despite relatively low Kennel Club registrations and numbers of Greyhounds exhibited at shows, there have been several dogs that have received high accolades in the show ring. Indeed there have been several notable breeders who have been dedicated to the Greyhound and have reaped their just rewards.

In her very first Greyhound litter, whelped in 1951, Judy de Casembroot produced Ch Treetops Hawk, thought by many to be the most influential sire in the Greyhound world today. He sired twenty champions during the 1950s. Judy de Casembroot and Bobbie Greenish's Treetops Golden Falcon won Best in Show at Crufts in 1956. Later this dog was sold to Prince Hussain, going to live in Pakistan where he lived until the ripe old age of fourteen years.

Other notable dogs went through to win Groups at Crufts in later years, Ch Shalfleet Sir Lancelot in 1973, Ch Solstrand Double Diamond in 1978 and Ch Mistweave Making Waves in 2003. At general and single Group Championship shows there have been several other Group and Best in Show winners over the years, but to this day none has yet beaten the record number of thirty-three Challenge Certificates won by Ch Royal Portrait. Clearly despite its low numbers, the breed is strong enough to compete and succeed at the very highest level.

Greyhound rescue

Sadly racing Greyhounds are frequently moved on once their useful track life is over, so many an ex-racer seeks a new, long-term, loving home. How sad it is that many are put to sleep long before their time is due, hardly just reward for the pleasure and reward they have given their keepers!

The plight of Greyhounds needing 'rescue homes' is now widely known and an enormous amount of work is done all over the country by people who do their very best to look after their welfare. Kennelling and -

Figure 55 A Rescued Greyhound and rescued lurcher enjoy a day out with their new owner

veterinary treatment, especially for injured and ill-treated hounds, costs an enormous amount of money and treatment for a hound with an injured limb, or for one that is seriously ill can need a four-figure sum to settle the bill. Funds are raised through having stands at Crufts, the Hound Show and such like, merchandise is sold and there are events such as sponsored walks. The Greyhound Club has also supported Greyhound Rescue, but provides its own support for any show Greyhounds that fall on hard times.

When one considers that around 15,000 dogs are imported to the UK annually from Eire, it is not difficult to see why so many racing Greyhounds end up in rescue. They may not have come up to scratch on the track, or have injured a limb, or maybe their career is simply over. Although it must be said that some owners and trainers do care for and retain their hounds, there are many who do not. Some are passed on for illegal coursing, and incidentally some pet hounds have been stolen for this very purpose.

Greyhound Rescue is also underway in the USA, where conditions can be appalling, and in several states racing has actually been banned.

In the words of Angela Collett, Founder and Trustee of Greyhound Rescue West of England:

Up until fairly recently there were so many hard-held prejudices regarding Greyhounds that few people would entertain the idea of having one as a pet. Habitually pictured muzzled, and considered impossible to de-institution-alise, they were shut away in back blocks of rescue kennels where staff, knowing little about them, had no confidence to home them and would deter anyone who asked. Thankfully, they are now recognised for the delightful characters they are – lazy couch potatoes, not needing the great long walks some thought, sweet and loving, ideal for older people (many work as PAT dogs visiting hospitals), great with kids, many good with cats and very easy to house-train.

Those who take on ex-racers will have taken on a hound that is just as loving as any other Greyhound, but they will need some exercise, for this is what they have been used to. A home with other small, family pets, such as cats and rabbits, may not be suitable, but advice should be taken on this concerning the hound in question. Several rescue societies pre-test ex-racers to determine whether or not they might be suitable for such a home.

Kennel Club registrations for 1908–1934 and at five-yearly intervals from 1950–2000

1908	84	1917	10	1926	212
1909	44	1918	9	1927	650
1910	67	1919	5	1928	842
1911	60	1920	39	1929	506
1912	62	1921	83	1930	365
1913	61	1922	110	1931	224
1914	41	1923	156	1932	232
1915	28	1924	173	1933	162
1916	19	1925	188	1934	206
1950	86	1970	85	1990	57
1955	72	1975	72	1995	89
1960	60	1980	50	2000	80
1965	30	1985	83		

Breed clubs

There is only one Greyhound Club in the UK and sadly the minutes of many of the early meetings were destroyed by mice in someone's loft, so there are gaps in the documentation. Before the present Greyhound Club, there had been others, amongst them the Greyhound Club of Great Britain which was closed down in the 1930s, and the South Western Greyhound Association (SWGA), which closed at the outbreak of the Second World War.

The current club was formed on 18 September 1946 at a meeting held at the Lion Hotel in Camborne, Cornwall. Several of the enthusiasts present had been members of the SWGA. Of the forty or so members at that time, it appears that only Dr Monica Boggia-Black is still active in the dog-showing world. This was a time at which numbers of Greyhounds registered with the Kennel Club ran into three figures each year and since when the numbers have dropped.

In 1976 the club held its first independent Open Show, judged by Angela Sturgess. Championship status was gained in 1978 and this show was judged by Dorothy Dicks and won by Eve Young's Ch Wenonah Goosander who took the same accolade at the club's next Championship Show under Judy de Casembroot. In 1983, 1984 and 1986, the club show was won by Ch Harestreak Arrow of Ardencote.

Membership has increased over the years since the club's formation, and has strong overseas support. The club celebrated its Golden Jubilee in style in 1996, holding special shows and giving mementos to members and exhibitors. The Championship Show that year drew a record entry of 139 exhibits for judge, Peter Jones.

Apart from regular breed shows, the Greyhound Club holds seminars and assessments for judges of the breed, so that every assistance is given to those who wish to learn more about Greyhounds, whether or not they are owners themselves.

Ten

The Irish Wolfhound

The Irish Wolfhound in history

There is pictorial evidence of large, powerful and swift hounds dating from around 1400 BC, some of which are hunting boar and are somewhat similar in type to the 'mastiff wolfdogs' as described by Lord Altamount, about whom we shall read more later. There is another hound seen on a fresco at Tiryns depicting a large Greyhound-type dog beside horses and a man drawing what is presumed to have been a carriage. If the proportional heights are taken as having been drawn with relative accuracy, the shoulder measurement of the dog would have been well over 40 inches, which makes the comments concerning size made later by Buffon seem credible. The skull would have been almost as large as that which was taken more recently from a bog and measured 17 inches, making the length when alive and clad in flesh about 19 inches. It has to be said that there were doubts as to the authenticity of this skull, some believing it to have been that of an extinct animal resembling a bear.

Undoubtedly very large hunting dogs with shaggy coats were used in the eighth century BC by the Celts and these dogs accompanied them to Britain and Ireland, as well as to northern Spain, in the years between the fifth and first centuries BC. Yet another early representation of a very large hound of similar type to that mentioned above is a statue in Athens dating from about the sixth century BC. Although it has a smooth coat it has a massive neck and would be about the size of a present-day Irish Wolfhound.

The view of Arrian (AD second century) was that the Greeks did not have any hounds swift enough to catch hares until after the invasion of the Celts in 273 BC. There was definitely substantial contact between Greece and the various Celtic nations and so it follows that there could well have been some exchange of members of the canine race. His description of the 'veritable grew' ('vertagi', 'vertragi' or 'vertahi'), a swift hound of the Celts, demands our consideration: 'There is nothing more beautiful to see, whether their eyes or their whole body, or their coat and colour. In those that are pied there is a wonderful variegation, and the whole-coloured ones are no less pleasing to the sight.'

Arrian tells his readers that they may be rough- or smooth-haired and recommends that they are not used for hare-coursing until two years old. This indicates that they were rather large hounds. Indeed Arrian kept a Celtic grew, a blue-grey bitch, and he describes her as 'willing and spirited . . . swift and neat on her feet, so that when she was in her prime she was able to take four hares in succession single-handed'. He goes on to say how gentle and affectionate she is with him and, 'She is so conversational that, whatever she wants, she will ask for it with her voice: and, even if she has done nothing wrong, if you mention the whip she jumps up and clings about your neck until you cease from your anger.'

It has been said that Irish Wolfhounds were introduced to the Roman arena where they vied with the Mastiffs in tackling lions but it is often diffi-cult to distinguish romantic legend from fact. The Romans were indeed familiar with large dogs, Symmachus writing thus to Flavianus before AD 393:

> You provide what is usual and unusual for helping on our display; you think out everything for winning the favour of the people to our quaestor, being both a generous provider for our annual ceremonies, and a discoverer of new things. And this is proved by your offering seven Scotic dogs (or hounds of the Scots) at which Rome was so astonished on the day of the rehearsal that they thought they must have been brought in iron cages. Therefore both for this, and also for your other presents, I render you the greatest possible thanks.

Phyllis Gardner, writing in 1931, said that she had seen an 'ancient repre-sentation of a lion-hunt with large greyhound-like dogs, different from the Assyrian bull-mastiffs'. Unfortunately she was unable to tell her readers where she had seen this, but she did quote a line from one of Joseph Addison's poems, 'And dauntless wolf-dogs shake the lion's mane'. There is also a miniature painting on a casket of the same period as Tutankhamen which shows a large, rather slender hound with pendant ears tearing at a lion which appears already to have been slain by an arrow. Much later, Conrad Gessner, in his *Icones Animalium* (1606) (translated into English in 1607 under the title *Book of Foure-Footed Beastes)*, refers to Greyhounds that:

> will not only set upon Buls, Boars and such like beastes, but also upon Lyons . . . The noblest kind keep home, unless they be led abroad, and sildom barke. They will not run after every trifling beast, by secret instinct of nature discerning what kind of beast is worthy or unworthy of their labour.

It is said that hounds were regularly exported from Ireland in early Christian times but it seems probable that the hounds in question were simply the inseparable companions of their masters. There is a picture on a tenth-century cross at Kells showing two men with spears watching two hounds pursuing deer. Again, on the assumption that the proportions are roughly correct, the larger of the two hounds would appear to be at least the size of an Irish Wolfhound of today.

Members of the breed appear as supporters on the arms of Irish kings, along with the motto 'Gentle when stroked, fierce when provoked.' It was in 1335 that a huntsman in the employ of Edward III was sent to Ireland to bring home some of these dogs. He had a staff of boys with him, each of whom was paid 3½d per day and ½d per day was allowed for food for each dog. Still in the fourteenth century, there was, in 1371, a duel fought between a gentleman and an 'Irish Wolfhound', the latter being the victor. Then, in 1545, we learn that four 'Greyhounds' were sent from Ireland to England by order of the government and Henry VIII was reported to be in danger of being disappointed because 'Irish dogs promised by him to a Spanish nobleman had not been sent'. The Marquis of Desarrya had four 'greyhounds' annually from King Henry VIII and two were sent by Shane O'Neill to Queen Elizabeth I in 1562.

We are told by Campion in 1571 that wolves were to be found in Ireland and that the dogs used to hunt them were Greyhounds which were bigger in bone and limb than a colt and the men with them were of 'great stature'. 'A brace of good wolf-dogs, one black and one white' were sent by Lord Deputy Perrott to Sir Francis Walsingham in 1585.

As we can see, Irish hounds were in much demand as gifts for nobles and royals in the sixteenth and the seventeenth centuries, great numbers going to Spain and others to Sweden. King John of Poland was said to have procured as many as possible and this was believed to have contributed to the breed's subsequent rarity. Thomas Wentworth, Earl of Strafford, was in Ireland between 1633 and 1639. There is a portrait of him by Van Dyck which also shows the head of a hound, albeit a powerful, smooth Greyhound or perhaps a Mastiff, which has been described as 'the last of his race'. Concern was such that in 1652 a declaration was issued against exporting hounds from Ireland but in 1653 Dorothy Osborne writes to her lover about the kind of dog she desires:

> You shall do one favour for me into the bargain. When your father goes into Ireland, lay your commands upon some of his servants to get you an Irish greyhound. I have one that was the General's; but 'tis a bitch, and those are always much less than the dogs. I got it in the time of my favour there, and it was all they had. Henry Cromwell undertook to write to his brother Fleetwood for another for me; but I have lost my hopes there. Whomsoever it is that you employ, he will need no other instructions but to get the biggest

he can meet with; 'tis all the beauty of those dogs, or of any kind, I think. A masty is handsomer to me than the most exact little dog that ever lady played withal.

Within a few weeks another of her letters tells of her hopes having been fulfilled:

I must tell you what a present I had made to me to-day. Two of the finest young Irish greyhounds that ere I saw; a gentleman that serves the General sent them me. They are newly come over and sent for by Henry Cromwell, he tells me, but not how he got them.

The term 'Wolfdog' was sometimes used in Dorothy Osborne's day and later in relation to the Irish dogs which hunted the wolf and this is borne out in the writing of Nicholas Cox in 1675 when in *Gentleman's Recreation* we read:

Although we have no wolves in England at the present, yet it is certain that heretofore we had routs of them, as they have to this very day in Ireland; and in that country are bred a race of greyhounds which are commonly called wolfdogs, which are strong, fleet and bear a natural enmity to the wolf. Now in these greyhounds of that nation there is an incredible force and boldness, so that they are in great estimation, and much sought after in foreign parts, so that the King of Poland makes use of them in his hunting of great beasts by force.

In 1657 Lord Conway received a communication from Major George Rawdon saying, 'I have your Lordship's two wolfdogs still, and must send a messenger with them, as no one will take charge of them on the journey. I have two more that are kept to hunt the wolf upon every occasion where he commits spoil, and then the people come still to borrow them out.' Just seven years later, in 1664, Mrs Katherine Phillips who had been in Ireland wrote the following poem about an 'Irish greyhound':

Behold this creature's Form and State
Which Nature therefore did create
That to the World might be exprest
What mien there can be in a Beast,
And that we in this shape may find
A Lion of another kind,
For this Heroick beast does seem
In majesty to rival him:
And yet vouchsafes, to Man, to show

135

Both service and submission too.
From whence we this distinction have,
That Beast is fierce, but this is brave.
This Dog hath so himself subdu'd
That hunger cannot make him rude,
And his behaviour doth confess
True Courage dwells with Gentleness.
With sternest Wolves he does engage
And acts on them successful rage.
Yet too much courtesie may chance
To put him out of countenance.
When in his opposer's blood
Fortune hath made his vertue good,
The Creature from an act so brave
Grows not more sullen, but more grave.
Man's Guard he would be, not his sport,
Believing he hath ventur'd for't:
But yet no blood or shed or spent
Can ever make him insolent.

One of the names given to the hounds which concern us here was 'Alaunt' and there was a tune called 'The Irish Alaunt' written around the close of the seventeenth century. Medieval writers describe the word 'alaunt' as meaning very large and powerful and willing to attack on the command of his master any creature, be it human or otherwise.

By 1732 we are told that such dogs were numerous in Ireland and were 'of the make of a Greyhound' but soon afterwards the wolf ceased to exist on Ireland's shores. The date of the last known wolf has been variously reported but it is known that wolves were killed in County Cork in 1710, in County Wexford in approximately 1730 and in the Wicklow Mountains in 1770. It has been said that the last wolf was killed in County Carlow in 1786 by a Mr Watson who kept hounds described as 'coarse, powerful animals, no way resembling the grand old giant rough greyhound, commonly known as the Irish Wolfhound'.

The fact that the wolf ceased to exist in Ireland ties in with the fact that thirty years after they were said to be 'numerous' they were reported by Harris to be on the decline. Harris gave the theory that this was so because so many of them had been sent as presents to monarchs of other countries. Oliver Goldsmith, whose mother had apparently been saved from a ravenous wolf by Bran, an Irish Wolfhound, wrote in 1774 that he had seen more than a dozen of these dogs. His description of them in his *History of Animated Nature* is interesting:

... the most wonderful of all that I shall mention is the great Irish wolfdog, that may be considered as the first of the canine species. This animal, which is very rare even in the only country in the world where it is to be found, is kept rather for show than for use, there being neither wolves nor any other formidable beasts of prey in Ireland that seem to require so powerful an antagonist. The wolf-dog is, therefore, bred up in the houses of the great, or such gentlemen as choose to keep him as a curiosity, being neither good for hunting the hare, the fox, nor the stag, and equally unserviceable as a house dog. Nevertheless he is extremely beautiful and majestic as to appearance, being the greatest of the dog kind to be seen in the world. The largest of them I have seen, and I have seen above a dozen, was about four feet high, or as tall as a calf a year old. He was made extremely like a greyhound, but rather more robust, and inclining to the figure of the French matin, or the Great Dane. His eye was mild, his colour white, and his nature seemed heavy and phlegmatic. This I ascribe to his having been bred to a size beyond his nature. ... The greatest pains have been taken with them to enlarge the breed, both by food and by matching. This end was effectively obtained, indeed, for the size was enormous: but, as it seemed to me, at the expense of the animal's fierceness, vigilance, and sagacity. However, I was informed otherwise: the gentleman who bred them assuring me that a mastiff would be nothing when opposed to one of them, who generally seized their opponents by the back: he added, that they would worry the strongest bulldogs in a few minutes to

Figure 56 Lord Altamount's Irish Wolfhound – 1794 *(E A Ash)*

137

death. But this strength did not appear either in their figure or their inclinations; they seemed rather more timid than the ordinary race of dogs, and their skin was much thinner and consequently ill-fitted for combat.

By 1790 it was reported that only eight such dogs existed in Ireland and these all in one kennel, that of Lord Altamount. But a picture of one of this gentleman's dogs in 1794 depicts something described by Edward Ash as a cross between a Slowhound and a Greyhound. It certainly does not resemble the Irish Wolfhound as we know it today.

In 1790, Ralph Beilby's *A General History of Quadrupeds* describes the 'Irish Greyhound' as 'the largest dog of its kind, and its appearance the most beautiful and majestic'. We learn of the rarity of the breed which was, by then, kept 'rather for show than use, being equally unserviceable for hunting either the Stag, the Fox, or the Hare'. Interestingly the dogs are described here as being three feet high, 'generally of a white or cinnamon colour, and made somewhat like a Greyhound, but more robust'. With their 'mild aspect' and gentle, peaceable disposition their strength was considered to be 'so great, that in combat the Mastiff or Bull-Dog is far from being equal to them. They mostly seize their antagonists by the back, and shake them to death, which their great size enables them to do with ease.'

Figure 57   The 'Irish Gre-hound' as depicted in the *Encyclopaedia Britannica* in 1791

Figure 58
The Irish
Greyhound as
depicted in *A General
History of Quadrupeds*
by Ralph Beilby,
1790.

Gemlin, in 1792, mentions the Irish Greyhound, describing it as 'nearly as large as a Mastiff, having an arched body, and narrow, projecting snout'.

Around the turn of the century there are a few recorded instances of the 'Irish wolfhound' being brought up with wolves for the purposes of experiment but in most cases it would appear that the dog eventually killed the wolf. Certainly Buffon brought up a female wolf with a 'braque' (resembling a lightly marked Dalmatian) and he successfully bred their hybrid offspring for several generations.

According to W. Taplin, by 1803 it was doubtful if any of the breed were to be found in Ireland and this is the point at which the breed seems to have disappeared into oblivion. Some light may be thrown upon this disappearance by a comment made in 1815 and referring to the proposed destruction of those dogs found unmuzzled in Newfoundland, 'it will be the means of an indeferant business as ever the killing the Doggs in Ireland was before the rebellion'. This comment could be highly significant.

The name Irish Greyhound had by now fallen into disuse and any of the breed which did still remain were known primarily as 'Danes' but in illustrated papers and cheap editions of natural history books the breed was variously described as Great Dane, Russian boarhound, German'are dog and bullcross deerhound. Interestingly Buffon had considered the Great Dane to be a variety of the Irish Wolfhound. In 1837, Thomas Bell told his readers that the breed of Irish Wolfhound or Greyhound was no longer to be found pure in Ireland. The reader will note that in all the references given thus far, other than the very early comment about shaggy-coated dogs of the Celts in the eighth century BC, there has been no mention of a rough coat.

The beginning of the modern Irish Wolfhound

The year that marked the beginning of the Irish Wolfhound as we know it today is 1841. In a publication called the *Irish Penny Magazine* a certain Mr H. G. Richardson wrote an article on the breed and gives an illustration of two large dogs with rough and possibly slightly curly coats. Whilst advising his readers that the Irish Wolfhound breed did indeed exist he admitted that he was unable to distinguish between the Irish and Scottish dogs. He equally had difficulty in deciding which were Irish and which were Welsh, though he thought the former were 'thicker, and not so high on the leg'. Mr Richardson stated that the breed had been kept in existence by crossing the 'old pure breed' with the Scottish and Welsh dogs. He had great difficulty in finding the pure breed because it no longer existed although, conversely, he did say that a Mr Rowan, a breeder of Great Danes, had 'another pure strain'. Owing to his difficulty in locating the 'pure breed' he fell back on the Scottish Deerhound for he was of the opinion that when Scotland was peopled from Ireland he felt sure they would have taken their Irish Wolfhounds with them. Folklore was once again revived and the animal hero, whatever he might originally have been, was stated to have been an Irish Wolfhound.

Despite my previous comment in which I say that 1841 marked the beginning of the breed as we know it today, in 1861 John Meyrick tells us that the breed was entirely extinct. The short section concerning the breed in his *House Dogs and Sporting Dogs* makes interesting reading:

> This animal is entirely extinct. I only mention the breed to prove what astonishing results careful selection of breeding can produce. There is even some doubt as to what variety this famous dog belonged to, but it is certain that to have caught and coped with the wolf, he must have been of the greyhound form. Indeed, both Ray and Pennant have described him as a tall, rough greyhound of extraordinary size and power. Ray says it was 'the greatest dog he had ever seen'. Evelyn, when describing the sports of the bear-garden, says, 'The Bull-dogs did exceedingly well, but the Irish Wolf dog exceeded all, which was a tall Greyhound, a stately creature, and did beat a cruel Mastiff.' Oliver Goldsmith, no very reliable authority perhaps, says, in his loose way, that one was about four feet high, or as big as a yearling heifer. Another account represents them as sufficiently tall to put their heads over the shoulder of a person sitting down.
>
> But the most singular, and perhaps the most reliable proof of the gigantic size of this extinct breed, is a skull, evidently, from its shape, that of a greyhound, discovered by Mr. Wylam at Dunshauglin. This skull, now preserved in the Royal Irish Academy, measures 11 inches in length. As the skull of a

common greyhound is not more than 7 inches long, the ancient dog, if his height was in proportion to the size of his skull, would have been upwards of 40 inches in height at the shoulder, a size exceeding by one-fourth part that of the tallest Deerhound, and quite justifying the descriptions of Ray and Pennant.

In the latter part of the nineteenth century we find Dr Fitzinger stating without hesitation that, 'The Irish Greyhound, next to the Indian and Russian Greyhound, is the largest specimen of greyhound type, combining the speed of the greyhound with the size of the Mastiff.' He also described another type which he called 'the Irish coursing dog', saying that it was a cross between the Irish Greyhound and Mastiff or bandog, being shorter in the neck, coarser in skull and with a broader chest and heavily flewed lips.

Captain George Augustus Graham, who was born in Scotland in 1833 and had a great interest in Deerhounds, owned his first Irish Wolfhound, Faust, in 1853 when he was living in Gloucestershire. He had already noted that some of his Deerhound stock seemed to throw back to the heavier Irish Wolfhound type. In 1862 he returned from India where he had kept 'rough

Figure 59 'Irish Greyhound', from J. G. Wood's *Illustrated Natural History,* 1861.

Greyhounds' and upon his return he set about rebuilding the Irish Wolfhound. He was convinced that the breed had, indeed, existed and that some of the cross-bred Irish dogs might still carry genetic traces of the original breed, on which he might build. He believed that there were three strains to be found in Ireland but that none of them were so large as the 'Wolfe Dogge' mentioned in early writings, there having been a deterioration both in bone and in substance. The breeders of the three lines to which he referred were Sir J. Power of Kilfane, Mr Baker of Ballytobin and Mr Mahony of Dromore. Using bitches obtained from the first two of these kennels he crossed them chiefly with Scottish Deerhounds, later introducing other large dogs including the Russian Wolfhound. It has frequently been reported that he also used the Great Dane but it has also been said that this was not a breed which he, personally, used. In 1885 he wrote, 'Whilst I freely allow that the Great Dane is an extremely fine and imposing looking animal, I fail to perceive his claims to elegance of form and beauty.' Certainly the Earl of Caleon used a harlequin Dane and Graham had some of his hounds. A Dane cross was also used by Major Granier who had bred the grandsire of Brian II.

Captain Graham kept very careful records not only of his own breeding but also the breeding of others and his Irish Wolfhounds bred true to type within only a few generations. The Deerhound outcrosses used in his breeding programme were primarily of the Glengarry strain though he also introduced Borzoi blood. One Irish Wolfhound line includes a black Borzoi which can also be found in Deerhound pedigrees. He also used a 'Tibetan' which I believe to be the Tibetan Sheepdog, a picture of which is to be found in my article about some of the lesser known Tibetan breeds in the May 1990 issue of the *Kennel Gazette*. It is possible that it is the introduction of the Tibetan which, at least in part, is responsible for the woolly coat which appears occasionally in the breed. The cross with the 'Tibetan' also tended to throw double dewclaws. The Tibetan was obtained from a London 'livestock provider's shop' and Graham quoted his height as 33 inches (though it has been said by others to have been 36 inches). According to Graham he measured 'tip to tip 74 ins., covered with a profuse shaggy coat of lion-coloured hair. His limbs are as straight as gun-barrels, and he is exceedingly active and playful. Like all big creatures, he has a perfect temper, and is docile, affectionate, and intelligent.' His tail was carried down in a manner which would not have been wrong for an Irish Wolfhound.

The name of the Tibetan was 'Wolf' and this has led to some confusion for it was thought by some that an actual wolf had been used. To further complicate the issue there were at least three other hounds bearing the same name. It seems unlikely that Graham used a Pyrenean, although he is reported to have done so (some people possibly believing the 'Wolf' was a

Pyrenean) but this breed was very probably used by H. G. Richardson.

In 1879 Captain Graham wrote in *The Country:* 'It has been ascertained beyond all question that there are a few specimens of the breed still in Ireland and England that have well founded pretentions to be considered Irish wolfhounds, though falling far short of the requisite dimensions . . . This blood is now in my possession.'

The Irish Wolfhound in the show-ring

Thanks to Captain Graham, in 1879 a class was arranged for the breed in Dublin for 'The Nearest Approach to the Old Irish Wolfhound'. Captain

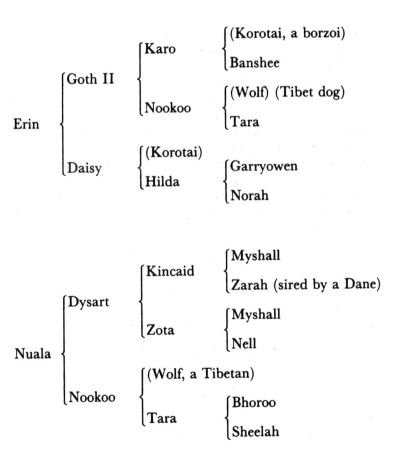

Figure 60   Pedigrees of Irish Wolfhounds showing how outcrosses with other breeds were introduced.

Graham had agreed to be the judge but the result was disappointing, for the dogs differed widely in type and none represented the old breed, as he would have described it. He awarded first prize to what he described as a 'Deerhound of unusual size' by the name of Brian and which he said 'needed nothing more than bone and substance to be our ideal of an Irish Wolfhound'. In making this statement he was effectively saying that what was required for the breed was a Deerhound with more bone and substance. It was Captain Graham who was responsible for the inauguration of the first breed club which came into existence in 1885 and of which he was the first President, remaining so until 1908. He wrote that the Irish Wolfhound Club hoped to produce a dog that 'shall have the stature and the power of the Great Dane, combined with the looks and beauty of the Deerhound'.

Irish Wolfhounds were first registered with the Kennel Club in 1886, the year in which the Kennel Club scheduled classes for the breed at its own show for the very first time. There were around twenty hounds entered and the judge, Mr M. B. Wynn, commented that there was a 'deficiency in height and bone'. Although there were very few breed classes at that time the few that there were were rarely well supported and prizes were sometimes withheld due to a lack of sufficient quality.

Figure 61　Irish Wolfhound (after Reingale, 1803).

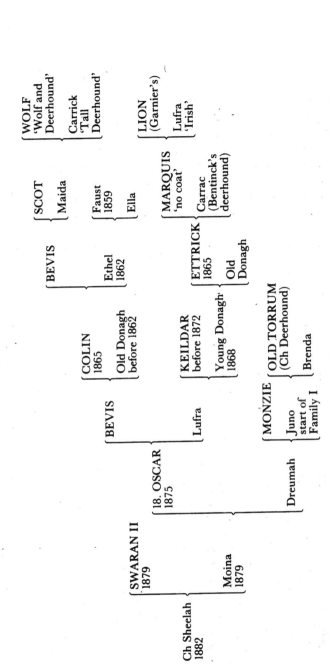

Figure 62 Pedigree of Ch Sheelah, as noted by Captain Graham.

It was in about 1888 that Vero Shaw asked Captain Graham to write an article on the Irish Wolfhound for the first edition of *Cassell's Book of the Dog.* In his article, although he was unable to claim that the breed had any direct lineage with the original Irish dog, he did say that the breed 'as they were producing it' was 'actually the type' of the ancient breed. He referred to a work of 1630, called *Antiquities of Ireland,* stating that the breed of his time bore a strong resemblance to the two dogs on the frontispiece. Edward Ash later traced the book of 1630, however, and discovered that the two dogs on the frontispiece were none other than smooth-coated Greyhounds of normal size. Another book, dated 1665, shows an illustration of a smooth-coated, heavily built Greyhound, with a muzzle resembling that of a Great Dane and called 'An Irish Greyhound'. There may, though, be an explanation for the confusion with dogs of distinctly Greyhound type at that period in the seventeenth century, for earlier, in either 1617 or 1618, a guest of the Earl of Mar's hunting party described a hundred couple of 'strong Irish Greyhounds' let free upon deer as they were driven out of a wood. The fact that there were other journalistic inaccuracies leads one to suspect that the writer had not been accurate in his nomenclature of the dogs in question. Indeed in 1803 there was an illustration by Reingale of what was clearly a dog resembling today's Irish Wolfhound, labelled Irish Greyhound. Still more confusion was caused by one Revd Hogan, who used the term Irish Wolfhound in connection with many different dogs which had been bred over the centuries.

Captain Graham showed a dog named Brian who stood only 30 inches at the shoulder and a bitch, Sheelah, who gained the title of Champion and measured 27½ inches. Later he campaigned an important stud dog, Dermot Astore, which he then sold in 1896. Sheelah aroused a great deal of comment in her day and was said to be 'a little heavy in bone for her height', as was her well-known son, Dhulart. Two others shown by Graham, though less well known, were Banchee and Fintragh.

The dog reputed to be the best dog the breed had seen was O'Leary, bred by Mr Crisp and sire of another quality dog, Kilcullen, who won the Championship at the Kennel Club Show at Crystal Palace in 1902. O'Leary was also sire of Mrs Percy Shewell's Ch Cotswold, described by Robert Leighton as 'undoubtedly the grandest Irish Wolfhound ever bred'. The height at shoulder was 34½ inches, making this perhaps the largest dog of any breed whose measurements had been recorded. But still there were varying types within the breed, ranging from those resembling Mastiffs to those which could be more closely associated with the Greyhound. As time went on extremes of type grew less and more uniformity could be seen.

There is an interesting little story of an Irish fancier who had heard much about the breed and picked up a puppy for sixpence in Covent Garden, London, thinking it a bargain whatever it turned out to be. It grew into an Irish Wolfhound and the lucky gent won many prizes with it, refusing the princely sum of £30 which he was offered should he decide to part with it. The selling price for a dog named Wargrave was listed in the catalogue of the 1897 Gloucester Show as £25. This belonged to Mr F. M. Birtill and, being recognised as one of the best of its breed hitherto seen, there were many prospective buyers. Eventually he was sold by public auction for £47 5s. Wargrave went on to sire a bitch, Atara, who was 'practically unbeatable' and a dog, Wolf Tone, who became an important sire.

At the beginning of this century Captain Graham, with the Irish Wolfhound Club, drew up a scale of points, each with a numerical value.

Figure 63
Irish Guard with his
Irish wolfhound
mascot

The head was considered most important because it gave the dog character; a short curly tail was to be deplored as it ruined a hound, a long, straight tail being essential to give balance when turning. Head and height together scored twelve points; coat, ten; loins, hocks and forelegs nine; feet and ears had seven points; and tail scored five. Smaller details including beard, eyes, teeth and nails scored up to three points maximum.

However, despite the fact that these values had been set Captain Graham did not consider them to be a good guide for judges as we can see in the following letter: 'Though I have stated the points, please do not quote me as setting any great value on such a method of judging.'

In 1902 Captain Graham and two other judges were asked to choose an Irish Wolfhound to be presented, in the name of the Irish Wolfhound Club, to the Irish Guards as their mascot. The dog they chose was Rajah of Kidnal, more information about which is to be found in the next chapter. His breeder, Mrs A. Gerard of Malpas, owned one of the largest kennels in England and bred Rajah's dam, Cheevra, who also whelped a bitch who was to stand 33 inches at the shoulder, Ch Cotswold Patricia.

Another highly successful breeder was Mr I. W. Everett of Felixstowe whose Kilronan and Yirra were perhaps the best of his early hounds, though Kilgerran and Pota were later thought to be better specimens. Other early breeders of note were the Revd C. H. Hildebrand and Mr R. Montagu-Scott. Demand for the breed certainly declined on these shores until after the First World War, though there was a market for the breed in the Dominions and in foreign countries where they were prized, not only for their great strength but also on account of their ability to tackle marauding animals including the wolf and the coyote.

The following standard of points was drawn up by the Irish Wolfhound Club in the mid 1880s:

GENERAL APPEARANCE: The Irish Wolfhound should not be quite so heavy or as massive as the Great Dane, but more so than the Deerhound, which in general type he should otherwise resemble. Of great size and commanding appearance, very muscular, strongly though gracefully built; movements easy and active; head and neck carried high; the tail carried with an upward sweep, with a slight curve toward the extremity. The minimum height and weight of dogs should be 31 inches and 120 lbs, of bitches 28 inches and 90 lbs. Anything below this should be debarred from competition. Great size, including height at shoulder and proportionate length of body, is the desideratum to be aimed at, and it is desired firmly to establish a race that shall average 32–34 inches in dogs, showing the requisite power, activity, courage and symmetry.

HEAD: Long, the frontal bones of the forehead very slightly raised and very little indentation between the eyes. Skull not too broad; muzzle long and moderately pointed; ears small and Greyhound-like in carriage.

NECK: Rather long, very strong and muscular, well arched, without dewlap and loose skin about the throat.

CHEST: Very deep, breast wide.

BACK: Rather long than short. Loins arched.

TAIL: Long and slightly curved, of moderate thickness, and well covered with hair.

BELLY: Well drawn up.

FOREQUARTERS: Shoulders muscular, giving breadth of chest, set sloping, elbows well under, neither turned inwards nor outwards.

LEGS: Forearm muscular and the whole leg strong and quite straight.

HINDQUARTERS: Muscular thighs, and second thigh long and strong as in the Greyhound, and hocks well let down and turning neither in nor out.

FEET: Moderately large and round, neither turned inwards nor outwards; toes well arched and closed, nails very strong and curved.

HAIR: Rough and hard on body, legs, and head; especially wiry and long over eyes and under jaw.

FAULTS: Too light or heavy in head, too highly arched frontal bone, large ears and hanging flat to the face; short neck; full dewlap; too narrow or too broad a chest; sunken and hollow or quite level back; bent forelegs; over-bent fetlocks; twisted feet; spreading toes; too curly a tail; weak hindquarters, cow hocks, and a general want of muscle; too short in body.

Following the Second World War

An American import, Rory of Kihone, was introduced to this country by the Irish Wolfhound Club following a serious drop in registration after the war. By 1950 all the bloodlines could be traced back to Clonboy of Oughborough and it was felt necessary that new blood be introduced. Despite this introduction and Rory's use at stud, registrations remained low and dropped to only thirteen in 1954 and to five in 1956. This serious drop could well have affected the Kennel Club's allocation of CCs for the breed as twenty registrations per annum was the minimum number stipulated by the Kennel Club for a breed to have CCs. Gradually, however, registrations increased and CC status for the breed was retained. Soon after, in 1960, Mrs Florence Nagel's Sulhamstead Merman was awarded Best in Show at Cruft's at the age of only eighteen months. This was the first time that a member of the breed had had this honour and to this day the achievement has not been repeated.

Fact or fiction?

There is a wealth of early literature about the Irish Wolfhound and before closing this chapter I would like to share with you just a couple of the many stories.

In Edward Jesse's *Anecdotes of Dogs*, 1846, we hear of a Wolfhound that accompanied an Irish officer at the hard-fought battle of Aughrim or Vidconnel:

> This gentleman officer was killed and stript in the battle, but the dog remained by his body both by day and night. He fed upon the other bodies with the rest of the dogs, yet he would not allow them or anything else to touch that of his master. When all the other bodies were consumed, the other dogs departed, but this used to go in the night to adjacent villages for food, and presently to return again to the place where his master's bones were only then left. This he continued to do from July, when the battle was fought, 'till the January following, when a soldier being quartered near, and going that way by chance, the dog, fearing he came to disturb his master's bones, flew upon the soldier, who, being surprised at the suddenness of the thing, unslung his carbine, he having been thrown on his back, and killed the noble animal. He expired with the same fidelity to the remains of his unfortunate master, as that master had shewn devotion to the cause of his unhappy country.

In Father Hogan's *Irish Wolfdog*, dated 1897, we learn of one 'in the first century of our era' who seemingly defended an entire province and 'filled all Ireland with his fame'. The price of '6,000 cows and other things' was offered for him by the King of Connacht and the King of Ulster offered something similar. This resulted in the inevitable: 'Ulster and Connacht fought for him. The dog joined the Ulstermen, made great havoc of the heroes of Connacht; he seized the axle-tree of the Connacht King so firmly that his head, when cut off, held its grip on the axle.'

ELEVEN

THE IRISH WOLFHOUND TODAY

Temperament and adaptability

The Irish Wolfhound has been a versatile breed over the years and has been used in working trials and for coursing. He is a brave animal, used originally to protect his master from predators, and has been described by some authors as 'even fierce', but this has almost always been qualified by the fact that the breed is extremely gentle, despite its size, and Irish Wolfhounds are utterly trustworthy with children. So often one sees pictures of children with their arms flung around the dog; indeed advertisements in the canine press, especially during the 1930s, frequently portrayed a hound, great in stature, with a child who was little more than a toddler. Even so, parents of children should always be sensible when introducing children to dogs and the hound's sheer size and weight must be borne in mind at all times. Young Wolfhounds particularly have a habit of jumping up to express their friendliness. This can cause problems, especially if the dog is fully mature, and so it is sensible to discourage this habit whilst the hound is still young.

The breed's size and stature is probably sufficient to deter any would-be intruder but the Wolfhound is not a noisy breed, although he has a melodious bay when sounding a warning. He is happy to please his owner and easy to train in new routines. It is not normally necessary to use anything more than a slightly severe tone of voice for, if one does so, there is danger of upsetting this large but relatively sensitive hound. Firm persuasion is all that is needed. Under no circumstances should a Wolfhound ever be hit or beaten, for great damage will thus be done and it would take a considerable amount of time to win back his confidence.

The Wolfhound is not a naturally aggressive dog but there is no denying that he is capable of being fierce if provoked and it is wise to remember this. For this reason training must begin at a young age so that the dog knows what is and what is not permissible before damage or injury occurs. Having said that, the breed has proved itself to be very satisfactory with elderly and handicapped people and has been used as a hearing dog for the deaf, as well as a 'PAT' dog. It is to be hoped that this breed will never be considered for use as a guard dog for its very size and strength could make it lethal if trained to be aggressive.

Thankfully most representatives of the breed are consistently kind with children, even those with which they are unfamiliar; were they not to be so then their enormous power and strength would make them problematic as household companions, another reason to begin sensible training in the early stages of a puppy's life. I think it relevant to recall here that, the Deerhound having been used in the creation of the Irish Wolfhound as we know it today, the exemplary temperament of the Deerhound is in the blood of the Wolfhound too. A word of caution though. Irish Wolfhounds, and Deerhounds for that matter, because of their hunting instincts, have been known to chase and kill cats. In the heat of the chase he does not always give enough consideration to what his quarry actually is. Even so, most Wolfhounds, following sensible and supervised introductions, will live happily with house cats belonging to their owners.

Thankfully, especially in view of his size, the breed is easy to train and

Figure 64   Pictured after winning Best in Show at the Hound Show 2005, is Mrs A. S. Macaulay's Irish Wolfhound, Ch. Gartlove Galenkelso.

desires greatly to please his owners. A growing young puppy can be something of a handful, but he will undoubtedly calm down as he matures. It is important that owners of such a large breed have complete control of the dog when on the lead and a 'Halti' can be very useful if one has any difficulty in this regard. The adult Wolfhound enjoys his comforts and owners must ensure that adequate exercise is given or is available. To keep the adult in the peak of condition both roadwork and free running are necessary and for the latter purpose either a large garden or a paddock is highly desirable.

As with any large dog, and especially one as large as the Irish Wolfhound, size must be taken carefully into consideration when deciding whether or not the breed will fit in with one's own family and its lifestyle. Taking on an Irish Wolfhound has to be a decision made between all parties concerned. There is no denying the fact that such a breed does take up a substantial amount of space and is in no way suitable for someone living in a small flat.

If he cannot live in the house he will undoubtedly appreciate having his kennel as near to the home as possible so that he can see what is going on. A Wolfhound will almost certainly mope if left alone without anything to do.

The breed not only needs large amounts of food but also an extremely well-balanced diet if his large frame is to develop as it should. Generally he travels well and seems to enjoy accompanying his owners on a journey; most also enjoy the sorts of environment they encounter at shows or lure-coursing meetings.

Over the last couple of decades, especially, there has been concern that the Wolfhound has got into the hands of breeders who have not given careful enough consideration to their breeding plans, sometimes through lack of experience. It has taken much time, enthusiasm and expense by conscientious enthusiasts of the breed to bring it to the high standard it is today. Those who do care about the breed are strong in their resolve to keep it as one of which they are proud and which meets with the Kennel Club's Breed Standard both in its physical attributes and in temperament. In this way it can remain the great, graceful breed we know with the balanced personality needed by one possessing such enormous size and strength.

Kennel Club Breed Standard © The Kennel Club

GENERAL APPEARANCE: Of great size, strength, symmetry and commanding appearance, very muscular, yet gracefully built.

CHARACTERISTICS: Of great power, activity, speed and courage.

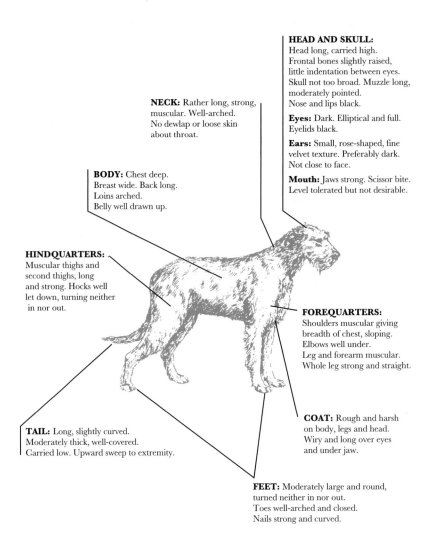

HEAD AND SKULL:
Head long, carried high.
Frontal bones slightly raised,
little indentation between eyes.
Skull not too broad. Muzzle long,
moderately pointed.
Nose and lips black.

Eyes: Dark. Elliptical and full.
Eyelids black.

Ears: Small, rose-shaped, fine
velvet texture. Preferably dark.
Not close to face.

Mouth: Jaws strong. Scissor bite.
Level tolerated but not desirable.

NECK: Rather long, strong,
muscular. Well-arched.
No dewlap or loose skin
about throat.

BODY: Chest deep.
Breast wide. Back long.
Loins arched.
Belly well drawn up.

HINDQUARTERS:
Muscular thighs and
second thighs, long
and strong. Hocks well
let down, turning neither
in nor out.

FOREQUARTERS:
Shoulders muscular giving
breadth of chest, sloping.
Elbows well under.
Leg and forearm muscular.
Whole leg strong and straight.

COAT: Rough and harsh
on body, legs and head.
Wiry and long over eyes
and under jaw.

TAIL: Long, slightly curved.
Moderately thick, well-covered.
Carried low. Upward sweep to extremity.

FEET: Moderately large and round,
turned neither in nor out.
Toes well-arched and closed.
Nails strong and curved.

Figure 65 The Irish Wolfhound breed standard in brief.

TEMPERAMENT: Gentle, kind and friendly nature.

HEAD AND SKULL: Head long, carried high, the frontal bones of forehead very slightly raised and very little indentation between eyes. Skull not too broad. Muzzle long and moderately pointed. Nose and lips black.

EYES: Dark. Elliptical (regular oval) and full. Eyelids black.

154

EARS: Small, rose-shaped, of fine velvet texture. Preferably dark in colour, not hanging close to face.

MOUTH: Jaws strong with a perfect, regular and complete scissor bite, i.e. the upper teeth closely overlapping the lower teeth and set square to the jaws. Level bite tolerated but not desirable.

NECK: Rather long, very strong and muscular, well arched, without dewlap or loose skin about throat.

FOREQUARTERS: Shoulders muscular, giving breadth of chest, set sloping. Elbows well under, turned neither in nor out. Leg and forearm muscular, and whole leg strong and straight.

BODY: Chest very deep. Breast wide. Back, long rather than short. Loins arched. Belly well drawn up.

HINDQUARTERS: Muscular thighs and second thighs, long and strong, good bend of stifle with hocks well let down and turning neither in nor out.

FEET: Moderately large and round, turned neither in nor out. Toes well arched and closed. Nails very strong and curved.

TAIL: Long and slightly curved, of moderate thickness and well covered with hair, carried low with an upward sweep toward the extremity.

GAIT/MOVEMENT: Easy and active.

COAT: Rough and harsh on body, legs and head; especially wiry and long over eyes and under jaw.

COLOUR: Recognised colours are grey, brindle, red, black, pure white, fawn, wheaten and steel grey.

SIZE: Minimum height for dogs 79 cm (31 inches), bitches 71 cm (28 inches). Minimum weight 54.5 kg (120 lbs) for dogs, 40.9 kg (90 lbs) for bitches. Great size, including height of shoulder and proportionate length of body is to be aimed at, and it is desired to establish firmly a breed that shall average from 81 to 86 cm (32–34 inches) in dogs.

FAULTS: Any departure from the foregoing points should be considered a fault and the seriousness with which the fault should be regarded should be in exact proportion to its degree and its effect upon the health and welfare of the dog.

NOTE: Male animals should have two apparently normal testicles fully descended into the scrotum.

Judging the breed

Keep in mind the breed's history and consider that the dogs you are judging should have had the speed and stamina to wear down the wolf and to dispatch it. The head of the Wolfhound should not be as fine as that of the Deerhound. Look for a weather-proof coat and small ears and a slightly arched loin. Despite the large size, keep in mind at all times that the breed should have retained the graceful curves so typical of a Sight Hound. Shoulders need to be well laid back and the forechest should be prominent. The Wolfhound is deep-chested and there should be width between the elbows. The breed standard gives a minimum height but in reality the average height seems to be between 32 and 35 inches.

Grooming

The Wolfhound's coat is not difficult to manage, especially if grooming is carried out on a regular basis. However, if left too long without proper grooming it will become heavy and out-of-hand. The most suitable grooming tools are a wire brush to remove loose undercoat, for the breed is double coated, a pure bristle brush or a comb for the top coat and a pair

Figure 66
Chris and Julie
Amoo's Irish
Wolfhound puppy,
Sadè Porryk

of thinning scissors. There is a certain amount of tidying to do to the breed by way of hand-stripping the ruff down the neck and the long guard hairs on the ears, so that the latter look smooth and velvety. The underline, too, needs to be kept discreetly in order so as to accentuate the outline. In the case of a tail which looks somewhat 'clumpy' at the base this also can be hand-stripped, and thinning scissors can be used on the hair on the elbows and feet. It is thought that a Wolfhound which is given sufficiently frequent roadwork will not need to have his nails clipped but should they, for whatever reason, need to be clipped, for a breed as large as this I would strongly recommend the guillotine type of nail clippers rather than straight-sided ones, or a heavy duty electrical nail file can be helpful.

Kennel Club registrations for 1908–1934 and at five-yearly intervals from 1950–2000

1908	41	1917	24	1926	176
1909	38	1918	3	1927	176
1910	39	1919	14	1928	202
1911	43	1920	30	1929	200
1912	36	1921	49	1930	199
1913	24	1922	58	1931	123
1914	21	1923	78	1932	130
1915	24	1924	115	1933	103
1916	21	1925	127	1934	112
1950	53	1970	258	1990	679
1955	79	1975	643	1995	637
1960	63	1980	794	2000	601
1965	122	1985	700		

The Irish Wolfhound in sport today

Originally the Irish Wolfhound not only protected his master but also provided skins to make clothing and supplied meat for the table. He was therefore used in the chase of large game and not for coursing hares.

In the 1920s hound-trailing was practised with the breed. This involved hunting by scent as well as by sight and by the following decade the Irish Wolfhound Coursing Club had come into being. It seems that there had been some discussion about the breed being dropped from the Hound

Group and several breeders were therefore at pains to prove that the Irish Wolfhound was, indeed, worthy of its status within this Group. The Brabyns and Sulhamstead kennels especially played a large part in promoting the breed in sport. Nonetheless there was little activity in this sphere from the time of the Second World War but interest in coursing the breed saw something of a revival in the 1970s.

The hare-coursing season ended in March but lure-coursing, introduced to the breed in this country in 1980, could take place throughout the year. By the very next year it seemed to have taken over almost completely from hare-coursing, to the undoubted delight of the hare who would presumably much rather the breed chase a mechanical lure!

Breed clubs

The Irish Wolfhound Club, the oldest club for this breed in the world, was founded in 1885 by Captain George Augustus Graham. Only a year after the Club's foundation the Kennel Club scheduled classes for the breed at its own show for the very first time. As interest in the breed grew during the early years of this century the secretary of the Club was often asked for technical information and as a result the Club published a letter in *Our Dogs* describing the breed and explaining how the various points were valued. Club members, too, were invited to list their own personal values for each of the points and these were then compared with Captain Graham's, which had been drawn up prior to the voting.

By 1902 membership of the Club had increased to forty-three but, even so, more members were needed if the Club was to be a financial success. In an endeavour to increase the breed's popularity it was Captain Graham who proposed that an Irish Wolfhound be presented by the Club to the newly raised Irish Guards. The Club donated ten guineas and a special fund was created to enable the Club to raise the further 20 guineas to cover the purchase price of a hound. One of the ways in which money was raised was by a Guards' Presentation Hound Competition at the Kennel Club Show at which Captain Graham was judge for the breed and Messrs Gresham and Hood-Wright assisted him in judging the special class. The judges were given the following guide to use in their judging: 'The hound best fitted in their opinion, by age, promise, quality or appearance, to be presented to the Irish Guards, keeping in view the fact that it has to be trained for Regimental purposes.'

The winner was Mrs Gerard's 2½-year-old Rajah of Kidnal who was presented to the Guards and was re-named Brian Boru. Mrs Gerard duly received her thirty guineas.

By 1904 three further judges had been included on the Club's judging lists, bringing the total to eleven, more shows by now scheduling Irish Wolfhound classes. The method of choosing judges for shows was then very different from the way it is now and I feel it will interest readers of this book.

A list of shows which scheduled the breed was drawn up by the Club Secretary and this was sent to each of the judges on the Club's list. Each judge was asked which judging appointment would suit him best. Upon receipt of the replies the Secretary would then write to the show committees advising them that the Club would be prepared to support breed classes at that show provided that such-and-such a judge were appointed. Those shows which did not agree to invite the suggested judge were, in consequence, not supported by the Club and as a result no special prizes or trophies were offered.

The Club managed to stay active throughout the war and by the early 1920s had become involved in hound trails and hare-coursing events. A coursing club was later formed which maintained the Irish Wolfhound breed standard, any attempt to use smaller, more lightly built dogs being stopped by the Club when it set a minimum height limit of 29 inches.

Another club, the Irish Wolfhound Association, was formed in 1924 but after a short while, and bearing in mind that the Irish Wolfhound Club was not in as healthy a state as it would have liked to have been, the two united, becoming the Irish Wolfhound Club (with which the Irish Wolfhound Association is united).

Soon the Club was able to produce a Year Book, which was deemed a great success, and, over the years, has provided an excellent record of the breed's history.

In 1930 Princess Mary, Countess of Harewood (later the Princess Royal) became the Club's Patron and when the Club's President, the Marquess of Dufferin and Ava died it was decided not to appoint another President during the time of Her Royal Highness's patronage. Since her death there has been no Patron and the President has been the Irish Guards' Regimental Colonel.

The Second World War had a greater effect on the breed than the First and it was evident that new blood needed to be introduced. Following a visit to America Miss Croucher recommended that Rory of Kihone would be suitable as a sire for British bitches and the result was that Miss McGregor, who had bred Rory, offered him to the Club as a gift. His passage, quarantine costs and insurance amounted to £84 13s, which was quickly repaid out of his stud fees between 1952 and 1954.

Registrations though were still low and the Club found it necessary to urge their members to register all puppies born as there was danger of having CCs withdrawn for the breed. By the 1960s registrations were climbing again and, with them, membership of the Club so that social activities and seminars needed to be organised. Pet owners and their hounds were encouraged to attend the Club's annual Summer Meeting to learn more about the breed. This event later went on to become a Club rally, still held annually and now with a special class for Rescue hounds, judged on their condition rather than their conformation.

The Irish Wolfhound Rescue Trust Fund was set up because although at first very few hounds seemed to need rehoming, the numbers steadily increased for a variety of reasons and there are many who prefer to find new homes for their dogs through the rescue scheme rather than selling them commercially.

The Club's first open show drew an entry of 150 dogs for breed specialist Miss N. Twyman, who came over from Ireland to officiate. At the beginning the breed club's championship event was held in conjunction with the Ladies' Kennel Association but later it held its own championship shows, Judy de Cassembroot having the honour of judging the first such show which brought with it an entry of more than 180 dogs.

Something I find to be a particularly interesting feature of the Club, introduced in the early 1970s, is that of associate membership. It was found that in a numerically growing breed it was not always possible for some people, especially pet owners, to obtain the necessary sponsors if they were to join the Club as full members. The situation was alleviated by the introduction of associate membership which allowed them to take part in all the activities of the Club except that they could not vote for judges nor for the committee. After three years as an associate, a member can apply for full membership if sponsored by two members. The Club now boasts extremely healthy membership figures, quite an achievement when one looks back to the formative years of the Club!

The Club has a goodly number of trophies, some of which are very valuable, not least the splendid Graham Shield depicting a Wolfhound head study. Originally known as the Silver Shield it was renamed in 1910 in memory of Captain Graham. The purchase price of this shield in 1886 was £43 but today it is said that valuation is impossible. This highly acclaimed trophy is presented on an annual basis to the winner of Best in Show at the Club's championship show.

The Club has always supported research into canine health and social events are organised under the guidance of area social secretaries. A judges' training scheme was also introduced in 1984.

In 1985, the year of the Irish Wolfhound Club's centenary, a letter was received from the Queen in which she conveyed her congratulations and good wishes for the future. Indeed, 1985 was a year to remember!

There are presently three breed clubs for the Irish Wolfhound, these being:

Irish Wolfhound Club
Irish Wolfhound Club of Northern Ireland
Irish Wolfhound Society

Names, addresses and telephone numbers of the Honorary Secretaries of these clubs can be obtained from the Kennel Club.

Twelve

The Saluki

Even a student of nations finds that the Saluki helps sometimes
to join together threads of various civilisations. The artist sees
in the Saluki form and atmosphere, and these hunting dogs of
the desert supply the glamour of tradition and the mystery of
the ages to the poet and dreamer. But most of all, those who
seek a true friend will find one in the Saluki.

HON. FLORENCE AMHERST

Early history

Some claim that the Saluki is the oldest pure-bred sporting dog, with early
references dating back to predynastic times, long before the Pharaohs,
somewhere between 6000 and 5000 BC. There is a Saluki head carved in
ivory from this period and later, at Karnak, on a carving in the tomb of the
Pharaoh Wahenkh Antef (2271–2222 BC), are shown four Salukis, called
White Gazelle, Greyhound, Black and Firepot. It is interesting to note that
the Saluki actually pre-dated the camel, for the latter did not arrive in the
Middle East until about 2000 BC. Dogs of Saluki type were depicted in wall
paintings in ancient Egyptian tombs. For instance, a painting in the tomb
of Rekh-Ma-Ra in Western Thebes (c. 1400 BC) depicts Salukis, golden
cream and white in colour, being led in the train of the conqueror. Other
examples are to be found at the tomb of Kenhetep at Beni Hasan and a
pair appear on one of the enamelled funeral boxes in Tutankhamen's tomb.
Many mummified bodies of Salukis have been found, especially in the
tombs in the Valley of the Kings, near Luxor, sometimes still wearing their
jewelled collars. Held in veneration in Egypt, their bodies were prepared
by embalmers, wrapped in linen and put in tombs at public expense with
equally public displays of lamentation and grief! It is interesting to note that
the long foot of the Saluki, so characteristic of the breed, clearly features in
these early records of the breed.

In AD 800 Abu Nuwas, court poet and jester, describing in his writings
the grace of the coursing Saluki, tells his readers that as the dog ran 'one

162

Figure 67
Dogs which are
seemingly of
Greyhound and
Saluki type attacking
game, Thebes,
c. 1450 BC.

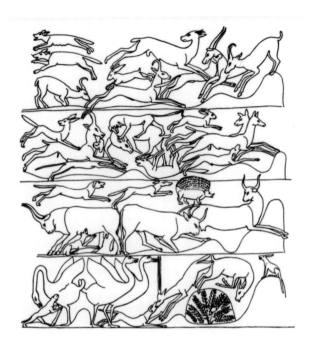

could join his head and feet in his collar', meaning that as the dog ran the legs were lifted high and fast. Nuwas also said that the 'dog peels the skin of the earth with four feet', an indication of the lightness of his gait and, 'His master is to him as a slave; at night he is the nearest to his cradle, and if the dog is naked he covers him with his cloak.'

It is also probable that the Saluki was introduced to China, possibly via the Persian stock, before AD 600. There is a report in the history of the Tung

Figure 68   Hounds resembling Salukis, from a wall painting in the tomb of Rekhma Ra in Western Thebes, *c.* 1400 BC

163

Dynasty that a 'Persian Dog' could run 700 li (about 200 miles) in a day. This dog was said to be as gallant as a horse and some were white in colour whilst others were brown.

Considered a nobleman among dogs the Arab term *slughi (slugi)*, or *saluki* in classical Arabic, means a dog or hound which is respected and it is clear that the Arabs bred the Saluki with care. The feminine forms of these words are *slughiya* (classical) and *silaija* (colloquial). A completely different word, *kelb*, is used for the pariah dog. It has been suggested that the word 'saluki' is derived from a post-Alexandrian Greek empire between Syria and India, by the name of Seleucia. Other historians have said that the name is derived from a long-vanished city in southern Arabia called Saluk which was noted both for the making of armour and for the breeding of swift hounds, described by some as the best hunting dogs. An Arab poem, over a thousand years old, contains the line, 'My dog brought by Kings from Saluk'. In other Arabic writings we find the Saluki described as 'my butcher: he make me independent of imports and importers'. In Persia the term used for this breed was *Sag-i-Tazi* which can be translated as 'Arabian Hound'.

The pedigree was transmitted from generation to generation by word of mouth and no mongrel-breeding was ever allowed. It is here relevant to

Figure 69 This interesting canine, described as a 'Greyhound' is from the time of the Han dynasty (China), AD 210.

point out that Moslems have always had an abhorrence of ordinary dogs which they have, since time immemorial, considered to be unclean. Croxton Smith told of a situation when a man was enjoying the hospitality of a sheikh and enquired of the skeikh how it was that he could eat meat which had been killed by a dog. The sheikh respectfully reminded the man that Salukis were not dogs but hounds. Indeed, the Arab regarded the Saluki as a spiritual hunting symbol and the great Islamic hunter, Yazid II, who lived in the eighth century actually allotted a slave to each of his Salukis, clearly signifying the great esteem in which they were held. Undoubtedly the breed has always been treated with very great respect. Even now, as an acknowledgement of his dignity, the Saluki is sometimes taken to the chase on the back of an Arab horse.

Sahara Desert tribes called the Saluki *Barake*, or 'Specially Blessed' and nowhere in North Africa or Arabia was the Saluki ever sold between tribes, being given as a gift of honour to friends or eminent guests. In Libya the Saluki was referred to as *el Hor*, meaning 'the Noble One' and they said the same of their hounds as they did of their horses, 'Are not these the inherited of our fathers, and shall we not to our sons bequeath them?'

Treated by the Arab in an entirely different manner from ordinary herding or sheepdogs, Salukis were highly prized by the Bedouins because the dogs provided food for the families; the Saluki was the only dog allowed inside the sheikh's tent. It has been said that Arabian dogs could exist for two or three consecutive weeks on milk alone. Puppies were often brought up by the women of the tribe and, indeed, were even suckled by them in difficult times. Indeed, a Saluki was never let out of sight and when a bitch whelped her owners played host to a number of visitors, many of whom hoped for a gift of one of the puppies. When the Bedouin tribe moved on the Salukis were allowed to travel on the backs of camels so that the hot sand did not blister their feet. Very probably it was the vast expanse of desert sand with its inaccessibility which helped to keep the breed pure. Some were presented to princes of other lands than Arabia and this is probably how the breed arrived in Persia where it was highly prized.

Despite the fact that the Saluki was so well cared-for, the dogs from the Arabian Gulf region were usually small and not particularly well nourished. Their coats were quite sparse, usually with feathering on the ears and tail only. Examples of the breed from Persia and Syria carried rather more coat and were generally larger in frame and heavier, enabling them to function in a cooler climate.

Terence Clark, who in recent years has had considerable experience with the breed in Iraq, believes that the Arabs make no distinction in their speech between the short-haired and feathered Saluki, although they would add the adjective *amlat*, meaning hairless or *aryash*, meaning feathery, when distinguishing between the two principal strains. In Iraq, he says, there are four distinct strains but the Arabs rarely differentiate between them, using only the term *Slughi*. In his travels, Mr Clark noticed a wide variety of strains, some of which were highly localised, others common to several different areas. In a most interesting article published in *The Saluki* (winter/spring 1990) he describes the four distinct 'types', which he categorises as smooth-haired, semi-smooth-haired, lightly feathered and feathered. Another observation he makes is that in Iraq it is common practice for bitches to be mated with more than one dog because breeders are keen on thus mixing the progeny and reducing the dangers of inbreeding.

Hunting with the breed

Bedouins certainly have always had a love of the Saluki and have hunted it with the hawk. It seems that the Saluki has more stamina than other Sight Hounds and is quite capable of coursing quarry for hours at a time. A gazelle is capable of moving at 45 miles an hour and yet it is said to tire sooner than the Saluki. Sometimes, though, in an endeavour to wear down the gazelle more quickly, more than one pair of dogs is taken out so that fresh pairs can be slipped. When the prey goes into less open country the hawks are sent after it and the dogs follow the hawks, subsequently holding the gazelle until the hunters arrive to kill it. The Sheikh of the Anezeh, though, preferred to run down the gazelle with his hounds for 'therein there is more sport'.

Often the Saluki was used without the hawk, the sportsman keeping hold of his dog up-wind until within about 500 yards of the prey, from which distance the dogs found it easy to catch the prey, running over desert hare in 'almost a moment'. Another method was to place dogs along the track where the prey was likely to pass and yet another involved the use of 'throwing-sticks', aided by the Saluki. It is most interesting to note that Salukis were known to 'gallop over country that was boulder strewn' and in Arabia were described as being capable of coursing hares 'over ground that would have broken every bone in an English Greyhound, without hurting themselves'.

At the age of six months the youngsters were used to hunt desert rats and jerboas, coursing the desert hare as they matured and then, finally, the gazelle. The gazelle can move at anything between 45 and 52 miles an hour and yet the Saluki's speed rarely exceeds 40. Often, therefore, a gazelle was separated from the herd and coursed down until it was tired out, often being hunted in a circle, the killing taking place near the spot at which the hunt commenced. Any Saluki which did not hunt well by the age of two years was 'got rid of'.

Writings of the early thirteenth century tell of the prized and favoured 'Tazi' of a huntsman prince and in 1506 Affonso d'Albuquerque, the Portuguese adventurer and navigator, said that in the Persian Gulf there were 'many who hunt with falcons and take by their aid creatures smaller than the gazelle, training swift hounds to assist the falcon in catching the prey'. From the sixteenth and seventeenth centuries there are a number of Mughal and Persian manuscripts depicting the Saluki engaged in the chase.

Well-trained Salukis also hunted winged game such as the desert partridge and bustard, startling it into sudden flight and then leaping from

Figure 70
16th century
painting of Salukis

the ground to catch it in the air at a height of several feet. Suitable vegetation for hunting with Salukis has, however, deteriorated over the years, largely due to overgrazing by goats.

Despite the fact that Salukis were much prized, they still suffered from a certain amount of traditional ignorance such as being strapped around the stomach to prevent overeating and being treated by the branding iron if they suffered from pneumonia.

It has been said, at least since the tenth century if not earlier, that when a man loses his way in the desert he barks like a dog. This causes the Bedouin dogs to bark back so that he can follow their noise until he arrives at the encampment. In modern times the Saluki is still used in the chase but is frequently transported by car until the quarry is close by, something which smacks of entertainment rather than sport, I fear!

Coursing matches

Coursing matches for Salukis were also arranged in the East as were races such as that described in the July 1932 issue of the *Tail-Wagger* magazine. Sheikh Uthman of Kifri apparently guarded his fawn and silver Saluki like a child; called Beloved, it was to race against the three-year-old Shitan, owned by a rival neighbour. The race took place at dawn and was heralded by the falconers, Beloved trotting to heel in leash, jacketed against the chill winds of the upland plains. After half an hour's ride the group of rival horsemen was sighted. Upon the sighting of gazelle the falcon was unhooded, the wager of 500 rupees agreed upon and at the signal the Salukis 'were off like twin arrows from one bow'. The sad end to the escapade is that in his excitement the neighbouring sheikh fired his rifle wildly and shot dead his own Saluki. Beloved took the prize and Sheikh Uthman gallantly made a promise that his rival should have one of Beloved's offspring when next she whelped.

How the Arab judged the Saluki

The first thing looked at by the Arab was the chest, which had to be deep and strong. The following points were to be considered and it is interesting to compare these with today's breed standard in the UK.

HEAD: There should be two fingers' width across the top of the head between the ears. There should be plenty of loose skin in the cheek. Ears should be long and finely feathered.

Figure 71   Slughis in the Egyptian desert 1907

FORELEGS: Elbows should be difficult to press together. Wrists should be small, and paws point forward at a small angle.

LOINS: Should be very narrow. There should be a width of three or four fingers between the two hip bones on the top of the back; a deep hollow between these bones is thought very good.

BACK LEGS: Hock must be very pronounced, and the lower the better.

REAR PAWS: There should be a pronounced flatness here, showing easy, quick turning at speed.

TAIL: Feathering must be fine and regular. The tail when pulled down between the legs and round up the back should reach the point between the hip bones.

GENERAL: The main slope of the body should be from tail to shoulder, giving an impression of speed, the hindquarters being higher than the shoulders. An arched back with spine showing is considered a sign of speed.

The Saluki in Europe

It is thought that the first Salukis imported into Europe were brought from Persia, now known as Iran, having gone there originally from Arabia.

There is a magnificent picture in the Dresden Art Gallery in which Duke Henry the Pious is shown with a Saluki. In the picture the Duke wears a pilgrim's collar to prove that he has visited the Holy Land. Salukis and Arab horses are shown together in many paintings.

Although it is the Afghan Hound that is usually claimed to be the breed Noah took into the ark, a splendid painting by Jacopo Bassano (1515–1592), entitled 'Animals Entering the Ark', shows two dogs of Spaniel type, one resembling a smooth Saluki or possibly a small-framed Greyhound and one which is clearly a Saluki. The Saluki is somewhat heavy in foreface but has a typically feathered tail with slight feathering at the back of the second thigh and just a touch at the elbow. It is well muscled and has slightly less tuck-up than the Saluki we know today. It is depicted glancing down fondly at rabbits and the painting is dated as approximately 1555. There are several other paintings depicting the breed, including a number by John Wootton, and in G. F. Reidel's *Icones Animalium* (1798) there is an engraving of 'Aegypticus Turkisher Hund', translated as Egyptian or Turkish Hound, which is a feathered Saluki. James Ward painted a red-grizzel Saluki belonging to Lady St George, this being exhibited in 1807, and thirty years later appeared a painting of a black and tan bitch, 'Zillah', by C. Hamilton. Both these paintings were engraved and, as such, appeared in the *Sporting Magazine*.

It is remarkable that the Saluki has been bred to type throughout the ages, as can be seen in many of the early paintings of both the Middle East and Europe.

The Saluki in England

It appears that the first Salukis came to England with the Arab horses in the early part of the eighteenth century. The first to be recorded with the Kennel Club was a bitch, Tierma, in 1877, she being only the seventeenth 'foreign dog' ever to be registered thus. Owned by Mr Allen and exhibited at shows, it was said that never had so graceful a dog been seen in Europe. Still described as the 'Persian Greyhound' the breed was said to be much like the English Greyhound except that the ears and tails were like those of a Setter. The differences were, none the less, very much greater for the Saluki head is not like any other head besides that of its close cousin, the Afghan Hound.

In 1895 two Saluki puppies were obtained by Mr W. Jennings-Bramley from the Tahawi Bedouin tribe in Egypt's Selia and Ismalia districts. This particular tribe was famous for its horses, hawks and hounds, and the two puppies, bred by sheikhs, were given the names Laaman, meaning 'the swift

Figure 72 'Persian Gazelle Hound' drawn by Arthur Wardle and published early last century. Compare with Wardle's drawing of an Afghan Hound on page 19.

glance of a lady's eye', and Ayesha, so named after the second wife of Mohammed. These were given to the Hon. Florence Amherst who worked with her father in the exploration of Egyptian tombs and antiquities and had much admired the breed. So taken was she with these two beautiful and graceful dogs that they formed the foundation of her Saluki kennel. Indeed, Miss Amherst shouldered the responsibility of bringing the breed to the notice of people in Great Britain whilst anxiously protecting the Saluki from those who wished to alter it from its original type. In her search for dogs of pure breeding she was supported by the Foreign Secretary who very kindly encouraged Iraq's High Commissioner to assist her.

Miss Amherst began exhibiting in 1906 and two varieties were soon to become recognised. The Shami was smooth-coated with feathering on ears and tail and light feathering between the toes and down the backs of the legs. The Njdi, on the other hand, was perfectly smooth with no feathering at all.

Imports came in from Syria and the Western Desert of Egypt. Miss Lucy Bethel imported Reish from Wadi Surhan, the Valley of the Wolf; Reish was mated to Laaman and produced Riechan amongst others. Another of

171

Figure 73 A 'Persian Greyhound' depicted in J. G. Wood's *Illustrated Natural History*, 1861. Compare this with the Russian Greyhound on page 42 and Scotch Greyhound on page 81.

Miss Amherst's noted dogs was Ch Zobied who was bred by Mr Vereker Cowley, he having brought in Salukis from the warlike Arab tribe of Montific. Brigadier-General Lance and his wife were also instrumental in the growth of the breed in this country, importing an important and beautiful pair of black-and-tan hounds called Sarona Kelb and Sarona Sarona. The Brigadier also imported a pair of goldens named Kataf and Reesham. Sarona Kelb, born in 1919, was from desert stock, a reputedly splendid hunting hound who had coursed and killed gazelle in the Middle East. He had the honour of winning the breed's first CC at the Kennel Club Show in 1923 and sired ten Champions, one of which, Orchard Shahin, was the first bitch to pick up a CC in the breed. She went on to become the first Saluki Champion in 1924 having won her three CCs at the first three shows awarding CCs for the breed. She was the result of a brother-sister mating (Sarona Kelb x Sarona Sarona) and won ten CCs in all. Only a month after his daughter had gained her crown, Sarona Kelb was also awarded his third

CC, going on to obtain twelve CCs, the last one awarded when he was eleven years old. Kelb lived to be twelve. The third Champion in the breed, a striking gold named Zobied, belonged to Miss Amherst but we must not forget such dogs as her Sultan who was shown prior to the First World War and was in much demand as a sire. Miss Amherst went on to become President of the Saluki or Gazelle Hound Club and the breed made steady progress. Occasionally at Club shows the owners of Salukis appeared in full eastern dress.

Miss Joan Mitchell was familiar with the Saluki in its native home and imported to this country her El la Bruse strain, usually of a 'wolf colour' and with dark eyebrows. Another who brought Salukis back to England after the war was Major Benetick.

Two early major landmarks in the breed's history came in 1937. Ch Sarona Gemil, a black and tan, was awarded Best Opposite Sex in Show at the Kennel Club Show in October of that year and followed this only two weeks later by a Best in Show win at Birmingham National.

As I mentioned earlier, it was not easy to get Arabs, nor indeed Persians, to part with their Sight Hounds and it often took much persuasive power before a dog was obtained. Colonel Mackenzie, after much difficulty, obtained a dog of the royal Persian strain, Shah by name, in exchange for an Arab pony desired by the prince who owned him.

During the Second World War breeding was carried on on a very reduced scale and this prevented famous strains from completely dying out. Sadly the Orchard kennel, amongst others, failed to continue. The first Championship Show to be held after the war was in 1946 when the two CCs were awarded to Mrs Parkhouse's Selim of Shammar and Mrs McLeish's Fukara of Shammar.

Salukis in the USA

The first Saluki to be imported into America arrived in 1861 but no offspring were ever recorded. Not until 1927 did imports from the English kennels, Sarona and Grevel, bring any real recognition for the breed. The breed experienced difficulties through the war years, just as it did elsewhere, but the minimum American Kennel Club requirement of twenty-five registrations per year was maintained so that the breed could retain its status.

Following the war a desert import arrived by the name of Abdul Farouk; he had cropped ears and was to become the only crop-eared Champion. His new blood was much needed at the time but afterwards the situation was eased by the importation of stock from Europe and the Middle East.

Fact or fable?

A story which so closely resembles that of the infamous Gelert is told of a gentleman whose wife had died, leaving one young son. The child was left alone in the house with a dog which had been reared personally by the man, but upon returning home one day he found the dog in the porch of the house, his muzzle dripping with blood. Thinking that his dog had killed his son and eaten him he killed the dog, only later to find the child asleep in his cradle with the remains of a viper that had been killed by the dog. Full of remorse, the father gave his hound a proper burial.

So many of the stories told revolve, in one way or another, around death. Another tells of a gentleman, al-Harith, who had some drinking companions with whom he spent a good deal of his time and for whom he had great affection. One of these friends, however, was in love with his wife and on one occasion he stayed behind whilst the husband went off with his companions – which was his undoing because the man's hound also remained behind! The couple, having eaten and drunk, 'lay together' and the dog killed them both. Upon his return, al-Harith realised what had happened and told his friends. He wrote a poem about what happened. The poem, in translation, reads hardly like a poem at all but its gist is that the dog was always loyal to him, guarding his honour when betrayed by wife and friend. It expresses his amazement that his friend should violate his honour and amazement that his dog should give him such protection. The story quickly became legend among the Arabs and al-Harith wrote yet another poem saying that a dog is, indeed, better than a faithless friend who seduces his wife whilst he is away. He vows to keep his dog as a drinking companion as long as he lives and to give him his affection and unadulterated friendship.

There are so many stories that I should like to relate from Arab literature but let me close this chapter with one of a slightly different nature. When plague struck the inhabitants of a particular house the local people felt certain that none had survived it and so blocked up the entrance. Some months later one of the heirs went back to the house to open it up and in the courtyard found a young boy, playing with a puppy. The puppy's dam appeared and the boy, who seems not to have been fully weaned at the time the plague struck, crawled to her, she allowing him to suck from her. The young child had copied the bitch's offspring and, in doing so, had survived the death of his own mother.

THIRTEEN

THE SALUKI TODAY

Temperament and adaptability

The Saluki makes a gentle, devoted and elegant companion and enjoys participating fully in family life. Despite the breed's sporting abilities and its coursing instincts, Salukis can be trained to live peaceably with other domestic animals. Most at ease when living in the home, they are quiet and unobtrusive, without any 'doggy smell'; this makes them a pleasure to have around, apart from their beauty!

Firm but gentle treatment, with mutual respect, will usually result in an obedient, well-mannered hound. The Saluki's temperament differs from that of other breeds and one should not expect a Saluki to be overtly welcoming to all and sundry. Whilst not noisy or aggressive dogs, they will give warning when strangers approach their home territory. Indeed the

Figure 74
Saluki, Ch. Kasaque
Hyperion of Saruk

175

breed needs careful and sensible management and, in the hands of a caring and sympathetic owner, is a most charming breed.

The Saluki has a strong homing instinct and it has been said that when a Saluki goes to a new home it must be impressed upon the dog that it is expected to live there. If this is not done, it may decide to return to its previous owner, however far away that may be. Numerous stories have been told about Salukis returning to their old homes via deserts and intricate city streets.

A reasonable amount of exercise is important to keep a Saluki in the peak of condition and it will be found that two Salukis together will, by playing, give each other a good deal of exercise. This is especially useful when free running is not possible. For those who ride horses, the Saluki is able to keep up at full gallop and rarely tires, thoroughly enjoying the outing.

A thin-skinned and single-coated breed, the Saluki is understandably conscious of cold weather and a coat will be needed for use in inclement weather. Otherwise he is a perfectly hardy breed and not delicate in the least, being well able to withstand all climes, given sensible management.

For its size, the Saluki has a remarkably small appetite and can remain in good health on a surprisingly small quantity of correctly balanced food. A Saluki in the peak of condition should be well muscled but without superfluous fat so that the first two or possibly three ribs can be seen very slightly under the skin. The haunches of a Saluki are meant to be seen and in a dog that is well constructed they should be visible and not covered by a thick layer of fat!

Grooming

Salukis are instinctively clean animals and are therefore easy to maintain in a clean condition. Even a bitch in season is very discreet about her condition and keeps herself clean at such a time. The type of brush favoured by the majority of Saluki owners is pure bristle, set into a soft cushion and care must be taken to avoid breaking the hair of the feathering. The feathering can mat and this should never be permitted to happen. At shows a light comb and 'polish' is sufficient to tidy the coat for exhibition. The Saluki is often bathed prior to a show and this is a relatively easy task.

Kennel Club Breed Standard © The Kennel Club

GENERAL APPEARANCE: Gives impression of grace, symmetry and of great speed and endurance, coupled with strength and activity.

CHARACTERISTICS: Great variation in type due to wide geographical area of origin. There are both feathered and smoth varieties. The expression should be dignified and gentle with faithful far-seeing eyes. Light flowing movement.

TEMPERAMENT: Reserved with strangers but not nervous or aggressive. Dignified, intelligent and independent.

HEAD AND SKULL: Head long and narrow, skull moderately wide between ears, not domed, stop not pronounced, whole showing great quality. Nose black or liver.

EYES: Dark to hazel, bright, large and oval, not prominent.

EARS: Long and mobile, not too low set, covered with long silky hair, hanging close to skull. Bottom tip of leather reaches to corner of mouth when brought forward. Provided ear is covered with silky hair which may grow only from top half, the standard is complied with but longer hair also correct.

MOUTH: Teeth and jaws strong with a perfect, regular and complete scissor bite, i.e. the upper teeth closely overlapping the lower teeth and set square to the jaws.

NECK: Long, supple and well muscled.

FOREQUARTERS: Shoulders sloping and set well back, well muscled without being coarse. Chest deep and moderately narrow, when viewed from front not an inverted V. Forelegs straight and long from elbow to wrist. Pasterns strong and slightly sloping. Not round boned. Humerus sloping slightly backwards.

BODY: Back fairly broad, muscles slightly arched over loin, but never roached backed. Brisket long and deep, not barrel-ribbed or slab-sided, with good cut up. Sufficient length of loin important.

HINDQUARTERS: Strong hip bones set wide apart. Stifle moderately bent with well developed first and second thigh. Hocks low to ground.

FEET: Strong, supple, of moderate length, toes long and well arched, not splayed out, but at the same time not cat footed. Feathered between the toes (except in smooth variety). Front feet may point outward, at very slight angle when standing.

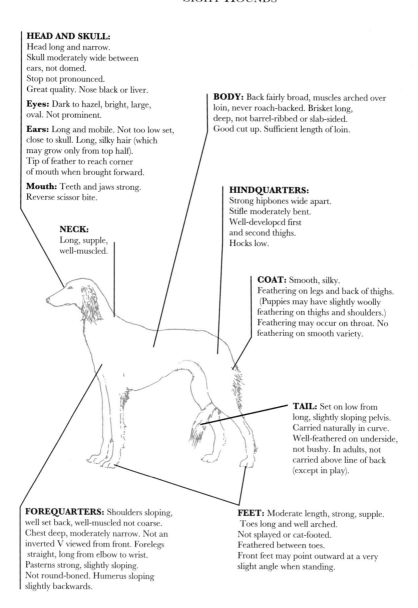

HEAD AND SKULL:
Head long and narrow.
Skull moderately wide between
ears, not domed.
Stop not pronounced.
Great quality. Nose black or liver.

Eyes: Dark to hazel, bright, large,
oval. Not prominent.

Ears: Long and mobile. Not too low set,
close to skull. Long, silky hair (which
may grow only from top half).
Tip of feather to reach corner
of mouth when brought forward.

Mouth: Teeth and jaws strong.
Reverse scissor bite.

NECK:
Long, supple,
well-muscled.

BODY: Back fairly broad, muscles arched over
loin, never roach-backed. Brisket long,
deep, not barrel-ribbed or slab-sided.
Good cut up. Sufficient length of loin.

HINDQUARTERS:
Strong hipbones wide apart.
Stifle moderately bent.
Well-developed first
and second thighs.
Hocks low.

COAT: Smooth, silky.
Feathering on legs and back of thighs.
(Puppies may have slightly woolly
feathering on thighs and shoulders.)
Feathering may occur on throat. No
feathering on smooth variety.

TAIL: Set on low from
long, slightly sloping pelvis.
Carried naturally in curve.
Well-feathered on underside,
not bushy. In adults, not
carried above line of back
(except in play).

FOREQUARTERS: Shoulders sloping,
well set back, well-muscled not coarse.
Chest deep, moderately narrow. Not an
inverted V viewed from front. Forelegs
straight, long from elbow to wrist.
Pasterns strong, slightly sloping.
Not round-boned. Humerus sloping
slightly backwards.

FEET: Moderate length, strong, supple.
Toes long and well arched.
Not splayed or cat-footed.
Feathered between toes.
Front feet may point outward at a very
slight angle when standing.

Figure 75 The Saluki breed standard in brief.

TAIL: Set on low from long and gently sloping pelvis. Carried naturally in curve. Well feathered on underside but not bushy. In adults not carried above line of back except in play. Tip reaching to hock.

GAIT/MOVEMENT: Smooth flowing and effortless, showing both reach and drive, without hackney action or pounding.

COAT: Smooth and of silky texture, feathering on legs and back of thighs. Puppies may have slight woolly feathering on thighs and shoulders. Feathering may occur on throat. In the smooth variety the coat is the same but without feathering.

COLOUR: Any colour or combination of colours permissible other than brindle.

SIZE: Dogs 58.4–71 cm (23–28 inches) at shoulders; bitches proportionately smaller.

FAULTS: Any departure from the foregoing points should be considered a fault and the seriousness with which the fault should be regarded should be in exact proportion to its degree and its effect upon the health and welfare of the dog.

NOTE: Male animals should have two apparently normal testicles fully descended into the scrotum.

Judging the breed

Owing to the different terrains, climates and prey in the Saluki's native lands, a great variation in size is permissible. A graceful breed in every way, and one looks always for that far-seeing expression which is so typical. Despite their grace and beauty, the body needs to be well constructed and the neck length must be sufficient to allow the hound to reach down to its prey. The foot of the Saluki allows it to cope with desert conditions both on rock and hot sand, and it should be long, well arched and slightly webbed and feathered between the toes (except in the smooth variety). Hind angulation should not be exaggerated. A smooth Saluki is permissible in the show-ring.

Points to consider

The Saluki's usefulness to man was in its ability to run fast over extended distances; for this it needed keen eyesight and a physique which would allow

179

Figure 76 Mrs M. Bryce-Smith with her Saluki, Ch. Nefisa Bushrah of Saruk JW, who went on to win the Hound Group at this show

it to carry out the work for which it was used. For sound, efficient movement the shoulder blade must be long, slanting and well laid back, allowing it to absorb the force of violent exercise over what may be rough terrain. Upright shoulders, usually coupled with a short neck, will only allow stilted movement without the long, low stride so necessary for this breed. Correct angulation in the hindquarters, with strong muscular development, is also important, for a dog with insufficient angulation cannot gallop freely. The Saluki, like all the Sight Hounds, needs plenty of heart and lung room so that the chest must not be too narrow and the brisket should reach down to the elbows. Though they can be gentle in repose, when in the field the eyes must be keen, bright and alert.

Figure 77 Saluki moving

Eastern imports of note

British breeders have been keen to keep eastern bloodlines in their stock and even today the Saluki and Gazelle Hound Club includes 'Import' classes at its shows. In 1957 Mr and Mrs Henderson (Kumasi) brought in from Iran (then Persia) two Salukis, one of which, Kumasi Dhiba, was smooth. Her name is to be found behind most of the smooths bred in this country. Dhiba came from Sheikh Chassib Miftim who was at Nazimyah on the Iraqi/Persian border and to make the journey to the Hendersons at Amarah, Dhiba was escorted by eight fully armed Arabs.

The dog brought in by the Hendersons was a feathered one and came from an Iraqi sheikh. He belonged to Sheikh Shakker Kommondan and was apparently one of his favourites, having, by the tender age of eighteen months, killed more than forty gazelles.

Miss Watkins's Windswift kennel was based on Sabbah the Windswift who had been bred in Riyadh, Saudi Arabia, by the Emir Mohammed Ibn Saud. In actual fact Sabbah had originally been presented to the Saudi Ambassador in London but did not seem to enjoy life in the big city so went to live with Miss Watkins, who was then in Kent, where he was mated to Windswift Yasmin.

In 1962 a dog and bitch were imported from Kuwait by Mr and Mrs Heard of Bridport. They came from Sheikh Sabah al Nasir of Kuwait and produced a litter when they came out of quarantine, the Heards retaining a dog, Taufaan Sharqi, and a bitch. Another dog, Sabah al Kuwait, was bred the same way in Kuwait by the Heards and he came to England before moving on to Libya. Before his departure he was used at stud by several of the prominent kennels.

It is a high compliment to the breeders in this country that, in return, several Arab sheikhs have imported dogs from Britain.

Coursing in the UK

Saluki-coursing in the UK began in 1925 when it was organised by Brigadier and Mrs Lance and in Scotland it was restarted in the 1950s. By 1955 there were annual three-day meetings on the moors outside Inverness when the blue-mountain hare was coursed by both Salukis and Deerhounds, although the owners of the latter ran their own stakes. The hares provided some long and thoroughly spectacular courses on terrain that included boulders, bogs and heathers on steep hillsides, despite the fact that unlike the brown hare they go to ground. Such three-day meetings are said to be as much a test of endurance for the owners as for the hounds as they are run over ground on which no Greyhound would ever be coursed. Mrs Hope Waters and her Burydown Salukis were instrumental in the recommencement of coursing in 1955.

The Coursing Section of the Saluki or Gazelle Hound Club now operates under rules based on those administered by the National Coursing Club. Although the rules have been modified over the years they are still very similar to those drawn up by the Duke of Norfolk in the sixteenth century.

It is reassuring to know that the Saluki that is being coursed today differs very little from that which was bred and coursed for centuries by the Bedouin tribes and that as a breed it continues to retain not only its alertness but also its stamina and speed. Another very important factor is that over the years many of the top coursing hounds, who have therefore proved that they are still capable of performing their natural function, have won regularly in the show-ring, although in other breeds, such as the Greyhound, the same cannot be said.

Kennel Club registrations for 1908–1934 and at five-yearly intervals from 1950–2000

1908	–	1917	7	1926	126
1909	7	1918	–	1927	146
1910	5	1919	–	1928	131
1911	6	1920	–	1929	70
1912	17	1921	–	1930	131
1913	6	1922	14	1931	55
1914	2	1923	21	1932	65
1915	–	1924	81	1933	54
1916	–	1925	85	1934	69

1950	73	1970	215	1990	159
1955	144	1975	249	1995	140
1960	152	1980	199	2000	125
1965	154	1985	213		

Breed clubs

The first meeting of the Saluki or Gazelle Hound Club was held in 1923 at Crufts Show in London. There were fourteen interested people at that meeting, one of whom, the Hon. Florence Amhurst, was elected President. Events moved with remarkable speed and in the space of only two weeks a standard of points and a set of Club rules had been set up and approved and by April of the same year the Kennel Club had given approval for official recognition of the Club. In July CCs were approved and the Saluki became a recognised breed.

At that same Crufts Show in 1923 the five Salukis present were entered in the Foreign Dogs section but by April eleven entries had been mustered at the Kensington Canine Society. The winner of the Open Dog class at this show was Sarona Kelb who, as we have already read, was to become the first male Champion in the breed and whose name is to be found behind a high proportion of Salukis in this country today. During the following year members of the Club bred nineteen litters between them and representatives of the breed were exhibited at fourteen shows, five of which offered CCs. The breed was making splendid progress and two further sets of CCs were awarded in 1925. Club membership was continuing to rise steadily and numbered sixty-seven by 1926.

The following year was an historic one for it saw the inauguration of the Saluki Racing Club and also the formation of the Saluki Club of America.

In 1928 there was a change of Secretary and the lady who took over from Mrs Lance, Mrs Holt, compared the Club to 'a large, unanimous family, with the welfare of the breed at heart'.

Until then, classes at shows had always been guaranteed by individual Club members but as the breed moved into the 1930s there was a drop in registrations, and entries at Championship Shows had levelled to an average of around twenty. It was decided that Club members should be asked to donate 10 per cent of any prize money they might win to a Guarantee Fund. This would, hopefully, have the desired effect of Saluki classes continuing to be offered.

In 1939, with the outbreak of war, Club activities were suspended and all assets were frozen. During the war the Hon. Treasurer, Mr Parkhouse, personally made any payments necessary to keep the Club in existence and indeed Mr Parkhouse became the Club's Secretary in 1949.

By 1969 the Club boasted a membership of almost 300 and Kennel Club registrations for the breed were also continuing to rise substantially. The Club was already holding its own Sanction, Limited and Open Shows, as well as successful rallies, but in 1969 the Kennel Club gave permission for the Club to hold a Championship Show. This took place at Ascot on 20 September and brought in an entry of 110 dogs. That same year saw the publication of the Club's first magazine which has grown to become a publication of extremely high quality and is well known by Saluki and other hound enthusiasts throughout the world.

There are presently only two breed clubs for the Saluki, these being the Saluki or Gazelle Hound Club and the Northern Saluki Club. Names, addresses and telephone numbers of the Honorary Secretaries of these clubs can be obtained from the Kennel Club.

FOURTEEN

THE WHIPPET

The Whippet affords a remarkable illustration of
the talent, not to say genius, of the dog-fancier,
and his ability to manufacture new types of dogs.

HERBERT COMPTON (1904)

The Whippet, often referred to in the past as 'the poor man's greyhound' was originally developed by the colliers and other artisans
for rabbit-coursing; later they were to become involved in track-
racing and this, too, proved very popular. As Croxton Smith said, the
Whippet 'mastered the secret of annihilating time and space'. Prior to the
First World War, when public houses could legally stay open all day, many
had a track at the back as a means of drawing in an extra and lucrative
income. Beer was cheap and the betting heavy.

Described as a 'piece of canine art' the Whippet was created by the
working man and many have considered it remarkable that a dog with such
a dainty design could have been created by the mill-hands, factory workers
and miners of the North, typified at the beginning of this century as 'heavy-
limbed, huge-framed, grimy delvers into the bowels of the earth'. Indeed
the North contributed not only to the creation of the Whippet but also
breeds such as the Airedale, Bedlington, Manchester, Yorkshire and
English terriers.

The breeders' requirements were for a small but very fleet Greyhound
which was more hardy than the small Italian Greyhound, an alliance of
swiftness and grace with both pluck and tenacity. Judicious breeding eventually produced an animal which combined the staying powers of the
working terrier with the speed and symmetry of the aristocratic Sight
Hounds, the physical outline having been gradually refined into closer
harmony with that of the Greyhound. Although initially used with the
rabbit, the Whippet was soon to become a dog which could be trained to
race without being led by fur, a more difficult task than at first glance it
might seem, but such competition came within the means of the poorest

185

Figure 78   Whippet and his catch

and the north-countryman took to the idea with avidity. Indeed, from a humanitarian point of view, a race dog which could be excited to great exertion without the scent of blood or sight of fur, well deserved its popularity.

The Whippet was known at first by several different names, amongst which was 'Snap Dog' because when running along the track or meeting a strange dog they would snap at one another. They were also sometimes known as 'Hitalians', an indication of their origin, for this new breed of small Greyhound often came about by crossing Italian Greyhounds with terriers or the Italian with the Greyhound. Others were Greyhound Terrier crosses and it was sometimes the old white English terriers that were used. Some of those involving terrier crosses, including the Bedlington on occasion, were rough-coated and later became known as long-coated Whippets. There has long been speculation as to which breeds were used in the development of the Whippet and the Manchester Terrier is also said to have played his part. Interbreeding gradually began to take place and soon what had been produced was a remarkable little 'Greyhound' which was exceptionally fast and also highly active.

The first Kennel Club registrations for the breed were made in 1891 but only five entries appearing in the Stud Book was a disappointing number, indicating that owners of Whippets were little interested in registering their dogs, most thinking it a waste of both time and expense. A highly acclaimed

Figure 79   The Whippet, often called 'the poor man's Greyhound'.

book about the breed appeared in 1894, written by Mr Freeman Lloyd, and it was largely thanks to his efforts that the Ladies' Kennel Club held a Whippet race, honoured by the presence of members of the royal family. However, dog-racing did not raise as much interest as was hoped at the time. Clearly considered a 'working-class sport', the more wealthy canine enthusiasts did not participate easily in the free and easy atmosphere surrounding it. The breed was to have different requirements if it was to be used for the track alone. The Whippet used both for the rabbit and the track needed to turn quickly and to be neat in using its head and teeth as well as being capable of good speed. For the track it needed to have the power to get off quickly and, without interfering with the other runners, to move at speed to the end of the track.

Before enclosed rabbit-coursing meetings were stopped the procedure often followed was that a number of rabbits was caught by netting and taken to the track as soon as possible afterwards so that they were fresh. The competition took the form of a knock-out, dogs either being handicapped according to their form or their names simply drawn from a hat to decide the pairs. No complicated points system was operated, the Whippet who caught the rabbit being the clear winner. In these early days a rabbit was

Figure 80
Mrs Oughton-Giles
with her Whippets
1902

held by the loose skin on its back and was placed on the predetermined 'spot' which was a small patch of sawdust, circular in shape and used on each occasion so that the rabbit was always released from the very same place. The dogs were slipped with great skill, in much the same manner as you will find described below in relation to track-racing. Each of the two dogs wore a ribbon around his neck and the judge also wore ribbons of the same colour, one around each arm. Depending on which dog caught the rabbit the judge would raise the appropriate arm so that the bets could be paid out as necessary. Tracks at the back of public houses were used for various different trials and occasionally there were mixed matches. Phil Drabble told his readers of one in which a famous pigeon was matched against a Whippet over the distance of 100 yards, though neither competitor was to rise more than six feet above the ground! But it was not long before the breed was used only for the track and for catching rabbits in the open.

188

Figure 81   Weighing in for a Whippet race 1907

Dogs frequently fought one another whilst on the track and on some tracks nets or canvas divided the tracks as a measure for avoiding this problem, and sometimes they were just divided by strings. Other than at Championship events all handicapping was based on known performances, weight and sex. The handicapping was closely studied by exceedingly skilful handicappers and it was known for two dogs to make a dead heat from different marks on at least four successive occasions. The most usual handi-capping scale at championship events was for dogs over 23 lbs, one yard for each pound; 23–18 lbs, 1½ yards to each pound; 18–12 lbs, 2 yards; 11 lbs and under, 3 yards. The 'standard' distance was 200 yards, although some races were run over as few as 100 yards. A fast dog was described in 1931 as being capable of covering 200 yards in twelve seconds which ties in with the published speed of White Eye, a black dog with one white eye, who, in 1888 held the world record for a 21 lbs dog over 200 yards; his speed was twelve seconds which, for purposes of calculation, is equal to a mile in 1¾ minutes. The dogs progressed by an astonishing series of strides or 'jumps' and it seems that the jumps of a dog of about 18 lbs could exceed 15 feet.

Heavy betting took place and much time, trouble and money was expended in getting a dog into the peak of condition. They were fed, exercised and trained with considerable care. Lancashire was the home of

Figure 82 Whippet Racing – 'starting' (c.1904) *(Edwards and Smith)*

Whippet-racing and dogs bred in the county were considered to be of greater importance than those from elsewhere. Cinder-tracks were said to be three or four yards faster than grass and some such tracks in Lancashire were 'world known'.

In the early days of track-racing each dog was held at the starting line by the root of the tail and the scruff of its neck. Upon hearing the starting pistol the slipper would swing his dog forward and throw it as far as he could in such a manner that he would (hopefully) land on his feet. Clearly a good slipper gave the dog he was handling a great advantage and the ability of the slipper was therefore taken into account so that effectively it was the best dogs which won the races rather than the most skilful slippers! There was a great deal of shouting and yelling from onlookers whilst the race was in progress and as the dogs drew to the end of the track their owners would be a few feet beyond the chalk, shouting their dogs to come to them and often waving a piece of material or a towel for which the dog would aim. Sometimes, however, it was a dead rabbit or even a dead pigeon that was waved. Whippet racing continued, though the methods of starting became more and more refined as the years progressed. One dog named Moley Rat was said to have been one of the fastest around 1930 and weighed 25¼ lbs. When only ten months old he won a £100 handicap at Newcastle as well as winning other £100 stakes later. He was a black dog, sired by what was then known as the greatest running dog sire of all time, Tom from Heyside.

As a comparison of the time, the most preferred weight for the show dog was around 16 lbs.

Training of dogs began at a very early age and puppies were called to their food by waving a rag so that they soon learned to come to the rag when called. Great importance was attached to the training of these dogs with roadwork of between 12 and 20 miles per day to perfect the feet and the muscle tone, and a ball was used to give strenuous exercise. Food was to be of the best quality available and it was frequently said that the Whippets ate better food than the families which owned them. Some of the best dogs were said to have been fed only on Scotch beef which had been sent down especially for them, for that obtainable from the butcher's shop was not considered good enough. However, as diet had to be carefully controlled many dogs were kept muzzled to prevent them from eating food which was not intended for them. When not being raced, many were kept almost entirely in the dark and were fed and attended to by one person only so that they were effectively deprived not only of their liberty but also of human company, other than that of one person. That is not to say that these highly prized Whippets were not treated kindly in other respects.

'Rag-racing', as it was often known, was not considered socially uplifting and there was frequently concern about what the neighbours might think if one were to begin participation in such a sport. But this did not stop puppies from being purchased from notably fast strains and eventually being accepted into the home, albeit having first to overcome initial reluctance from the lady of the family. So began the career of another Whippet on the race track.

At the risk of repeating any of the information which has already been covered I believe that readers will find the following article of great interest, despite its considerable length. Written by Mr J. R. Fothergill, President of the Whippet Club, it was published in 1904:

> The whippet has often been called 'the poor man's race horse', but it can also be the rich man's race-dog. It is true that, with a few exceptions, only working men in England have ever attended to whippet-racing, but I shall endeavour to show that, although it is the cheapest form of sport, it is far from being the meanest.
>
> Although whippet-racing finds its patrons amongst some of the narrowest intellects in England, there is no doubt that the simple miners and mill-hands of the North have a genius for the breeding, running, and educating of their dogs. I have visited Lancashire more than once, especially to investigate whippet-racing there, and have come away full of admiration for their scientific methods, their keenness and honesty.
>
> The best racing whippets are bred like race-horses, through a long line of

winners. To be of any use the dog must begin its education very young. As soon as it has been weaned it is kept aloof from his fellow-puppies and other dogs. From this day forward it lives the life of a hermit, having no friends and no enemies. The reason for this is that the dog will have to do his racing unjockeyed, so to speak, over a 200 yards' course, and from the moment he leaves the 'slipper's' hands he must never take his eyes off the 'rag' which another man (the walker up) has carried before him up to the end of the course. If, then, he has been in the habit of chivvying playmates, or fighting with strange dogs, there are ten chances to one that he will prefer to indulge in these games up the course instead of honestly 'running to the rag'. If, on the contrary, he has never known the society of other dogs, it will rarely occur to a whippet to molest them. Those who turn out 'slappers', as they are called, are useless for racing, as they will never run in front. At the first Lancashire whippet-race I attended a friend told me he was bringing out a whelp for the first time. It was twelve months old and had never run in company. I suggested it was a toss-up whether it would 'run honest' or not, and he was quite surprised at my doubts. But the whelp turned neither to right nor to left, and in the company of five screaming dogs, and between some thousand onlookers, ran straight as a line from start to rag.

During the first six months or a year a puppy requires much attention and patience; he is generally, therefore, handed over to an experienced 'walker', who, for two or three shillings a week, will keep and educate him. The puppy at once takes up his quarters in the man's kitchen and bedroom, where he plays and sleeps till his master has left work for the day, when he is taken for a walk. It is comical to see a little puppy walking on a lead, muzzled and coated. They always muzzle whippets to prevent them picking up bad food when in training; many of them even sleep in their muzzles.

The puppy is now encouraged to tear and worry rag paper, even though he destroys, at times, some of his master's belongings. The taste for the rag once developed, he is held by one man in the proper slipping fashion, whilst another worries him with a rag. He is let loose at it, and then, by increasing the distance from a yard to thirty or so, the puppy will dash at the rag with all the speed he can muster. Great care is taken not to give the puppy too much exertion, as this would damp his fire. He is taken to whippet-races, where he hears the people shout, accustoms himself to the starter's pistol and the noise of the dogs yelping. No dog shows more nerve than the racer; he is indifferent to everything save his rag, and afraid of nothing. The experiment was once tried, for a wager, of lighting a line of straw across the track; the dogs ran through it quite blindly. I have been asked whether a dog was brought to such a pitch of keenness by starving him; and again whether he was taught by the whip! The reader will already have understood there is no need for such curious means to prick the courage; nay rather, the dog, whatever be his offence, is never chastised. The fearlessness of the race-dog is due entirely to the fact that he has never known suppression or defeat from man or beast. He lives by rule, is daily given his runs and walks, and his only diversion is to witness a dog-race, or to visit the public house of an evening in his master's arms or on the lead. Here he will attract a circle of whippeters, who will handle him and maul him about on the table, much to the satisfaction of the walker.

When the whelp is about ten months old he bids good-bye to his first keeper, and starts life with a trainer. Of course the greater number of dogs are brought up by their owners and trained by them, but most of these will spend six weeks, at some time, with a trainer. But the successful dogs, as a rule, are those that are under professional care, which is by no means expensive.

The dog is now walked regularly from 5 to 15 miles a day, according to his size, and does a 200 yards' course twice a week, or even shorter distances. When he is quite hard, and his feet in condition to stand the cinder track, he runs his first race. It is impossible to lay down hard and fast rules for training, as trainers differ so much in method, and dogs in constitution; but the chief points observed are these. The dog must have enough slow work for hardening him to give him stamina, say, for three races in an afternoon, and enough running to develop his speed; by observation and timing the trainer is able to see how much exercise, fast and slow, he needs. It is important, moreover, that the dog, when walking, should go on a lead at his trainer's pace, and that, when he runs, the distance shall never exceed 200 yards. As for feeding, the bantam's eggs, the first slice off a shoulder of lamb, old sherry, and other delicacies that one hears is the race-dog's bill of fare, these are vain imaginations! The dog usually gets a basin of broken bread, gravy and pudding; very often tea and ale, and, in fact, has just what the family has. Meat he is not given until the last few days before a race. Of course if he has to run for £50 match he is somewhat more expensively fed for a week or so. (From *The Twentieth Century Dog (Sporting)* edited by Herbert Compton)

Mr Fothergill tells us that there were no more than four 'crack slippers' in Oldham and that they took between £3 and £5 for slipping the winner of a handicap; he stresses how important it was to secure a good slipper for some of them could procure as much as three or four inches by the skill used in their methods. A really good slipper might slip as many as thirty dogs in one Saturday afternoon. Having explained the handicap system in some depth, Mr Fothergill goes on to say:

I cannot but think with regret how many bad dogs are exterminated every year, but as the whippeter is a poor man he cannot afford to keep bad stock.

On the other hand, there are feelings almost romantic between the owner and a successful dog; it is always the centre of love and affection in the family, and deserves to be when, perhaps, it has supported them from time to time by its winnings. And when it gets too old it lives for the rest of its life by the fire, and the family gets another winner to run for them. Of course betting is with the whippeters the sole aim of dog-racing. At the winning end of the course there is a stand erected for 'clockers'. These stand with watch in hand and time the winners of the first heats before they and their friends put down their money on the ultimate winner. The dog-timing watch is expensive, costing about £9 or £10; the hand travels round the dial once in two seconds. Thus a dog can be timed easily to a sixteenth of a second, which represents a yard.

Twice a month all through the year there is a handicap of £25 or £40 at Oldham itself, at which some two or three hundred dogs are entered. After the first round one can generally get 6 to 1 or better on the field. Sums of £300 or £400 are frrequently won at these handicaps, and I once saw a dog backed by its owner to win £3000, but he lost by a nose! Needless to say the owner was a well-to-do innkeeper.

Tricks of the trade and disrepute

We have already discussed the influence that the slipper could have on the success of a Whippet and there were indeed a number of tricks which were regularly practised. Money being involved there were undoubtedly wrangles, one of which was to enter a good dog under the name of a less successful one. Dogs being known in other districts only by name and not by sight, such a practice was possible and if the handicap was on form rather than on weight a good dog under the guise of a poor one had an obvious advantage. This misdemeanour was aided by the fact that the dogs were kept well rugged-up until the very moment at which the race was to commence so that with a little devious skill even the colour could be changed so that one dog might pass as another. There was even a case of a dog being entered as a bitch. Apparently it was sometimes considered necessary to increase the odds on a good dog and so he might be deliber-ately undertrained or might even have had an elastic band around his muzzle so that he might not catch the rabbit. Sometimes 'holding' was employed, which meant that the dog was not slipped immediately on the gun, and it was not unknown for a dog to have one of his feet trodden on so as to lame him. The tricks were seemingly endless and must, I suspect, have required a good deal of skill on the part of the dogs' owners and handlers!

Mr Fothergill, again, gives us a clear insight into some of the less ethical side of Whippet-racing:

There are many ways of acting fraudulently, so that the favourite cannot win. Doping and other tricks are uncommon; they are too elaborate. But where there is no careful supervision of the start, – on the London running grounds, for instance, – the slipper gets the dog off with a bad start. This is so common a practice in London that on occasions the pistol has been fired and none of the dogs have been slipped, the reason being that each man was betting on others' dogs. This of course reduces the sport to robbery and absurdity. But if the stewards insist on fair starting, there are left fewer ingenious tricks in whippet-racing for cheating the betting than there are in horse-racing; for it is possible to see if a man has held his dog, however momentary the delay may have been, whilst it is never quite obvious that a jockey is pulling.

Unfortunately there were, indeed, those who were only interested in the financial profit to be gained from Whippet racing and this often brought the sport into disrepute. It was actually known to have an effect on the working conditions of some of those who owned successful racing dogs if, for example, their foreman was also involved in the sport in some way. Even school children had a vested interest for they would often be quizzed by their teachers as to which dogs were due to run when.

A breed for the ladies?

Around the turn of this century it was thought that Whippet racing, 'suitably conducted', was a sport in which ladies might find great delight for it offered 'the quintessence of excitement crystallised into a few seconds'. It was possible that it might be conducted in private enclosures, thus adding an attraction to dog-breeding which was not to be obtained 'in the same innocent conditions' in any other breed. Added to this there was no bloodshed but a great deal of fun. In Mr Fothergill's view, 'A lady looks better with a whippet than with most other dogs; they are so ornamental. Though if for this purpose a foil is required, a bulldog certainly serves best.'

Whippets in the show-ring

Born in 1891, Zuber was to become the breed's first Champion in the show-ring, a title he claimed in October 1896 at the Kennel Club Show. He had won his first CC at Bath in 1894 and his second at Crystal Palace in 1895. Bred and owned by Mr Vickers, he was by White Eye out of Herndell and it is interesting to note that White Eye, a black dog with one white eye, was described as a '21 lb racer'. Ch Zuber was a highly influential sire, as was

Figure 83   The Whippet as depicted by Scott Langley in Hutchinson's *Dog Encyclopaedia*, published in 1934.

his son, Ch Enterprise, also owned by Mr Vickers. The first bitch to gain her crown was Ch Manorley Model, an event which happened at the Kennel Club Show in 1897. Bred in 1893 by Mr R. Riley, she was owned by two brothers, Messrs F. and J. Bottomley who dominated the show-ring right up until the First World War. She was a red and white bitch, sired by Spark and out of Jenny. The Bottomley brothers did not breed many of their champions but they were adept at picking up hitherto unknown stock at the race track, re-registering them to carry the Manorley prefix, and then exhibiting them as show dogs, frequently with great success. Ch Seagift Seraph was the first Whippet to be shortlisted for the Best in Show award at a General Championship Show. It was at the East of England Ladies' Kennel Society in 1947 that she was beaten only by the Best in Show and Reserve Best in Show winners (there was no Group system in operation). Bred in 1944 by Mrs Barnsley and Mrs Whitwell, she was golden fawn and was the first post-war bitch Champion.

The following year, at Leicester Championship Show, the Whippet Ch Brekin Spode was awarded the honour of Best in Show, the first award of its kind for the breed. Spode, bred by Lady F. M. Danckwerts, had a very great influence on the breed and her dam was the highly acclaimed Ch White Statue of Conevan. Ch Fieldspring Betony was a highly acclaimed Whippet who gained his title in 1953 and sired five Champions as well as other winning stock. A small dog, of a size small enough for the poacher to carry under his coat, as the breed should be, he was owned by Mrs Cooke and is behind the majority of modern Whippet pedigrees. Incidentally, his litter sister, Ch Fieldspring Betony, also gained her crown in the same year. Others who sired a number of Champions were Mr Douglas Todd's Ch Wingedfoot Marksman and Mrs Chapman's Ch Pilot Officer Prune, whilst Mrs McKay's Ch Laguna Ligonier sired no fewer than twelve Champions. Multiple CC winners in the show-ring include Mrs Knight's Ch Dondelayo Roulette, with twenty CCs and Mrs Argyle's Ch Harque the Lark who gained nineteen. Ch Laguna Ravensdown Astri and Ch Sticklepath Saracen were also multiple CC winners of note. In 1958 Ch Robmaywin Stargazer of Allways won the Hound Group at Crufts and Reserve Best in show went to Mrs Knight's Ch Dondelayo Duette.

FIFTEEN

THE WHIPPET TODAY

Temperament and adaptability

The Whippet is a highly adaptable dog and is of such a size that he can fit in well with most household situations. Because the Whippet's history of coursing and racing are primarily of an amateur nature he has, over the years, been principally owner-trained and has therefore not developed the exaggerated muscle which can be seen on some of the Greyhounds bred for the race track. Whippets, however, retain their instinct for ratting, are quite capable of pointing game and will frequently not hesitate to flush rabbits, even though it may mean that they have to go through thick cover. Some are not averse to coursing hares or working with ferrets and they are rarely gun-shy. In short, one should never lose sight of the fact that the Whippet is a sporting dog, something it has always been. He was developed to cover short distances and has great stamina; these facts must also be borne in mind when selecting a breed.

A highly intelligent animal, in disposition the Whippet is loving and expresses great affection to humans. He is easy to house and his size, coat and habits make him easy to keep clean, added to which this is not a breed that is difficult to feed. Especially when sharing the home, the Whippet becomes a devoted companion and with children he is a gentle and generally tolerant companion.

He can, though, be somewhat sensitive to cold winds but is otherwise just as hardy and free from disease as the other Sight Hounds, although he is of smaller stature. It is not difficult to train a Whippet to use only those areas of the home designated for him, provided that a comfortable bed, raised slightly from the floor, is available at all times. As with all breeds the bed must be free from draughts and damp.

A sensitive and intelligent hound, there has, over the years, been some concern that the breed might be in danger of losing not only type but also some of its breed characteristics through becoming too commercialised. Registrations rose rapidly but during the 1980s eased off to a level which gave less cause for concern. As with all breeds, there is a terrible fear amongst specialist breeders when Kennel Club registrations climb unacceptably high but, thankfully, the majority of those who are genuinely involved in the breed stay the course and their bloodlines are still available for use when breed statistics are once again on an even keel.

Coat and general grooming

Despite the fact that the Whippet has a short, tight coat, it would be a mistake to think that it does not need grooming. Grooming is an important part of any dog's routine and apart from the bond that can be formed between dog and owner during grooming sessions it is essential if the coat is to be kept in good order. A Whippet needs regular grooming and although some people choose to bath their dogs infrequently others bath them with a certain regularity, usually at least a couple of days before a show so that the coat settles sufficiently. The aim is to have the coat looking sleek and 'satiny'.

A general brushing will loosen any dry dirt, following which a comb should be used and then a softer brush. A rubber-spiked brush should then

Figure 84 Pauline Oliver with her Whippet Ch. Spyanfly Says it's Bardo

be used all over, especially inside the thighs, on the underparts and the head; this has a massaging effect. Finally use a hound glove and then polish off with a soft cloth. Treat the ears with special care when grooming, using a small, moist sponge to clean the outside of the ear if necessary for there is a possibility that the ear tips may have come into contact with the content of the food bowl when eating and, if so, this needs to be removed as soon as possible.

Bathing is a simple procedure but care must be taken to thoroughly rinse out the shampoo, for which purpose a large soft sponge can be used. It is not wise to bath a single-coated dog only a matter of hours before a show as it takes a good few hours for the natural oils to return to the coat. It is possible to allow a Whippet to dry naturally in warm surroundings and indeed it is wise to keep him in a warm atmosphere for several hours after bathing.

Because he is a single-coated dog, as has already been mentioned, the Whippet does feel cold winds more than many other breeds and so it is advisable to have a coat to act as some measure of protection when exercising in cold weather.

Nails need trimming, and ideally filing, if your hound's feet are to look their best. If one does not wish to go to the trouble of filing I have seen many Whippets' nails kept in perfectly good order by slight trimming on a weekly basis, but always at least four days prior to a show so that the edges have had time to smooth off. For the show-ring it is wise to see that the coat down the sides of the neck is not too profuse and a good quality pair of thinning scissors can be used for this purpose. This should, however, only constitute 'tidying up' and the breed should in no way look as if it has been trimmed or scissored. Likewise, a certain amount of discreet 'tidying' can be carried out on the feathering of the thigh, the general area of tuck-up and on the tail if necessary. Several exhibitors tend also to the whiskers on the face, but this is simply a matter of preference.

Colour and size

Colour and size are two features of the breed which have changed more than other characteristics over the years. Height is perhaps that which has been of greatest concern so that the breed would not be confused either with a small Greyhound or a large Italian Greyhound. A Whippet which is too large runs the risk of being coarse and if too small there is that danger of its appearing somewhat like one of the Toy breeds.

For many years the height incorporated in the Kennel Club's Breed Standard was 18½ inches for dogs and 17½ inches for bitches although there was also a stipulation that 'Judges should use discretion and should not unduly penalize an otherwise good specimen.' This gave a certain degree of latitude and the breed standard now states that the height of dogs can range between 18½ and 20 inches and bitches 17½ and 18½ inches. It is interesting in relation to height to read C. H. Douglas-Todd's comment that those he described as 'older and more experienced breeders and exhibitors' were convinced that 'it would be a great mistake to make any changes'.

Exercise

Although the Whippet is capable of doing considerably more, a couple of miles roadwork each day is sufficient to keep the hound in good general condition and sufficiently muscled up. On occasions when roadwork is not possible, about thirty minutes' free exercise should be arranged instead. Because he is an active dog the Whippet will make full use of a good-sized run if given one and this will, to a certain extent, compensate for roadwork, although controlled exercise on a lead develops muscles in a different way, so a combination of both is the ideal.

Kennel Club Breed Standard © The Kennel Club

GENERAL APPEARANCE: Balanced combination of muscular power and strength with elegance and grace of outline. Built for speed of work. All forms of exaggeration should be avoided.

CHARACTERISTICS: An ideal companion. Highly adaptable in domestic and sporting surroundings.

TEMPERAMENT: Gentle, affectionate, even disposition.

HEAD AND SKULL: Long and lean, flat on top tapering to muzzle with slight stop, rather wide between the eyes, jaws powerful and clean-cut, nose black, in blues a bluish colour permitted, in livers a nose of the same colour, in whites or parti-colour a butterfly nose permissible.

EYES: Oval, bright, expression very alert.

EARS: Rose-shaped, small, fine in texture.

MOUTH: Jaws strong with a perfect, regular and complete scissor bite, i.e. upper teeth closely overlapping the lower teeth and set square to the jaws.

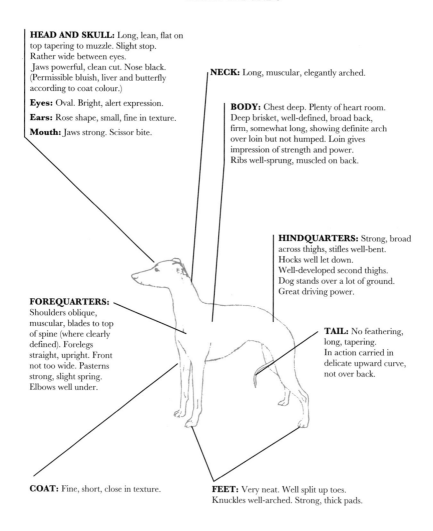

HEAD AND SKULL: Long, lean, flat on top tapering to muzzle. Slight stop. Rather wide between eyes. Jaws powerful, clean cut. Nose black. (Permissible bluish, liver and butterfly according to coat colour.)

Eyes: Oval. Bright, alert expression.

Ears: Rose shape, small, fine in texture.

Mouth: Jaws strong. Scissor bite.

NECK: Long, muscular, elegantly arched.

BODY: Chest deep. Plenty of heart room. Deep brisket, well-defined, broad back, firm, somewhat long, showing definite arch over loin but not humped. Loin gives impression of strength and power. Ribs well-sprung, muscled on back.

HINDQUARTERS: Strong, broad across thighs, stifles well-bent. Hocks well let down. Well-developed second thighs. Dog stands over a lot of ground. Great driving power.

FOREQUARTERS: Shoulders oblique, muscular, blades to top of spine (where clearly defined). Forelegs straight, upright. Front not too wide. Pasterns strong, slight spring. Elbows well under.

TAIL: No feathering, long, tapering. In action carried in delicate upward curve, not over back.

COAT: Fine, short, close in texture.

FEET: Very neat. Well split up toes. Knuckles well-arched. Strong, thick pads.

Figure 85 The Whippet breed standard in brief.

NECK: Long, muscular, elegantly arched.

FOREQUARTERS: Shoulders oblique and muscular, blades carried up to top of spine, where they are clearly defined. Forelegs straight and upright, front not too wide, pasterns strong with slight spring, elbows set well under body.

BODY: Chest very deep with plenty of heart room, brisket deep, well defined, broad back, firm, somewhat long, showing definite arch over loin but not humped. Loin giving impression of strength and power, ribs well sprung, muscled on back.

HINDQUARTERS: Strong, broad across thighs, stifles well bent, hocks well let down, well developed second thighs, dog able to stand over a lot of ground and show great driving power.

FEET: Very neat, well split-up between toes, knuckles well-arched, pads thick and strong.

TAIL: No feathering. Long, tapering, when in action carried in a delicate curve upward but not over back.

GAIT/MOVEMENT: Free, hindlegs coming well under body for propulsion. Forelegs thrown well forward low over the ground, true coming and going. General movement not to look stilted, high stepping, short or mincing.

COAT: Fine, short, close in texture.

COLOUR: Any colour or mixture of colours.

SIZE: Height: dogs 47–51 cm (18½–20 inches); bitches 44–47 cm (17½–18½ inches).

FAULTS: Any departure from the foregoing points should be considered a fault and the seriousness with which the fault should be regarded should be in exact proportion to its degree and its effect upon the health and welfare of the dog.

NOTE: Male animals should have two apparently normal testicles fully descended into the scrotum.

Judging the breed

Judges should not encourage exaggerations in this breed for it was built for speed and for work. The Whippet should combine power and strength with elegance. The body should be well arched-up (but not wheel-backed!) and overall the Whippet should be graceful in outline. Withers are prominent and the chest, allowing for plenty of lung and heart room, should be deep. Quarters should be broad across the thighs, the stifles well bent and hocks well let down. Effectively the Whippet stands over a large amount of ground for his size and on the move has great drive from the rear. According to the standard the maximum height is 20 inches but unfortunately there are too many over-sized specimens, which should not be encouraged. It is always useful when judging the breed to look at an exhibit from the back. In doing

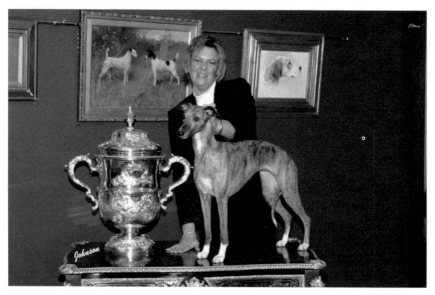

Figure 86 Whippet, Ch. Cobyco Call The Tune BIS Crufts winner 2004, pictured at the Kennel Club with owner Lyn Yacoby-Wright.

so, one can see clearly how the shoulders and elbows fit in with the general conformation.

Looking ahead

The Whippet is a versatile breed and has, over the years, been in constant danger of becoming too commercialised, falling into the hands of breeders who think more of commercial gain than of breed type. Possibly they have been attracted to the breed because it is easy to manage, relatively in-expensive to feed and easy to whelp. A great many breeders have, in the past, bred haphazardly and this has resulted in a large number of Whippets needing to be re-homed. In recent years Kennel Club registrations have dropped slightly but seem to be creeping up again, added to which far more puppies are actually bred than are registered with the Kennel Club, especially in a breed which is used also in sport. Responsible breeders must constantly seek to be certain of the integrity of those to whom they sell their puppies.

Despite the above comments, the Whippet has undoubtedly improved tremendously over the last thirty years or so and the UK breeders pride themselves on having the best bloodlines in the world.

The sporting Whippet

Developed to reach great speed over short distances, the Whippet has both a keen eye and a quick brain with a high level of intelligence. As a result it is capable of hunting, even for hours on end, and can catch both the hare and the rabbit. It has to be said, however, that although some Whippets are efficient at coursing hares, the hare is a large quarry for such a relatively small dog and frequently the Whippet is unable to dispatch the hare cleanly and quickly. Some Whippets will run beside the hare, seemingly for fun and without any intention of catching it. Whippets work well with ferrets and they are rarely gun-shy.

In hare-coursing there is also some element of danger to the dog. The hare can turn very sharply and if the Whippet should happen to catch hold of the hare at the moment of turn there is a risk of the Whippet's neck being broken. This may be one of the reasons why so many Whippets are injured when hare-coursing. Thus it takes courage for the owner of successful show stock to course their hounds for there is a very real risk of injury; nonetheless there are several bench champions who have competed successfully, amongst them being Miss Baird's Ch Sound Barrier, who won the top

Figure 87 Whippet puppies playing chase and displaying their natural ability to run

trophy for dogs, the Moonlake Cup, for two consecutive seasons. The coursing season, which is from late September to early March, runs concurrently with the show calendar for this breed, so life can get quite complicated. Apart from General Championship Shows, including Crufts, there are also breed club shows at this time and this means that one needs to look carefully at both calendars so that one can get the dog into show bloom and out of it at the appropriate times!

Because of the nature of their work, the Whippet's jaws must, of necessity, be strong so that the quarry can be gripped and held. Whippets in general have good mouths and certainly either an overshot or undershot mouth is a very serious fault.

At speed rabbits do not run in a straight line but dodge from side to side so that a Whippet may well be obliged to make a 'side catch'. His neck therefore needs to be both very powerful and very flexible if he is to catch and kill the quarry. The pads of his feet need to be thick and with well 'cut-up' toes to grip the ground when turning.

Kennel Club registrations for 1908–1934 and at five-yearly intervals from 1950–2000

1908	132	1917	16	1926	275
1909	121	1918	15	1927	314
1910	127	1919	26	1928	326
1911	121	1920	87	1929	288
1912	114	1921	116	1930	211
1913	150	1922	160	1931	162
1914	91	1923	207	1932	154
1915	40	1924	201	1933	196
1916	39	1925	247	1934	176
1950	675	1970	2038	1990	1581
1955	708	1975	1615	1995	1514
1960	1528	1980	1676	2000	1686
1965	2045	1985	1293		

It must be noted that the Kennel Club changed its registration to a single-tier system on 3 April 1989 and this is responsible, at least in part, for the sudden increase of figures in registration figures from 1989.

Breed clubs

The Whippet Club was the first of the specialist clubs for the breed and was founded for its betterment in 1899, standing alone as a breed club for thirty-seven years. It is likely that there were indeed clubs prior to that date but these were most probably only devoted to Whippet-racing. In the early years of the breed, right up until the mid-1930s, there were very few classes for Whippets unless they were guaranteed by the Whippet Club. Guaranteeing a class effectively means that if the entry fees do not amount to the prize money the guarantor makes up the difference. Even at Championship level Whippets were considered one of the lesser breeds. In an endeavour to keep the breed true to type, the Club kept a careful check on whether or not breed judges were judging according to the requirements of the breed and they regularly recommended judges for the larger shows. The system seemed to work well and it became a recognised procedure that show secretaries asked for the recommendation of the Whippet Club in this regard. It is interesting to note that, at a meeting in 1908, the Club asked the Kennel Club if the name of the breed could be changed from Whippet to 'Miniature Greyhound' but the name of Whippet has remained to this day.

Registration of the title 'The Whippet Club' was granted by the Kennel Club at a meeting held on 3 October 1898 and the *Kennel Gazette* of October 1900 tells us that a 'Whippet Handicap', promoted by the Whippet Club was held at Crystal Palace. Unfortunately, however, there are no records of the Whippet Club's first few years of existence for at a meeting in 1909 the Secretary, Mr C. B. Payne, confessed that he had left the minutes books on a train at King's Cross Station. As former Hon. Secretary of breed clubs myself, I can imagine how that unfortunate man must have felt. Could he possibly have committed a worse sin? Records do, however, go back to 1907, so someone at least must have retained copies of minutes for the previous two years. The Club's first chairman was Mr Fred Bottomley (Manorley) and many well-known breeders and exhibitors have served either on the committee or as officers throughout the years. In the early years two of the longest serving officers were Messrs Lewis Renwick and Bernard Fitter.

The Whippet Club did not function during the First World War but at a meeting in November 1919 it was decided that the activities of the Club should recommence. Even as late as the 1930s Whippets were regarded as one of the lesser breeds and the Whippet Club and individual members of the Club frequently stood as guarantors when classes were scheduled for the breed. The Club also kept a careful check on its list of recognised judges for the breed and was often asked to recommend judges, especially for the larger shows. This, in turn, played its part in keeping the breed true to type.

Indeed the Whippet Club had a substantial part to play in those early years for in 1921 it is recorded that the Kennel Club asked the Club which shows they recommended for the allocation of CCs, to which the response was Crufts, Birmingham, Cardiff, Taunton, Bristol and Reading.

There had been concern for several years that there should not be any division between show and working dogs for many of the Whippet-racing clubs ran small Lurchers and, despite the fact that they were not pure-bred, called them Whippets. The problem was exacerbated by the fact that the rules of many racing clubs stated merely that the dogs raced should be of 'Whippet type'. It is fair, though, to say that some of the clubs, especially in the south, ran pure-bred Whippets only. As a result, in 1968 a sub-committee was formed by the Whippet Club to set up rules for the racing of pedigree Whippets. This went on to become the Whippet Club Racing Association (WCRA), which ran several Championship meetings each year confined to Whippets holding WCRA 'passports'. To hold such a 'passport' a Whippet must be Kennel Club registered and must have five generations of breeding behind it, acceptable to the Association. No dogs under 16 lbs or over 30 lbs may compete and to qualify for the title of Whippet Club Racing Champion a dog has to have won two Championship finals. The first Championship meeting of this kind was held at Bracknell in 1970. Any change in WCRA ruling has to be put before the AGM of the Whippet Club for approval.

In its long history the Whippet Club has held two special anniversary celebrations. To celebrate the Club's fiftieth year Mr Leo Wilson and Mr B. H. Evans were the judges at its Jubilee Show and between them they drew a record entry. It seems that the National Whippet Association and the Midland Whippet Club lent their support and co-operation which the Whippet Club found very praiseworthy. For the eightieth birthday celebratory show there were parades of show and racing champions which endorsed the forming of the WCRA.

The Whippet Club provides its members with newsletters and has a Whippet Rescue Fund which, in the early 1980s, became a registered charity. It is interesting to note that member clubs of the WCRA are instrumental in raising funds in this regard. The Club now also includes classes for racing and coursing Whippets at some of its shows.

The National Whippet Association is another long established club, having been formed in 1936 and launched on a capital of only £2, with just six people in attendance at the Club's first meeting. Mrs Conway-Evans was instrumental in getting the Club off the ground and, indeed, for keeping alive an interest in the breed throughout the war years. There was an Open Show in October 1945 and the Club's first Championship Show was held at the Scottish Drill Hall, London, in 1946 with Mr C. G. Douglas-Todd as the judge, drawing an entry totalling 239. The Club became well known for its Members' Lunches, the first of which was held at the West of England Ladies' Kennel Society in 1948.

The Midland Whippet Club was formed in 1949 with the Northern Whippet Club and the Whippet Club of Scotland both following within the next decade. Many of the more recent breed clubs restrict their activities to geographical areas. As is the case with several of the breeds which are served by a number of different societies a Breed Council has now been formed.

There are presently eleven breed clubs for the Whippet, these being:

East Anglian Whippet Club
Midland Whippet Club
National Whippet Association
North Eastern Whippet Society
Northern Counties Whippet Club
Northern Ireland Whippet Club
South West Whippet Club
South Yorkshire Whippet Club
Whippet Club
Whippet Club of Scotland
Whippet Club of Wales

The names, addresses and telephone numbers of the Honorary Secretaries of these clubs can be obtained from the Kennel Club.

SIXTEEN

SOME OTHER CLASSIC SIGHT HOUND BREEDS

Azawakh

The Azawakh is named after a valley in north-east Mali, where this hound was first discovered. But for a long while it has lived across most of North Africa where it acted as a companion and protector of the Tuareg Bedouins, by whom it is valued as highly as a camel. This breed was developed for speed and for staying power, reaching speeds of up to forty miles per hour (sixty-four km per hour) and chasing sometimes for as long as five hours in an incredibly hot climate. Another name for the breed is the Tuareg Sloughi, and it is occasionally called Azi.

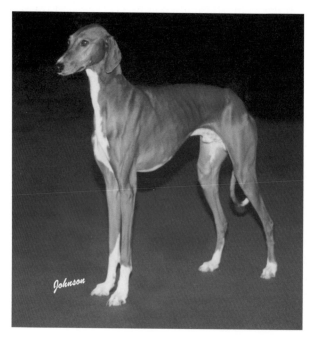

Figure 88
Azawakh

It assists the Tuareg Bedouins in hunting and even as puppies Azawakhs learn to chase animals. They are socialised by spending time with young members of their pack, for they can learn from them as they chase away or kill any intruders. When the Tuareg set off on a hunt, their dogs are usually carried with them on their saddles, then, when prey is sighted, they are released for the chase.

The genetic relationship with other Sight Hounds is still uncertain, but some images would lead us to believe that the breed may have been around for as long as three thousand years.

Introduced both to Europe and to the US in the twentieth century, this is a breed that some find aesthetically most pleasing, whereas it is not a breed that appeals to everyone. The Azawakh has a natural tendency to guard and is instinctively reserved with strangers, though thoroughly gentle with people it knows and loves.

A particularly slender and elegant hound, measuring 60–74 cm (23–29 inches) and weighing 15–25 kg (33–35 lbs), the Azawakh is full of refinement, with a fine, dry skin under which muscles are visible. This is a tall and racy dog, without coarseness and his frame fits into a standing rectangle. The Azawakh has a very distinctive 'dancing' gait and a pronounced fineness of outline. The smooth, taut skin is covered by a short, silky coat, the colours are red or sand, from the lightest to the darkest of these colours, also all brindle colours are acceptable, with or without a black mask and/or blaze. There are white markings on fore chest and/or throat, the tail has a white tip and there should be at least a trace of white on the feet; this can extend to 'stockings' high up the leg.

The Basenji

Although I feel it only fair to include the Basenji in this section, strictly speaking it is neither a classic Sight Hound, nor Scent Hound. So varied are people's theories about the breed that over time it as been described as both a terrier and a spitz breed, but today it is of course accepted as a hound.

It has developed from a diversity of canid types, and is probably most closely related to the pariah. Clearly its distant ancestors were those depicted on Egyptian rock carvings, dating back around five thousand years. Similar dogs to the Basenji were certainly in Upper Egypt, and probably in Lower Egypt too. The first domestic dog known in ancient Egypt, the Kufu dog, shows strong Basenji characteristics.

With the fall of the Egyptian Empire, trade routes opened up and the dogs that had been favoured in Egypt spread through various tribes of

Figure 89   Basenji

the Congo. As merchants travelled with their dogs, together they moved further into Africa.

In Africa the breed was reputed to be very attached to its master who reciprocated this deep affection. The Basenji was used for many different tasks, and was essentially a multi-purpose hound. The long-toothed reed rat was a great threat to homesteads and livestock, and this was common prey for the Basenji. It was also used as a beater of game and for hunting antelope.

Fast and agile, the Basenji is an exceptionally good jumper and is sometimes known as the *M'bwa m'kubwa M'mwa mamwitu* which translates roughly to 'jumping-up-and-down dog'.

One of the breed's most unusual features is that it does not bark, although contrary to popular belief it is by no means silent for it has its own special noise, something between a chortle and yodel. However because it does not use its voice when working, to create a noise hunters in Africa tie around its neck a dried gourd filled with pebbles.

The first Basenjis to arrive in Britain were two brought over from Africa in 1895. They were exhibited at Crufts under the name of 'Lagos Bush Dogs'. Sadly they both died of distemper soon after the show, but the early twentieth century again saw the breed in Europe and the Basenji still has a dedicated band of followers.

The Basenji is a lightly built, finely boned, aristocratic-looking dog, measuring 40–43 cm (16–17 inches) at withers and weighing 9.5–11 kgs (21–24 lbs). Its dark, almond-shaped eyes are far-seeing and have a rather inscrutable expression. With its wrinkled head, pricked ears and proudly carried head, the Basenji's deep brisket runs up to a definite waist, so that with its tightly curled tail it presents a picture of gazelle-like grace.

Colours are black and white; red and white; black, tan and white; black; tan and white, and also brindle. The distribution of these colours is clearly laid down in the breed standard.

Chart Polski

The Chart Polski, or Polish Greyhound, is an ancient Polish breed that came close to extinction, but has relatively recently been revived and was recognised by the Polish Kennel Club In 1981. A few have now even found their way to the US where the first litter was whelped in 1991.

This breed has been in Poland since the thirteenth century, as can be certified from old hunting literature. It is a hound of great size, 68–80 cm (27–31 inches) at withers, powerful, muscular and definitely stronger and less fine in shape than most other short-haired Sight Hounds. However, the Chart Polski must not be heavy or lethargic. The strong frame, short-coupled body, distinctly visible musculature and powerful jaws show that this dog has been used for hunting in the difficult conditions of the Polish climate. The breed has been used not only for hunting hare, fox, roe-deer and bustard, but also for the wolf.

This is a self-assured, confident hound, reserved and brave. When hunting, the Chart Polski is fast, highly skilful and untiring, and in action reacts quickly and brutally. Movement is flowing and energetic with a long, ground-covering stride, both at the walk and on the trot. The action of the hindlegs is one of the characteristics of this breed, for they can be placed on a single, straight line whilst on the trot and this is not a fault.

The coat is springy to the touch, rather harsh and yet neither wire-haired nor silky. Length varies slightly all over the body, being longest at buttocks and along the underside of the tail, where it forms modest 'breeches' and a brush. All colours are permitted.

Cirneco dell'Etna

The Cirneco dell'Etna, known also as the Sicilian Greyhound, has identical roots to the Pharaoh Hound and is remarkably similar in appearance, although much smaller, standing ideally 42–50 cm (17–20 inches) at withers and weighing 8–10 kg (18–22 lbs). It appears to have arrived in Sicily with the Phoenicians around three thousand years ago, since when it has bred true to type due primarily to its isolation. However, there are claims that similar dogs appearing on coins and engravings in the area prove that the breed was there many centuries earlier.

The Cirneco is certainly a Sight Hound, but is also capable of tracking, and additionally uses sound when out hunting rabbit and, because it works silently, also feathered game. It has been developed for hill-coursing on the slopes of Mount Etna, which may account for its smaller frame.

This is a breed that is not particularly easy to train and needs to be introduced carefully to other dogs and to children. Having said that, it is a lively and friendly companion that is gentle and affectionate.

The Cirneco dell'Etna is of square proportion with its depth of chest slightly less than the height from ground to elbow. This breed generally

Figure 90   Cirneco dell'Etna

moves at a gallop, with intermittent trotting phases. Its fine skin fits well to the underlying tissues in all parts of the body. In colour it can be a self-coloured fawn, more or less intense, or diluted, or it may be fawn with white. Some other colour combinations are tolerated, but the pigment must never show black patches, nor should it be depigmented.

Ibizan Hound

The Ibizan Hound, also known as the Podenco Ibicenco or Balearic Hound, was undoubtedly depicted on ancient Egyptian tombs and pottery. The breed takes its name from the island of Ibiza which was invaded by the Carthaginians in the sixth century BC. A century later they left behind their hunting hounds, the forerunners of the breed we know today. The breed is also said to have lived on the island of Formentora for around five thousand years.

The breed was also used for hunting in the regions of Provence and Roussillion, but it became so strongly connected with poaching that in time it was banned. The reason that this was such a valuable hound for poachers was that it worked silently, thereby enabling them to work in secrecy.

Figure 91   Ibizan Hound

In the 1950s a Spanish cynologist living on the island of Majorca began a controlled breeding programme, as a result of which the Ibizan Hound spread to the show rings of Europe and subsequently the US.

This is a breed that is reserved with strangers, but not nervous or aggressive. Dignified, intelligent and independent the Ibizan Hound is distinguished by its large, erect and highly mobile ears and its clear, amber, expressive eyes. The Ibizan Hound is a tall dog, but its height varies considerably from 56–74 cm (22–29 inches). Unlike the majority of breeds there should be a distance of 7–8 cm (2¾–3 inches) between the bottom of the ribcage and the elbow.

An agile, tireless, controlled hunter, it retrieves to hand and has the ability to jump great heights without a running take-off. It moves in a suspended trot, which is a long, far-reaching stride, with a slight hover before placing the foot on the ground.

Figure 92
Kangaroo Dogs in
Australia 1908

The white, chestnut or lion coloured coat, frequently a combination of these colours, may be smooth or rough, but it is always hard, close and dense.

Kangaroo Hound

In the Australian outback the Kangaroo Hound has been usefully employed to hunt wallabies and kangaroos, also to catch emu and to run down and kill native Dingoes. This is indeed heavy work and to create the right hound for the job Greyhounds were imported to cross with Deerhounds and Irish Wolfhounds, so this is certainly a large hound, weighing in the region of 36 kg (79 lbs).

The Kangaroo Hound readily became a firm favourite with Australia's outback farmers, enabling them to hunt and kill without guns, to provide them with meat and to allow their sheep to graze without encountering competition from the marsupials.

A few were seen in Britain during the nineteenth century. One arrived

Figure 93 Eleven month old Kangaroo Hound, Linthorpe Brutus 1902

at London's Zoological Gardens in 1839, and the Prince of Wales exhibited a pair as 'a curiosity' at a dog show in London in 1864.

The killing of marsupials was eventually restricted by law in Australia, but the breed is still maintained by some.

Magyar Agar

During the tenth century the ancestors of the Magyar Agar, or Hungarian Greyhound, went with the Magyars to the countries that have now become Hungary and Romania. The first specific mention of this hound appears between AD 895 and 907, in the writings of Count Arpad. During the nineteenth century both the English Greyhound and the Asian Sight Hounds played their part in the breed's development.

The Magyar Agar was originally used to hunt small game, but is now primarily used for hare-coursing and long-distance racing. Although this is a Sight Hound, it is a breed whose scenting powers are also noteworthy. Untiring, full of stamina, fast, tough and robust, on some distances the Magyar Agar proves himself even faster than the English Greyhound.

The nature of the breed is rather reserved, but it is not shy and is certainly sensible, intelligent and faithful. With a watchful instinct, this breed is a good protector of people, their homes and their property, but it is not aggressive or vicious. Height is 62–70 cm (24–28 inches) at withers and movement is described as a ground-covering elastic trot.

The coat, which comes in various colours with certain exceptions, is short, dense, coarse and smooth, and a considerable amount of dense undercoat may develop in winter time.

Mid-Asiatic Tazi

The Mid-Asiatic Tazi, commonly known as Tazi, is considered the indigenous breed of Kazakhstan, but is also found in Uzbekistan and Turkmenistan. More strongly built than the Saluki, it is similar in appearance with its short, soft, straight coat and fringing on tail and ears.

During the 1970s the Tazi was blamed for the disappearance of the local deer, the dzeinari, and was hunted almost to extinction in the USSR, using jeeps and helicopters. A few survived in remote areas but realising how few Tazis exist today, due to the toils of a handful of dedicated breeders, it seems incredible that in the early twentieth century there was an estimated population of six to seven thousand Tazis in Kazakhstan alone.

It was used to hunt wolf, which it could bring down single-handedly, and

Figure 94 Mid-Asiatic Tazi in Kazakhstan *(Juliette Cunliffe)*

also for gazelle, foxes, mountain goats, wild cats and badgers. Sometimes the Tazi is used with hawks to hunt hare. The Tazi used to be very highly prized, its hunting capabilities often meaning the difference between life and death for its owners. It has been said that at one time a single Tazi was worth forty-seven horses!

219

Pharaoh Hound

Dogs found in Ancient Egyptian art have been likened to the Pharaoh Hound, but it is believed that the Phoenician traders took their hounds to Malta, now considered the home of this magnificent breed, which is known locally as Kelb tal Fennec, meaning 'rabbit dog'. Known in Malta and Gazo for centuries, this is a hound that has been used in remote rural areas. A familiar sight on the island, although the Pharaoh Hound came to Britain in the 1920s, it did not really become established here until the 1970s after British enthusiasts recognised the breed's potential as a show dog.

The Pharaoh Hound is of medium size, standing 53–63 cm (21–25 inches) at shoulder and is of noble bearing, with clean cut lines. It is a graceful breed, and yet powerful with an alert expression. An alert, keen hunter that uses both sight and scent, it also uses its ears to a marked degree when working close. The Pharaoh Hound is very fast, with free, easy movement, covering the ground well and without any apparent effort.

The short, glossy coat ranges from fine and close to slightly harsh and the colour is tan or rich tan. A white tip on the tail is highly desirable and there may be white on the chest, called 'the star', and on the toes. There may also be a slim white blaze on the centre line of the face, but flecking or white in places other than those mentioned above are undesirable.

Figure 95
A brace of Pharaoh Hounds

Rampur Hound

Also known as the Rampur Greyhound or North-Indian Greyhound, the Rampur Hound was a favourite of the Indian Maharajas and was primarily kept in India to hunt the jackal, but was also used for wild boar and deer. However this is a breed that is also perfectly capable of tracking and killing wounded game.

Although the occasional specimen came to Britain decades ago, one of which was exhibited in London's Zoological Gardens in 1877, it is now unknown here, but there are just a few in the US.

The smooth-haired Rampur Hound, with a coat like that of a newly-trimmed horse, is substantially built with a broader head than that of the English Greyhound. The pointed nose has a characteristic Roman bend, ears are fairly large and high-set, and the bite is extremely powerful. This breed is known for its particularly fine sense of balance. There is webbing between the toes of its hare feet and it is said that it can stand on hard ground better than its English counterpart.

The coat is usually mouse-grey or black, but it is said that the black, which is more rare, is the better hunter. Friendly with its owners it can be aggressive with strangers and has something of a reputation of biting without giving warning.

Figure 96
Rampur Greyhound
1907

Sha-Kyi

The Sha-Kyi, or Tibetan Hunting Dog, is still found in remote regions of Tibet where it has long been used to hunt game, including musk deer. It is generally taken on a leash within sight of the game, and then slipped. This is a breed that does not kill its quarry, but barks to attract the hunter's attention so that he can close in for the kill.

It is also used for hunting bharal, a wild sheep, and serow, a wild goat. These it pursues toward cliffs where the prey stops to defend itself by trying to butt the dog over the edge, but the hound is trained only to keep the animal at bay and not to approach so close that it puts itself in danger.

The training of the Sha-Kyi is quite remarkable, because a puppy is tied to its dam while she goes after the game. As a result, it is dragged along after her, a method that seems utterly cruel, but that is reputed to make the hound fierce and keen.

To my knowledge, only one was ever imported to Britain, this in the early 1930s by an English breeder who had attempted to keep the dogs in Tibet, but they were 'tiresome in attacking strangers'.

Because of Tibet's harsh climate, the Sha-Kyi has some coat making it appear heavier than it actually is.

Figure 97
Sha-Kyi, or Tibetan Hunting Dog, pictured in the early 1930s

Sloughi

Another breed from North Africa, the Sloughi has its home both in the mountains and in the deserts. Because of this there are essentially two varieties of the breed. The desert type is more slender, light, graceful and elegant, whilst the mountain type is more compact, with stronger bone. It has been used over the centuries to hunt down hares, gazelles and small fennec foxes.

Many believe that it was the Sloughi that was depicted on the tomb of Tutenkhamen. It seems to have originated initially in the Middle East, then spreading westward across the Sahara Desert and along the coast of North Africa with the nomad tribes. Like most of the Arab Sight Hounds, the Sloughi is held in high esteem by its male owners. It has even been said that the Sloughi gains their respect more than female family members.

Because the Sloughi becomes attached to its owner and family at a very early age, it is generally reluctant to transfer its loyalty if ever a change of home becomes necessary. However, the author has witnessed undoubted exceptions to this general rule.

Elegant, racy and yet strong, without coarseness, the Sloughi is a dignified hound, marked by its muscular leanness. It is a quiet hound, of dignified

Figure 98　Sloughi moving in Hound Group at a Championship Show

Figure 99   North African Gazelle Hounds 1907

bearing, noble, haughty and extremely expressive. Loyal to its owners, but aloof with strangers, the Sloughi has a gentle expression, rather sad and wistful.

This is a breed that is capable of sustained effort over a long distance, moving with a free, effortless gait, without exaggerated extension. When moving the head carriage should not be too high. Height is 61–72 cm (24–28 inches).

The Sloughi has a fine short coat, and undercoat may grow during the winter months. Colour ranges from light sand to red sand (fawn), with or without a black mask, black mantle, black brindling or black overlay. Excessive white in the coat is undesirable.

Spanish Galgo

The history of the Spanish Galgo, or Spanish Greyhound, dates back to Roman times, but it unlikely to have arrived on the Iberian Peninsular until much later. Various Sight Hounds were bred together during the Moorish invasion of southern Spain, and amongst them was of course the Sloughi. Some Spanish Galgo are smooth, with very fine short hair all over the body, just a little longer at the back of the thighs, and yet others have longer, harder hair. The length of this hair can vary and tends to form a beard and moustache. All colours are accepted but well pigmented fawns and brindles, followed by blacks, are given the most preference.

The breed was exported in great numbers to Ireland and England, amongst other countries in the sixteenth, seventeenth and eighteenth centuries. It is described as having a 'serious' temperament, and on occasion is rather reserved, so needs to be well socialised to prevent this. However the Spanish Galgo shows affection for family members and generally gets along well with other dogs. Its head closely resembles that of the English Greyhound, whereas its muscle structure is closer to that of a Sloughi. The breed's ideal height is 60–70 cm (24–28 inches).

The Spanish Galgo has retained characteristics enabling it to run for long distances over rugged terrain. Although it has been used to hunt rabbits, foxes and boars, its principal use, and that for which it is generally employed at present, is to hunt the hare in open fields. This is indeed an energetic and lively hunter and its typical gait is the gallop. It is also used for racing, when it is sometimes crossed with the English Greyhound.

*   *   *

As many as fifty-three separate breeds are believed to fall into the category of Sight Hounds, more than half of which are in Asia, Africa and the Mediterranean regions, so understandably it would not be practical to include them all. There are also certainly other hounds that use sight when hunting, but some of them are all-round hunters and do not rely primarily on sight.

Neither should we overlook the lurcher, in the make-up of which several different breeds are used. However, many a Sight Hound has been used in the development of lurchers and this is another dog that is held in high esteem by many who love the Sight Hound breeds, so a special chapter has been devoted to the lurcher.

SEVENTEEN

LURCHERS AND LONGDOGS

It is not improbable that the hounds hunted by that celebrated Master of antiquity, Xenophon no less, in pursuit of the hare, resembled closely this despised companion of poachers, whom I am not ashamed to love.

JOHN BOARD

A book that covers the pure-bred Sight Hound breeds would not be complete without inclusion also of the lurcher, which always carries some Sight Hound blood.

The lurcher is a highly versatile hunting dog, said to be unsurpassed as both a hunter and companion. It is renowned for its gentle nature, and is happy to be either at its master's feet or at the hare's tail. This is a silent hunting dog that hunts and runs down game. However, it is not a specific breed of dog, but rather a 'type', for its breeding varies according to the particular needs of the owner.

Lurchermen, as they are usually known, hunt different species of game and so it is inevitable that they require slightly differing dogs according to the quarry and the terrain on which they work. Amongst the most popular combinations used in hare coursing are Deerhound-Greyhound, Saluki-Greyhound, a three-quarter cross and lurcher to lurcher. An all-round lurcher, which is expected to hunt, jump, kill and carry the game back, just as a retrieving breed would, is usually made up rather differently; perhaps Bedlington-Greyhound, Collie-Greyhound or Whippet-Greyhound.

The Bedlington-Whippet lurcher is popular amongst lurchermen who hunt rabbits on land where there is plenty of cover, whilst hunting the same terrain for the fox a Bedlington-Greyhound or Bull Terrier cross would probably be more suitable.

It is said that lurchers probably came into being because centuries ago ownership of the Greyhound was restricted to those of royal and noble blood. Indeed the Deerhound, too, was rarely to be found in the hands of the common people. So it was that crosses were made producing an

Figure 100
Rescued lurcher
believed to be
Bedlington-
Greyhound cross.
Although its ears are
usually flat to the
head, here they are
alert to every sound!
(Juliette Cunliffe)

efficient hunting dog that commoners could own for a good hunting dog
would be an invaluable asset in helping them provide food for the family
table.

In general a lurcher's blood is made up from one of the Sight Hound
breeds, mixed with the blood either of a particular terrier breed, or one of
another group of mixed breeds. Because the two groups of dogs used are
not as per the Kennel Club's Group system, I list them here for the sake of
clarity:

TERRIERS : Bedlington, Staffordshire Bull Terrier, English Bull Terrier, Kerry Blue Terrier, Soft Coated Wheaten Terrier, Irish Terrier, Jack Russell Terrier or Airedale.

OTHER BREEDS: Foxhound, Beagle, Golden Retriever, Setter, Spaniel, Labrador Retriever, Old English Sheepdog, Rottweiler, Dobermann, Rough Collie, Bearded Collie or Border Collie.

But different people choose to break them down differently. Lieut-Col E. G. Walsh, known familiarly at Ted Walsh, considers that the word 'lurcher' is used loosely to describe any cross-bred Greyhound-type of dog. He considers that a lurcher is an intentional cross between a coursing dog and a working dog, which may be a sheep or cattle dog, police dog, hound, gundog or terrier. Or it may be the result of the offspring of dogs thus bred.

The term 'longdog' includes hounds that are made up from two different types of coursing dog, usually Greyhound to Deerhound, Greyhound to Saluki or such like. This may again be the result of many generations of such cross-breeding. Technically the term 'longdog' can also be used to describe one of the larger coursing hounds, such as the Deerhound or Greyhound.

Perhaps less well known to those not closely involved with the lurcher world is what is known as a 'Norfolk lurcher'. This is usually considered a cross between either a Greyhound or Deerhound and a collie or cattle dog, or of course the offspring of such a cross. Norfolk lurchers are not always rough-coated but the coat is always weather-proof, so that the dog's working ability is not impaired.

Then we have the 'Smithfield' which is an old type of breeding that was a cross between a Greyhound or Deerhound and a drover's dog, producing a rather lanky, rough-coated dog that was used for cattle and sheep droving. The name presumably came about because such dogs were used by men from the Midlands and East Anglia when they drove their stock to Smithfield and other city markets.

The lurcher recounted in history

In 1668 John Wilkins, Dean of Ripon, wrote an essay for the Royal Society and in it appears the first mention of the lurcher in print when he talked of 'Greater Beasts: Greyhounds. Lesser Beasts: Lurchers'. From this we gather that the lurcher was known in the latter half of the seventeenth century, but that it was smaller than the Greyhound.

Just two years later, in 1670, lurchers are mentioned in the Act of Charles

II which authorises gamekeepers to seize them, as well as Greyhounds and setting dogs. A little while later a dog that must clearly have been very highly valued was advertised as a lost dog in the *London Gazette*. It was described as being pied, and somewhat shaped like a lurcher.

More and more references to lurchers subsequently crept into books and essays written about sporting dogs and field sports, sometimes referred to as a kind of 'mungril greyhound'. There is an interesting description of these dogs given in Thomas Fairfax's *Compleat Sportsman*, which came out in 1760.

> Lurchers is a kind of hunting dog much like a mongrel greyhound, with prickt ears, a shagged coat, and generally of a yellowish-white colour; they are very swift runners so that if they get between the burrows and the conies they seldom miss; and this is their common practice in hunting; yet they use other subtlilties, as the tumbler does, some of them bringing in their game and those are the best. It is also observable that a lurcher will run down a hare at a stretch.

It is probably helpful to clarify that a 'tumbler' was a dog somewhat resembling a small Greyhound. It would hunt alone and take home its catch and was so called because of its ability to turn and tumble, winding its body about with ease.

In 1804, William Taplin told his readers that the lurcher was originally produced by crossing the Greyhound and the shepherd's dog. Then, by breeding in and in with the Greyhound, little of the shepherd's dog was evident other than the docility and fidelity which were retained. The lurcher's height tended to be roughly three-quarters that of a Greyhound and they were of a yellowish or sandy-red colour. Their coat was rough and 'wirey-haired', the ears naturally erect but drooping a little at the tip.

Taplin said that Lurchers were little known in and around cities but were established favourites of small farm holders where they were often used instead of a shepherd's dog, but had both the speed and cunning to turn up a rabbit or, when the opportunity arose, a half or three-quarter-grown leveret. His skills often brought him into the possession of what he described as 'poachers of the most unprincipled and abandoned description'.

He thought the lurcher equalled or even exceeded any other dog in sagacity and that many were almost capable of the speed of a well-formed Greyhound. When poaching they were incredibly successful. They killed rabbits with certainty if they were any distance from their warren, and were proficient in the destruction of hares. When proficient in hunting, they were even capable of pulling down a fallow deer.

By 1867, J. H. Walsh, better known under the pseudonym of

'Stonehenge', said that although the lurcher was not used by what he described as 'the fair sportsman', it nonetheless needed to be recognised as a distinct and well-known cross. He felt that the lurcher was very little better than a pure-bred Greyhound that had the same amount of practice and was accustomed to the same kind of work. He knew of many a Greyhound that would not miss a hare when sighted, or even put onto the fresh scent, dropping their noses and hunting all out on the turns of the hare, nearly as well as the Beagle. From this he deduced that the lurcher's nose was not only derived from his sheep-dog ancestry.

But Walsh also drew his attention to the less happy side of being a lurcher in those times when he wrote:

> He is also a most destructive animal, showing speed, sagacity, and nose in an extraordinary degree, from which causes the breed is discouraged, as he would terminate all furred game in a short time. A poacher possessing such an animal seldom keeps him long, every keeper being on the look out, and putting a charge of shot into him on the first opportunity; and as these *must* occur of necessity, the poacher does not often attempt to rear the dog which would suit him best, but contents himself with one which will not so much attract the notice of those who watch him.

Walsh goes on to give a brief description of the lurcher and from this we learn that the tail was frequently docked so that it might not be recognised as a hunting dog.

> It is needless to describe the *points* of the lurcher, further than to remark that he partakes of those of the greyhound in shape, combined with the stouter frame, larger ears, and rougher coat of the sheep-dog, but varying according to the breed of each employed in producing the cross. Formerly these lurchers were invariably deprived of their tails, in order to pass muster as sheep-dogs, and some are still thus cropped; but as hundreds of these farmer's friends are now suffered to enjoy their full proportions, the lurcher, when he does exist, is also full-tailed. The colour varies greatly, and may be any one of those belonging either of the breeds from which he springs.

Moving into the twentieth century

Writing in 1948, John Board was one of the few canine authors of his era to write more than a few sentences about the lurcher, although later several authors devoted entire books to this remarkable canine that is loved by so many. Sadly, as this is not a pure-bred Kennel Club recognised breed, many Sight Hound lovers give the lurcher less attention than he deserves, though many of them are indeed secret admirers.

John Board believed the lurcher to be the most intelligent of all Sight Hounds, though he recognised that the lurcher's close association with the Romanies did not always help his reputation. Like the hunting dog employed by our remote ancestors, Board told his readers that the lurcher could be relied upon to kill and deliver his owner's dinner wherever game was to be found. He recounted the tale of his friend's lurcher, 'Springer', who, on autumn evenings following dinner, would travel in the car with is owner to Dunster Lawns where he would pursue innumerable rabbits startled by the glare of the headlights.

Although Board pointed out that the lurcher was, strictly speaking, a mongrel, he felt it had developed into a very definite type and should seriously be considered as a companion. But Phil Drabble OBE, the naturalist and broadcaster, did not see the lurcher as a mongrel at all, rather a deliberate cross-breed that was what he described as 'the traditional breed of Gypsies who want dogs more for pot-boilers than for sport'. He considered that the progeny of Greyhounds with diluted blood, traditionally a sheepdog cross, had more stamina and brains than Greyhounds. Unlike Mr Walsh, he believed that Norfolk Lurchers were effectively Smithfields.

The gypsy and the lurcher

Although it is perhaps commonly believed that all gypsies kept lurchers, at least until relatively recently, it is likely that only about half of them did so, and by no means all of these were breeders. A lurcher is unmistakable in looks, so set the alarm signals ringing for gamekeepers and policemen alike! Some gypsies preferred to keep terriers, some a guard dog, and others kept no dogs at all.

As motor traffic has increased, the old familiar sight of a roaming gypsy wagon is now rare indeed, but dating back to 1449 there is an old reference to what were described as 'masterful beggars' going about Scotland with their horses, hounds and other goods.

We have to consider that when gypsies first came to Britain it was very sparsely populated with numerous open heaths, forests and commons, with deserted tracks in which they could hide when necessity called. They had many different trades to bring in a little cash, but what food they did not buy or barter, their dogs helped them to obtain. Dogs that hunt by scent can be very noisy, and scent-hunting takes time, but those that hunt by sight do so quickly and, equally importantly, quietly.

Following the Second World War, with building and roads encroaching

231

on the countryside, even bringing with them street-lighting, many gypsies needed more static sites and their aesthetically pleasing horse-drawn carriages were overtaken by lorries and shiny caravans. Many of them needed to live near to populated areas so that they could better sell their wares, and the meat upon which they had been so reliant upon their dogs to provide, could now be bought in the butchers' shops.

Dogs were certainly still used for poaching, but coursing became more popular with large sums of money changing hands. Indeed many a hare was simply left to rot, so much had the gypsies' needs and life-style changed.

Breeding lurchers and longdogs

In simple terms, a lurcher may be described as a cross between a coursing dog and a working dog, whereas a longdog is a cross between two coursing dogs. Some British lurcher enthusiasts would only consider Britain's indigenous breeds amongst the coursing hounds they would use, but others consider, and indeed use, other breeds too.

As author of this book, I am the first to admit that I have absolutely no experience of the working lurcher, except that I found what I expect to have been a Bedlington-Whippet cross or similar many moons ago, and to this day I regret not having kept her as she was such an adorable lady, still so vivid in my memory. As a result I can only pass on the comments of others as to how suitable the various pure-bred hounds might be when planning one's lurcher or longdog breeding programme.

Personally I know that the AFGHAN HOUND is worked with great success in its homeland for rough hunting, but in Britain the breed seems not to impress the lurcher enthusiast. An Afghan coursing a hare apparently does not have suitable speed, action or turning ability, although I have to say the Afghan fraternity would doubtless not agree with this at all. Having owned Afghans in the past, I would indeed praise them highly for their turning capability, and I suspect most Afghan owners would agree with me. Afghans perform well on the race track, but they are very independent hounds and need close supervision with farm stock.

The BORZOI has historically been used for coursing dangerous game, but in Britain not for working, except in the coursing field. In America, however, Borzois, and Borzois crossed with either Greyhound or Deerhound, are used to control coyotes because of the harm they do to sheep and calves. In Australia Borzoi blood has occasionally been used to produce the Kangaroo Hound.

In a lurcher breeding programme the Borzoi is generally considered too tall and too thin to be of much use, but if the game is to be fox or deer, and if a Borzoi is crossed with a genuine working dog, then a cross might be of value.

The DEERHOUND is highly valuable in lurcher bloodlines, but despite his many attributes as a hunter, his sheer size is a negative factor for he needs space in which to turn, and the rabbit is often too small and too nimble. On the positive side, coupled with his remarkable eye-sight, the Deerhound has remarkable stamina, a weather-proof coat and sufficient nose to follow a blood spore. Several lurcher enthusiasts like to see a small amount of Deerhound blood in a Greyhound-Collie cross, and a Deerhound-Collie cross can also be worthwhile if not too big.

In the longdog, many a Deerhound-Greyhound cross is good and fast, but they don't always seem to turn a hare sufficiently well.

The GREYHOUND is understandably used frequently in lurcher and longdog breeding programmes, and usually to great advantage. To produce a longdog, often a fifty/fifty Greyhound mix is considered the combination that provides the best results.

Some owners of longdogs like to train Greyhound crosses to do some ratting as part of their education, especially if they lack a little keenness. A bite by a rat is almost certain to improve a dog's performance!

The show Greyhound is not really of interest to lurchermen who prefer a rather smaller hound that has been bred to work rather than for its beauty points. There are also subtle differences between track and coursing Greyhounds, but some interbreeding between the two goes on, and in Ireland there is hardly any difference at all. A Greyhound-Deerhound cross, especially if the latter is a coursing hound, produces a dog with remarkable physical ability and cunning, making it an ideal longdog. A Greyhound-Deerhound hybrid is usually capable of taking and killing a fox with little assistance, but it should be borne in mind that a hound capable of taking a fox is equally capable of taking another dog, so it is essential to consider this.

Along the borders of Wales, and in Wales itself, many gypsies bred the successful Greyhound-Bedlington cross, and also the Whippet-Bedlington cross. The latter is too small for hare coursing, but the former is a particularly good all-rounder, though lack of size can sometimes be a drawback.

The IRISH WOLFHOUND is not so fast as the other large Sight Hound breeds, such as the Deerhound, though is a sound and dependable hunting dog and incorporated in a breeding programme can produce a certain amount of staunchness. However this breed is really only worthy of consideration when hunting large game, such as hyena and leopard, so it not usually employed in Britain.

The SALUKI, like the Afghan, is unlikely to be entirely trustworthy with farm stock, so this is a negative aspect with regard to incorporating the

Saluki in a lurcher breeding programme. This breed is not so fast out of slips, nor does it have the speed of the Greyhound, but offset against that is its tremendous stamina.

The WHIPPET is a first rate rabbiter and many pure-bred coursing and working Whippets are perfectly capable of doing anything that might be expected of a small lurcher, and some will vouch that they even do it better. Whippets work particularly well when out hunting with a couple of terriers. For this reason, some lurcher enthusiasts do not see any reason to use a Whippet in a lurcher breeding programme, however a Whippet-Bedlington cross, or a Whippet-Collie cross does usually have a more weatherproof coat, which is of benefit.

Figure 101 A much loved lurcher

Lurcher rescues

Sadly many lurchers, like their Greyhound cousins, end up in rescue, which is especially sad for they, too, are wonderful companion dogs that are loyal to their owners. When kept as companion animals they really need no more exercise than other breeds of dog, just a ten minute walk and an opportunity to run around and burn off their excess energy. The rest of the time they are quite content to enjoy the comforts of their new-found home and to be given the love and care of which they are so deserving.

Sometimes it is necessary to build a bridge between a dog's working or racing career and its introduction to a loving home environment, especially if it has been living in kennels or sheds as is so often the case. For this reason, some are fostered for short periods until the right homes are found. During this period their characters are assessed and they are helped to come to understand and learn about so many things that other dogs take for granted. It is heartbreaking to part with a fostered lurcher, or indeed a Greyhound, after only a short while, but if the dog is moving on to a permanent loving home, and making way for another rescued dog to be fostered and on the road to happiness, then the heartbreak is worthwhile.

EIGHTEEN

WHELPING AND REARING

D eciding whether or not one should bring a litter of Sight Hound puppies into this world is a very serious matter, something not to be taken lightly. Before reaching your final decision I would urge you to give due consideration to a number of different factors, most of which are (or should be) applicable to any breed of dog.

The first question to ask yourself is whether or not your bitch is of good enough quality and breed type to warrant being the dam of a litter. Naturally, if you are deeply fond of her it is only too easy to overlook some of her faults and to concentrate only on her finer qualities. Whichever the breed, she should match up to the breed standard as closely as possible, and remember that a bitch which is 'sound' should be sound both physically and mentally. There are quite enough puppies being bred at present and one's aim should always be to improve the breed. Breeding from a bitch of less than good type and quality does not further the cause. If a bitch has a fault, that fault will rarely be bred out in the first generation and may indeed rear its ugly head to an even greater degree in the next or subsequent generations.

Having completely satisfied yourself that your bitch is suitable as a brood bitch, you can then ask the remainder of the questions that you must, of necessity, ask yourself. Firstly, it is to be hoped that your reason for wishing to breed is that you wish to keep one of the puppies yourself – but do you have sufficient suitable homes lined up for the others? Note the word 'suitable'. That your elderly aunt has said, 'Oh, I'd love one of her puppies if she whelps, dear,' is simply not good enough. Though some, undoubtedly, can prove to be excellent owners for hounds, family members and friends, in the main, do not always mean what they say when they assure you that they would love one of your bitch's puppies when the time comes! And even if they do mean what they say they may not be suitable owners for one of the Sight Hounds, especially the larger ones. Too many dogs end up with rescue societies because their owners were not selected with sufficient care in the first instance.

Now is the time to ask yourself whether or not you would be strong enough to cull any of the litter should it be necessary. As this chapter is clearly not intended for the experienced breeder perhaps I should clarify the meaning of the word 'cull'. Although its meaning is clear to me, I have come across people who have managed to misinterpret it because they could not allow themselves to believe that the word actually means what it does! To cull is to put down some of the whelps, ideally at birth or very soon after. This is not done in all breeds but in some, such as Deerhounds, until quite recently it was considered by most experienced breeders to be a necessity, unless the bitch happened to produce a small number of whelps. A bitch might produce ten, twelve or even as many as sixteen puppies and they thought it simply not fair on the bitch to allow her to rear more than eight. Thinking has changed somewhat over the last ten years or so, but still some breeders allow their bitches to rear only six or seven, which seems to them a manageable number. You may think of finding a suitable foster mother, but before this solution takes too strong a hold on you, I can assure you that finding a good and suitable foster mother is an enormously difficult task. It is probably kinder to make your decisions as to which puppies to cull at birth. Many breeders make their ultimate decisions on weight and sex alone, although nature may already have played its part in determining or indicating some of the losses for you.

Do you have the time available to devote to the correct rearing of the litter when it is born? A full-time job does not tie in well with owning a dog anyway, and is certainly out of the question if your bitch is due to whelp. Whatever your other commitments, you will need to keep yourself completely free for an absolute minimum of four days before and after the due date in case the litter does not arrive on time. The text books so often say that puppies can be born safely within three days before and three days after the due date of whelping, but I have quite frequently heard reports of perfectly healthy litters being produced one week early and many vets will wait a full week after the due date before considering a Caesarean operation.

On the subject of Caesareans, Sight Hounds are reasonably easy whelpers due in part to the puppy's elongated head shape and the general construction of this group of breeds. Having said that, one always has to be on the look-out for whelping difficulties, which we shall come to in just a moment.

On the assumption that you are still giving due consideration to whether you should or should not breed a litter, I would ask you also to consider whether you have sufficient finance and facilities for a fast-growing litter of puppies. You will need quite a lot of equipment if it is to be your first litter, you must be prepared to pay vet's bills, both the dam and the puppies will consume a goodly amount of high-quality food and you may well need to construct a suitable run so that the puppies can exercise sufficiently but safely. And don't forget that, depending on when the puppies leave home and the type of vaccine used by your vet, you may also incur vaccination charges, even though these may be subsequently passed on to the puppies' new owners. As I said earlier, ideally you should have owners lined up for all the puppies available for sale but, should this not be the case, or should a prospective purchaser's plans change at the very last minute, you may need to advertise, which will further increase the overall cost of producing the litter. Looking on the negative side, if for some reason your puppies are not all sold at what is considered to be the desired age for the breed (usually between ten and fourteen weeks), are you able to keep additional puppies in your home until suitable new owners are found — or forever, if necessary?

Give consideration to your bitch's age, and always keep in the back of your mind that the Kennel Club now usually refuses to register any puppies born to a bitch which is eight years old or more, though, naturally, a bitch should certainly not be mated for the first time at anywhere near that age, two to three years usually being considered the best age for a first litter though some breeders allow their bitches to have a first litter at four or even five. This, however, is not suitable for all breeds.

Lastly, please don't ever be tempted to believe the old wives' tale that a bitch *needs* to have one litter for her own good. Many bitches live perfectly happy, healthy lives without ever producing offspring!

Choice of stud

Naturally you will wish to produce puppies of the best possible quality, whether your interest in the breed revolves around showing, coursing or simply adoration of the breed. Whatever your interests, selection of the right stud dog is of paramount importance, given that your bitch is of good enough quality from which to breed.

The decision about which stud dog to use is a crucial one and deserves much prior consideration. Do not fall into the trap of selecting a Champion dog which happens to live in your own general area. He might, perhaps, be the right dog for your bitch but, on the other hand, there is every likelihood he is not. Unfortunately the stud which seems to be absolutely right often lives hundreds of miles away! One can select a dog based on phenotype (physical appearance), genotype (genetic make-up) or, more usually, a combination of the two.

Firstly, take yourself around to some Championship Shows where classes for your breed are scheduled and to breed club Open Shows, for these are the types of show which will undoubtedly attract the highest number of good-quality exhibits. Watch the classes with care and get some idea of which dogs appeal to you and which have qualities that are likely to complement your bitch. Look also at the offspring produced by the various sires for it is true to say that you should be taking notice not only of what the dog himself looks like but also what he produces. It is fair to say, though, that in many cases you will see in the show-ring only a very small proportion of what he has produced and frequently only the best of his progeny are exhibited at shows. At some breed club shows you will be lucky enough to see progeny classes, in which a stud dog is exhibited with those of his progeny, entered at the show, also in the ring with him. This can make a splendid display and is an ideal opportunity for the onlooker to assess whether or not the dog in question is passing on his good qualities or otherwise.

Look also at pedigrees and to do this you should ideally consult people who have an in-depth knowledge of the breed. They may well be able to point out some features further back in the pedigree that can be used to enhance the quality of your intended litter, even though they may not be apparent in the stud dog himself. If, for example, your bitch has a lighter eye than is required for the breed, you will preferably require a stud dog who not only has a darker eye himself but who comes from a line of dogs all or most of which had a similar depth of colour. You will appreciate that this example serves only to express what you should look for in the very simplest terms and that to read a pedigree fully takes a great deal of experience.

You should also give due consideration to whether, by using the dog which by now interests you most, you would be inbreeding, line-breeding or outcrossing. Very briefly, inbreeding involves the mating of close relatives such as father to daughter, mother to son, or brother to sister. Mating half-brother to half-sister, for example, is also considered by some to be inbreeding but a lot depends on the closeness of the breeding in other sections of the pedigree and it is often considered to be the closest form of line-breeding. Certainly inbreeding or close line-breeding should not be attempted by the novice for, although it can be very useful on occasion to the established and careful breeder, inbreeding, because of the close genetic link-up, is likely to bring out faults and abnormalities. Line-breeding is the method of breeding most commonly used and is most usually interpreted to involve the breeding of a pair which have a common ancestor within the first four or sometimes five generations; naturally, the dog or dogs to which one is line-breeding should have essential attributes and this is one of the subjects which you will undoubtedly need to discuss with a more experienced breeder who has first-hand knowledge of the dogs concerned. The novice breeder also has to use extreme caution when outcrossing for this means that there are no common ancestors within at least four generations. This effectively means that there are numerous different bloodlines within the pedigree and that one is usually basing one's decision for the proposed mating purely on phenotype. This method is often used by established breeders on occasion in order to bring in a feature they feel is lacking or could be improved upon in their own particular line. In doing so there is, however, always a risk factor, for when one is dealing with bloodlines with which one is not familiar the unexpected can occur.

Certainly if yours is a maiden bitch (i.e. one that has not yet produced her first litter) you would be well advised to use a well-proven male. If you are inexperienced yourself do not consider a dog that has not yet been used at stud and particularly if he is owned by someone who is inexperienced like yourself.

A word here to anyone who has a pet dog that he or she is considering using at stud. Please don't do it. Once a dog has been used his outlook on life will most probably change, he will seek out the ladies, become more dominant in his personality, especially in the company of other males, and may well forget his manners in the house – and the larger hounds can cock their legs a considerable distance up your furniture! There will always be sufficient top-winning show dogs available for those bitches that are to be bred and you are unlikely to receive more than one, or perhaps two, requests for his use at stud. It is simply not worth the trouble you will be caused.

Booking the stud

The stud dog should be booked well in advance of the date on which the bitch is due in season, for some dogs are in relatively frequent demand and their owners may stipulate that they cannot mate more than a given number of bitches in a certain period of time. It is always usual for the bitch to travel to the stud and the dog's owner may or may not be in a position to keep the bitch on his or her premises for a few days. An additional in-season bitch in one's home is often not easy to manage with anxious males about the place! Should it be agreed that your bitch may stay for a few days it is wise to check at this stage whether you will be charged a fee per day for her lodging, which is quite in order.

It is also usually wise to have a second choice of stud in hand should it perhaps not be possible to get a mating with one's first choice. It is not uncommon for one dog to choose not to have anything to do with a particular bitch, whilst another dog can be quite keen. When approaching the owner of your second choice, do be honest enough to say that their dog will only be used if the first choice fails for whatever reason. Most breeders, especially if you are honest with them, will understand, although it has to be said that others may take offence, so put your case clearly. If you are lucky, it may well be that the owner of your first choice has another dog of very similar breeding which could be used as an alternative and this possibility should, of course, be discussed at the time of booking the stud. Under no circumstances allow your bitch to be mated by two dogs during the same season as she could produce puppies by two different sires and you will not know which comes from which.

The fee for the stud service should be agreed at the time the booking is discussed. Different breeders and, indeed, different breeds each have slightly different ways of handling this. Remember that you are paying for a stud service, not for a litter of puppies, although some breeders may suggest that you pay a percentage of the fee at the time of the mating and a further sum upon production of a litter of live puppies. Other stud dog owners may perhaps prefer to have one of the puppies from the litter in lieu of a stud fee but in this case do be sure that you agree whether the stud dog owner is to have first, second or third pick or, as sometimes happens, more than one puppy. The exact arrangements should be set down in writing for it is all too easy to forget exactly what was agreed. Certainly the most usual arrangement is for a straight stud fee to be paid at the time of mating and, in most cases, should puppies not be produced on the first occasion, she may return to the same stud at her next season without additional charge, but, again, do agree this in writing from the outset.

The mating

Although a bitch is usually in season for something between three and possibly four weeks she is only receptive to the male for a few days, usually about three. Thus you will need to check her vulva regularly so that you can be certain when it is at its softest, this being the time at which she will be ready to be mated; she may have stopped losing colour at this time but not necessarily so. Most stud dog owners allow you to be present at the time of mating so that you can witness the 'act' but they may not wish you to be involved. Much often depends on the way the bitch responds to the male and in some cases either a bitch or dog can be put off by the presence of the bitch's owner. A lot also will depend on your own attitude. For this reason it is wise not to take the entire family along with you – the exercise is not to be used as an educational experience for your children! On occasion bitches have arrived at my own house with an entourage and I can assure you it is a nightmare for the stud dog owner.

You may, however, possibly be asked to hold the bitch steady whilst the stud dog owner takes care of the male. Always bear in mind that the stud dog is at a greater risk of injury than the bitch and one of those risks is that, however well-mannered a young lady, she can, especially if a maiden, be taken by surprise, panic and turn around to snap. For this reason be sure that you go along armed with a good, sturdy leather collar so that whoever is taking care of her can get a secure hold. This is another reason why it is most unwise (unless you are experienced and have very good reason) to allow a maiden dog to be used on a maiden bitch. Mating the smaller Sight Hound breeds is not usually especially problematic, but mating of the larger breeds such as Deerhounds is considerably more difficult, and it is absolutely essential that the human element involved is highly experienced.

If all goes well (and it doesn't always!) the two will tie for anything from about five minutes to over an hour. Between ten and twenty minutes is perhaps the most normal. During this time you will most probably find that the dog turns so that the two are back to back, and some are even known to lie down. Quite how they manage to perform such contortions, I have not yet worked out! I always like to have a drink of water to hand for them at this stage, although most will decline until the mating is finished.

It is usual for a stud dog owner to offer two matings, usually one day apart. Some even do three matings when possible but I do not advise this unless the first mating was a slip-mating (i.e. one in which the dog penetrated but no significant tie took place). Others prefer to do only one mating and this can frequently result successfully in a litter of puppies.

Care of the in-whelp bitch

You are unlikely to have a clear indication of whether or not your bitch is in whelp until the fifth week following the mating, at which time you should be able to discern a slight thickening around the loin. Earlier signs that the mating has been successful are slightly enlarged teats which are pinkish in colour soon after the mating, or that her appetite has changed somewhat. Some bitches, though by no means all, experience slight sickness. Several breeders now like to have their bitches scanned by a vet, although this does not always give an accurate indication of the number of puppies she will produce.

It is from the fifth week, when you are as certain as you can be that she is in whelp, that you will need gradually to increase her intake of food. As her bulk increases she will be reluctant to eat very large amounts of food at any one time so if you normally give two feeds per day, these should be increased to three. As her whelping time approaches she will probably be eating about twice as much food as normal. Do make sure that you increase the meat content of her diet, not only the bulk foods.

Whilst she should be given regular exercise throughout her pregnancy, especially after the fifth week, she should not be allowed to get involved in violent exercise with other dogs for fear of injury to her puppies. During the last few weeks – and the gestation period is about sixty-three days – she should not be allowed to do any galloping; nor should she be permitted to leap over fences etc.

If you have not already been absorbed in books about whelping (which I hope you have), now is the time to do all the reading you can so that you are well prepared. Your bitch will need a whelping box which must be adequate in size and must, of necessity, be raised at least two inches from the ground to avoid draughts. I would never use a whelping box without a guard rail, which, for preference, should be detachable so that it can be removed when the puppies are up and about on their feet so that there is more space in the box. I also like to have a flap at the front so that during the whelping process I have easy access to the bitch when necessary. There are various designs of box that you can buy or construct, but unfortunately there is not sufficient space here to go into the matter in great detail.

She should be introduced to her whelping box about a week or ten days before the due date so that she is entirely familiar with the surroundings in which you wish the whelping to take place. If she is not introduced to her quarters, you may well find that she would prefer to deposit puppies all over the sitting room carpet!

You will also need to fit a heat pad or erect a heat lamp over the whelping box, making certain that it is high enough not to be knocked over by the bitch when she stands up. It is safest to choose a lamp that has a wire guard below the bulb. I find those bulbs which give off a white light much too bright for the bitch and her whelps and would recommend that you either choose one with a red hue or one that gives off heat only, in which case do remember to leave a dim light on somewhere in the room. Whilst they are small the bitch always needs to see what she is doing so that she does not inadvertently sit on a puppy. Take care when positioning the lamp not only that it and its wires are entirely safe but that both whelps and dam can move out of the direct heat from it should they choose to do so, for your heat lamp will be left on twenty-four hours a day unless you happen to have your litter in an extremely hot summer.

You should collect an *enormous* supply of clean newspapers with which to line the box, for you cannot imagine quite how many times you will need to change the paper, during the whelping especially. A clean, soft bedding looks very nice but is not at all practical whilst the bitch is whelping and in any event bedding should always be placed on newspaper so that any moisture can be absorbed by it.

I am well aware that all breeders have different equipment preferences, but I have found by experience that the above equipment is entirely practical and something like it indispensable. Always remember that you cannot hope to raise a successful litter if you try to skimp on necessities.

Supplements to the bitch's diet

Personally, the only supplement I give is calcium and I prefer to give the liquid form rather than tablets. This should not be given until immediately after the puppies have been whelped. The actual amount given will depend upon the breed and the weight of your dog, but do follow the given instructions to the letter so that you neither over- nor under-dose.

Many people give additional vitamin supplements and such-like but I feel a well-balanced diet is quite sufficient. I have, in the past, given raspberry leaf tablets for ease of whelping but I found that the bitch delivered her puppies like shelled peas and failed to give me that all-important warning that she was about to start pushing, so I shall refrain from using them again unless I have a bitch I know is likely to have problems – and if I know she is likely to have problems, the chances are I shan't be breeding from her!

The whelping

As I have already said, Sight Hounds are relatively easy whelpers but problems can and do occur when a puppy is presented in an unusual position, such as a breech (i.e. rear first and upside down). A puppy may be lodged in the canal, or the umbilical cord of one may be obstructing the passage of another. For these reasons I would strongly recommend that you advise your vet roughly when you think your bitch will whelp so that he does not take unkindly to your emergency telephone call in the middle of the night. The maiden bitch may be distressed by the onset of her first puppy and may panic, so be sure that you are by her side to reassure her. Most Sight Hounds, however, sever their own umbilical cords and so you will very probably not need to interfere too much in the whelping process. Different breeders have differing ideas on whether or not the bitches should be allowed to eat the afterbirths; personally, I am happy to allow her two or three but I try to remove the remainder for if she eats too many she tends to have loose motions. As she will most probably not wish to eat any food for a little while I do feel that a couple of afterbirths give her some nourishment.

As the bitch can push quite violently with her legs when producing each whelp I think it wiser to remove at least the majority of those already born

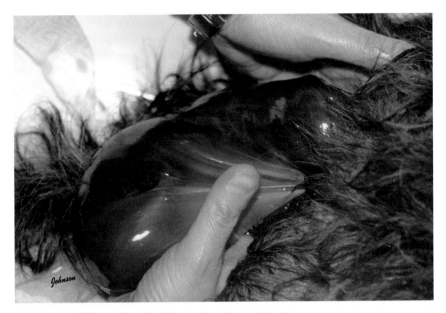

Figure 102   The author whelping a Deerhound bitch

whilst she is thus involved. You should therefore have a high-sided card-board box lined with comfortable, perfectly clean bedding, under which is a heat pad or a not-too-hot hot-water bottle. This will help to keep the puppies quiet so that she is not unduly distressed by their cries. Naturally I do not keep the puppies away from their dam any longer than I feel is necessary for their own safety and for her comfort. You will also need another lidded box or bin, to be kept just outside the room, or in a far corner of the room, so that any dead or malformed puppies can be removed discreetly.

Different bitches seem to expel their puppies with varying degrees of rapidity; sometimes the second is on its way before you have even had a chance to sex the first. But at other times there can be long gaps between the whelps and if ever you have a gap approaching an hour you would be advised to call your vet and at least to discuss the situation with him.

Personally I like to weigh and detail each puppy as it is born so that I can keep a careful record of each one's progress from the moment of birth. I fully appreciate that many other breeders do not do this, but I find that if it is done discreetly and with care it distresses neither the puppies nor their dam, for there is plenty of other activity going on at the time to distract them.

Although bitches are inclined to eat afterbirths so quickly that you can hardly notice, do try to count to be sure that you have a corresponding number of afterbirths to whelps. Should one be retained in the bitch your vet must be consulted immediately so that he can give her something which will enable her to expel it. If it is left inside it can so easily cause a problem.

When the whelping is over the bitch will have to be gently persuaded to go outside to relieve herself, and on the first occasion at least she must be very carefully supervised for there is always the danger that there is one more puppy inside her and it lands in the garden. Thankfully I haven't had it happen personally but I know that it can! If this outing away from the whelping room is at night, make sure that you are armed with a strong torch. Something else worth mentioning here is that if you have to take your bitch to the vet during her whelping because she is having difficulty of some sort, have the car well prepared with anything you might need. One of my bitches had an awkward whelp attended to by the vet and then proceeded to give birth to a further three in the back of the car on the short journey home. This, of course, took place in the middle of the night and it was difficult to distinguish whelps from placentas. By some minor miracle all puppies survived, I am glad to say.

Bear in mind that during the first few days the dam will be very reluctant to leave her puppies except for very short times to relieve herself. Never

Figure 103
Deerhound puppies suckling with gusto on day one

246

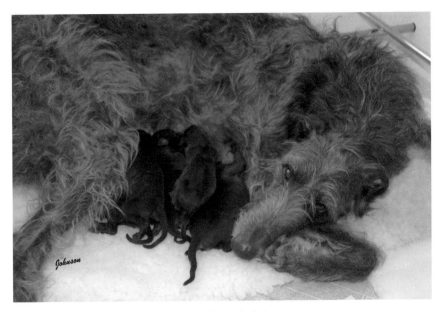

Figure 104   Deerhound puppies just after whelping

keep her away from the puppies longer than necessary but, on the other hand, do be sure that she does her toilet, for bitches can be stubborn and make themselves unnecessarily uncomfortable as a result. Likewise she will most probably be reluctant to eat much for the first day or so. I usually find that a couple of whisked raw egg yolks (never feed raw egg whites) go down well with a drop of goat's or cow's milk and in the mixture can be concealed the liquid calcium if you wish. It is usually necessary to tempt the bitch to eat something initially, and white meats or fish are the most easily digestible to begin with. Don't worry if you have to hand-feed her for a couple of days, she will soon return to her normal eating habits. You will, as before, have roughly to double the quantity of food you give her by the second week and she will probably require three times as much during the third week, this being the period of heaviest lactation. The food should be offered in small portions, four or even five times a day, and remember to keep up her intake of protein in relation to carbohydrates for protein assists greatly in the production of milk. As the puppies gradually get closer to becoming fully weaned you can gradually reduce her food supply to a more normal level.

It goes without saying that she must have constant access to water for her liquid intake is most important whilst she is feeding her puppies. I always put a dessertspoon of glucose powder in the water and most hound breeds can happily drink fresh milk, although if your bitch's motions tend to get a

Figure 105   Whippet dam and young whelp

Figure 106   The author's Whippet, Tintavon Gwen Torrence at Modhish (Swedish Imp), with her litter of only three, making for a very contented family! (Note the guard rails.)

bit loose (they will, in any event, be a bit loose whilst she is cleaning up after her whelps) you should decrease the milk intake, in which case make sure you keep glucose in the water. Be careful that the liquids are located somewhere out of harm's way from the puppies' point of view.

Removing dew claws

Many breeders of Sight Hounds have the puppies' dew claws removed but there is no hard and fast rule about it. There is a danger of the dew claws being torn if left on but it is debatable whether the puppies should be put through the trauma of having them removed. If it is done, it must be done by a vet on the third day after the whelping. Speaking from personal experience, I have had only one dog who experienced damage to a dew claw and, on balance, I prefer now to leave them on except on a smooth-coated breed such as a Whippet. Should you decide to have them removed it is preferable for the vet to visit your home and it is imperative that the bitch is kept well out of earshot. Small puppies can make an enormous amount of noise, albeit only for a few seconds. Should it be necessary to go to the surgery with the puppies your bitch will most probably wish to travel with you for she will be disturbed to be away from her litter for so long at such an early stage. Again, at the surgery make sure she is not within earshot whilst the claws are being removed and ideally keep her and the puppies in your car until it is your turn so that you avoid any unnecessary exposure to infection in the waiting room.

Weaning

The third week of a puppy's life is highly important and for this reason I feel that provided a bitch is coping sufficiently well with her litter and is continuing to provide sufficient food without too much strain on her own resources, it is wisest not to begin weaning until the fourth week. Having said that, I would stress that if you are in any doubt as to whether or not she can cope, especially with a large litter, then weaning can commence during the third week.

Every breeder seems to have a slightly different method of weaning and most, I am sure, are highly satisfactory. I am therefore highly reluctant to say that one method is better than another. There are now so very many carefully balanced dried foods on the market that if you take sensible advice from those who do bring up their puppies on this type of food you are sure to find one that suits; but, if you do choose to use a dried food, make sure that it is sufficiently well soaked according to the maker's instructions. Leading brands of tinned foods also offer one of puppy quality, although some breeders prefer to use scraped meat, gradually building up to a mince. A helpful tip for feeding puppies' first meals is that you do so when their tummies are empty so try to time the meals to be ready when they wake up from a long sleep; don't go into the room and disturb them before the food is prepared or they will have already begun drinking from their dam.

With all puppies I like to introduce one milk feed on the first day of weaning, followed by two on the second day. By the fourth day they are usually well ready to accept a 'meat' meal, this to be offered between the two milk meals. I usually create a tempting and nourishing milk meal from good-quality oats with warmed goat's milk and a little clear honey mixed in. Goat's milk is infinitely better than cow's milk for young puppies and, if you do not have a conveniently located fresh supply of it, it can be bought in frozen sachets. Alternatively there are plenty of proprietary milk mixes designed specifically for puppies. By the sixth day a fourth meal can be introduced so that one has, by then, established a pattern of milk, meat, milk, meat. Naturally, the quantity of food given will vary according to the breed and once again I would strongly recommend that you take the advice of established and successful breeders of your own specific breed. Especially with the larger hounds it is imperative that puppies are sufficiently well fed and have a correct intake of calcium, usually provided by the addition of bone-meal in the diet.

Figure 107   Deerhound bitch puppy at thirty-three days

As the weaning process goes on you will find that the bitch is spending longer and longer away from her puppies and by the time they are six to seven weeks old they should be fully weaned. Sometimes a bitch will allow puppies to suck for much longer than this but it is to be discouraged as by now each puppy will be so demanding that it will take far too much from the dam. In addition to this, constant suckling will never allow the bitch's milk to dry up. When fully weaned the puppies should still be allowed to spend time with their dam for she will continue to teach them the ways of the world.

Additional notes on puppy care and development

Dehydration

If you are able to gather up large amounts of loose flesh which, when released, do not quickly fall back into place it is possible that the puppy is suffering from dehydration. This can most easily be discerned by picking up the flesh at the back of the neck. This is cause for concern and a vet's advice should be sought without delay.

Ears

When a puppy is born its ears are sealed. The ears open between the thirteenth and seventeenth day.

Eyes

A puppy's eyes will usually have opened by the ninth or tenth day, at which time they will be of a distinct bluish colour. At this stage the eyes are not yet able to focus and the puppy should be kept away from strong light. Of course, you must never attempt to force the eyes open but if they are particularly sticky they may be bathed gently with a solution of warm, but very weak, tea. If, however, there is any sign of infection you must contact your vet.

Muscle twitching

This is a perfectly normal and essential part of the development of a puppy's muscles. As much as 90 per cent of a newborn puppy's life will be spent sleeping and this is when muscle twitching will most easily be seen.

Nails

The nails of tiny puppies can be very sharp and can cause the bitch some discomfort as they knead her teats when feeding. For this reason nails, which at this age are still quite soft, should be trimmed on a regular basis.

Poor suckers
Some puppies are inclined to hang on to the bitch's teats without actually sucking. This is often indicated by a puppy constantly crying, indicating that he is not getting as much milk as he needs. In such circumstances be sure that he is on a teat every couple of hours and, initially, gently knead the teat with your fingers to stimulate the milk flow. Check also that he is swallowing. This should be roughly at the rate of two swallows per second.

Safety
When the puppies start to move around on all four feet it is essential you see to it they are safely enclosed for it is all too easy for them to get injured because they have found their way into places not intended for such tiny youngsters. Electric cables should, of course, be kept well out of reach. It is useful to have an extension to the whelping box in which the puppies may play safely until they need to venture further.

Stimulation
It is essential that a puppy is stimulated to urinate and defaecate, this usually being done by the bitch by means of her licking. Should you have occasion to hand rear a puppy or if a puppy seems not to have been stimulated in this way by the dam you must, of necessity, simulate the dam's actions by rubbing both the tummy and the anus with a damp tissue.

Sucking due to teething
When teething, puppies will try to suck anything available and it need not necessarily be a teat! Occasionally it can be another puppy's leg, ear or, not infrequency, a little chap's penis! Such offenders must be discouraged before damage occurs.

Toxic milk
Signs of a toxic milk supply are that the puppies appear somewhat bloated, have a red swollen anus and greenish-coloured diarrhoea. It is essential that you contact your vet at once. As toxic milk can cause the puppies' early death, you may well find that you are obliged to rear the litter by hand or, a daunting task, find a foster mother.

Umbilical cords
Usually the umbilical cords will have shrivelled up and fallen off by about the second day. The umbilicus should have dried up neatly but if there is any sign of infection it should be bathed with antiseptic. In the event of healing not taking place immediately, contact your vet.

Umbilical hernias
Umbilical hernias can be inherited or can, sometimes, be caused by trauma at birth when, for example, a bitch has tugged too forcefully on the umbilical cord. Should you encounter a hernia it is always wise to let the vet check it to be sure that surgery is not necessary.

Urination
Sometimes a puppy will cry because it needs to urinate but has not been stimulated to do so by the bitch. Urination can be stimulated as mentioned above, following which the puppy should be passed back to the bitch, rear end first, and she will usually continue the task she should have undertaken a little while before!

A little extra advice

Failure of a bitch to clean up after her puppies
In the unlikely event of a bitch not cleaning up after her puppies before the weaning process begins a little vegetable oil may be smeared on the puppies and this should encourage her to begin. Once the puppies are being weaned the cleaning up falls to you!

Other pets
All other family pets should be kept out of sight of the bitch whilst she is rearing her litter. Most bitches do not welcome dogs or any other animals at this time.

Strangers
During the first two weeks following the birth of her litter the bitch should not be subjected to strangers. Litters of newborn puppies should not be brought into this world to entertain friends and neighbours. There will be plenty of time for socialisation later on.

Exercise
As the bitch begins to leave the nest for longer and longer periods be sure that she gets sufficient exercise so that she can build up her muscle tone. It is wise, though, not to allow her to walk where other dogs may have been, for there is risk that she may pick up infection which could be passed on to the puppies.

Regurgitation

It is only natural that a bitch may decide to regurgitate food for her puppies, for this is exactly what she would have done in the wild. It is not a pretty sight but you will find that the mass of food disappears almost as quickly as it appeared. In due course you will find, to your possible relief, that she has given up this little habit!

Mastitis

Always keep a careful check on your bitch's teats to see that the mammary glands are not becoming hot, hardened and inflamed for this indicates mastitis which is uncomfortable and distressing for the bitch. If caught in the early stages you may rectify the problem by holding a warm cloth to the affected teat and trying to express a little of the milk yourself. The puppies should then be encouraged to use that teat. If the symptoms have not cleared within twelve hours your vet should be consulted.

Eclampsia

Known in the human as 'milk fever', eclampsia, to me, is one of the most frightening things that can happen to a bitch. It develops with amazing speed and the bitch can die within a matter of hours. It is caused not, as many think, by a calcium deficiency but by the body's inability to transport the calcium from the body's reserves. The early outward symptoms are easy to miss. To begin with, she just seems a little strange and perhaps does a little nest-making, much as she did before she whelped. She may pant more than usual and seem a little on edge, and if you place your hands on her shoulder-blades you may be able to detect a slight tremble, which very quickly turns into a 'shiver'. Her legs then stiffen and she will have some difficulty in standing, probably wobbling over. By now her pulse will have become rapid and she will possibly have started to salivate; her temperature may be as much as 106°F (41°C). Time, now, is of the essence and the only way to save the bitch is by a massive dose of calcium given intravenously by your vet. The bitch will appear to return to her normal state remarkably quickly but your vet may well advise that she does not continue to feed her litter, which makes life difficult for you and distressing for her. Depending on the circumstances, your vet may say that she can continue to feed her puppies, in which case you should most certainly work towards weaning them at an early age.

Discharge

Following whelping some discharge from the vulva is normal and for the first day or two it will be malodorous and dark in colour, soon changing to blood red and then paling off to nothing more than a slight mucous discharge. This is all caused by bleeding from the surface of the uterus from which the placentas have broken away. Should you find that the initial thick discharge continues for more than two days you should most certainly seek veterinary advice.

Metritis

The earliest signs of metritis in the bitch are a lack of interest in her puppies and general lethargy. An inflammation of the uterus, metritis is often caused by the retention of a placenta or by an unborn whelp, this being the reason why it is so very important to know that she has produced the same number of puppies as after-births. Another cause can be bacteria intro-duced to the genital tract, which can be as a result of unclean fingers used to assist the whelping, or by unclean bedding. As with most illnesses it is important that metritis is detected in good time when it can usually be recti-fied by a course of antibiotics. In severe cases spaying may be necessary and in extreme cases metritis can cause death. Untreated metritis causes the milk to become toxic and this being the case the puppies have to be hand-reared or fostered.

Coat

For the first two or three days after the puppies are born the bitch will not wish to be interfered with more than necessary. Soon, though, she will probably welcome a little attention and will allow you to give her a very short grooming session on her way back from one of her essential visits to the garden. Her coat will be decidedly out of condition whilst nursing her litter and I am afraid you will not have to be surprised if she sheds coat in considerable quantities. If you have an Afghan it is essential that you keep her coat free from tangles for there is always a danger of the puppies becoming caught up in it.

NINETEEN

GENERAL CARE

I feel sure that you, the reader, will appreciate that it is not possible to be specific about exactly how and where your hound should be housed, for circumstances differ greatly and clearly arrangements made for one pet dog vary quite considerably from those made for a number of dogs living together in one establishment. An Afghan Hound exhibited in the show-ring will need an environment in which his coat will be kept in the best possible order, whilst this will not be so imperative for, for example, a Deerhound kept only for coursing. Indeed, most established Afghan Hound breeders and exhibitors would probably find it difficult to agree with established Deerhound breeders and exhibitors on the subjects of housing, feeding, exercise and preparation for show. Having been involved with both breeds I hope I am able to see both sides of the story, but I can also appreciate how very difficult it is for each to comprehend the reasoning of the other.

Let us begin from the time at which a young puppy leaves its breeder and takes up residence in its new home and, as we go through this chapter, I shall endeavour, as far as possible, to point out differences in care for the various breeds.

Where to buy your puppy

Whether your intention is to have a show dog, a pet or a working hound it is imperative that you buy from a reputable breeder who will have given all due consideration to the quality of the dam, choice of sire, care of the in-whelp bitch and the rearing of the puppies during those early, formative weeks. It is important that you do not simply look through the advertisement column of your local paper and buy the first puppy of the breed you have chosen which happens to be advertised. You may be lucky but, on the other hand, there is every chance that you will not!

Perhaps you are fortunate enough to have friends or acquaintances who already own the breed of your choice and so be able to acquire some valuable information through them. But still you must be on your guard for if it is a show dog that you seek your pet-owning friend may not be in a position to give you all the information you require. Initially you are probably best advised to contact the Secretary of one or more of the breed clubs, who will probably be able to put you in contact with reputable breeders in your general area and might be able to tell you who has puppies available or due to arrive shortly. You will have found the names of the various breed clubs listed at the end of some of the chapters in this book and the telephone numbers of the current Secretary can be obtained by telephoning the Kennel Club.

Another very good way of coming into contact with breeders is to visit one or more of the many shows held up and down the country, for this will give you a chance to see a number of mature dogs at first hand and to seek out the breeders of those dogs which have interested you most. The best shows to visit for this purpose are General Championship Shows (but, as they often span about three days, be sure to go on the correct day for the breed of your choice) and Breed Club Shows at either Open or Championship level. Of course, there are also local Open Shows but here you are less likely to find a sufficiently wide selection of your chosen breed. To find out about shows you will need to purchase either or both of the two weekly canine newspapers *Our Dogs* or *Dog World,* though unless you live in a large city and have access to the major stores you may well find that these need to be ordered through your local newsagent. These newspapers will also give you a great deal of information about the dog scene in general and each has a relevant breed note section keeping you up to date with happenings within your own breed. In these newspapers, as well as in some monthly magazines, you will also find advertisements from breeders but, again, I would urge you to work on recommendation if possible. Most importantly, always keep in mind that the puppy you eventually purchase will, hopefully, live with you for its entire life and it is therefore essential that you make wise and careful decisions from the outset.

Preparing for your puppy's arrival

Although you may have had to wait a good while for the puppy of your choice, especially if he is a potential show puppy, there will have been plenty to do and prepare during the period of waiting. It is to be hoped that you will have found out as much as possible about the breed and will have established contact with at least one of the breed clubs. You will also have organised your home so that it is suitable for a long-legged, probably boisterous young puppy. Sight Hounds are usually the most careful of creatures when they are mature, but as youngsters they have tremendous bursts of energy and, if you have any expensive ornaments which might be knocked off low shelving by a happy tail, you would be well advised to move them to a slightly higher level right now!

Bedding

Your puppy will need a bed he can consider his own. If you are a handy carpenter you can construct a sturdy, high-sided wooden box, one of the sides being lower than the others and the base of the box being raised from the floor or, if you are not of the practical type, one of the large, strong, oval-shaped pet beds will be suitable. In either of these your puppy can, if he wishes, curl up and feel secure. Sight Hounds do have a tendency to sleep with their legs stretched right out so make sure the sleeping quarters are of ample size or you may find, especially with the larger breeds, that the legs stick dangerously out of the box.

Of course, your hound may well prefer to spread himself, seemingly, all over the floor or, worse still, the sofa. Start as you mean to go on and if you don't wish your puppy to use the furniture make that quite clear from the outset. If you allow him on the sofa one day and not the next he will not know what is expected of him, Sight Hounds enjoy pleasing their owners, even from an early age, and it is important that you command his respect and give instructions kindly but firmly so that he understands exactly what you want. With any young puppy, there will be times when he seems to do everything against your will, but put that down to just being a youngster and continue to persevere. You must become the boss so that he looks up to you and treats you as 'top dog' in his little pack.

Should it be that you have decided that your hound is to sleep in an outdoor kennel it is essential, if it is a wooden one, that it be adequately lined and slightly raised from the ground to avoid dampness and draughts. Should you be using a brick-built kennel it would be wise to install an infra-red heat lamp to take off the chill in cold weather.

Bedding in a kennel is also a matter of preference. I know that some Sight Hound owners use straw but this can tend to harbour parasites and must consequently be changed regularly; it is certainly no use for the longer coated breeds such as Afghan Hounds for it gets tangled in their coats. A fine grade of wood wool is sometimes used by those who own very short-coated breeds, such as the Whippet, but care must be taken not to allow your dog into the kennel until the dust has settled once a fresh supply has been used. Especially if you have only one dog you may wish to consider one of the excellent, albeit none-too-cheap, paper beddings now available. I now keep all my dogs in my house, but when I did keep some kennelled out I kept a lining of clean newspaper on the base of the floor with comfort-able, washable bedding on top. Large supplies of clean, preferably unused, newspaper are not easy to come across but it is possible to strike up a friendly relationship with your newsagent or a newspaper wholesaler.

The run
The provision of a secure run for your hound is essential for Sight Hounds are renowned for being great escape artists. They seem to come in two basic categories, jumpers and diggers, but never mind what he appears to excel at, always keep in the back of your mind that he is probably as capable of the alternative method of escape if the fancy takes him!

Fencing should be six feet high, well bedded into the ground and should curve inwards at the top to beat even the highest jumper at his own game. As an alternative you could, of course, have an enclosed top which, if solid, can also be a great help on wet days. Chain link fencing, although quite expensive, is certainly the most secure, for cheaper forms can be chewed so that the links divide up and create holes. It is not wise to select any fencing with a plastic coating, particles of which can easily be chewed and swallowed. Should you decide that your dog is to have the run of your entire garden, so be it, but you will have to take the same precautionary measures for Sight Hounds are quite capable of seeking out the slightest chink in wooden fencing panels and squeezing through to the outside world.

The base of the run is again a matter of preference; it will also depend upon the amount and type of exercise your dog has when not in his run. A concrete run is perhaps the easiest to keep clean but, because they help exercise the muscles of the feet, some prefer chippings for Sight Hounds. The chippings must not be so small that they get caught between the pads, nor so large that they are uncomfortable on the feet. I have found Cotswold chippings to be the best and if purchased ready washed they do not give off the unpleasant red dust which takes a few weeks to wash off the unwashed variety. Such chippings occasionally contain fossils! If you choose to have chippings in the run your hound will need some roadwork. A hound, as indeed any breed, also needs access to interesting smells and so, if he does not have the free run of a paddock or part of your garden, it is good to have an area which is primarily grass; ideally this should be divided off from the hard surface so that your dog can be kept from turning it into a quagmire in rainy weather.

Feeding

Your hound will appreciate feeds at regular times and obviously whilst he is still a puppy you must be guided by his breeder as to what he is to be fed. If you do decide to change his diet to something which suits you better, do so gradually to avoid upsetting his stomach. It is most important to remember that Sight Hounds must not under any circumstances be fed immediately before exercise. Following exercise they should be allowed to rest for a short while after which time they will be anxious to feed.

There are so many complete meals on the market now that I shall refrain from giving any exact recommendations as to diet. All I would say is that a high protein intake is more necessary for an active dog than for one which rests at home most of the day, indeed too high a protein content given to an inactive dog can be positively harmful, so do bear this in mind when deciding on the best diet to suit your dog. Don't be afraid to spend a good while reading the ingredients lists on the various packets and if you shop in a store where all the dried foods are on display in containers only, never be afraid to ask to see details of content. Obviously, if giving a dried food if necessary it must be soaked in accordance with the maker's instructions and your hound should, in addition, have a constant and plentiful supply of fresh water. Should you decide to feed a meat and biscuit diet, balance these carefully for one is as essential as the other. Hounds enjoy a drink of milk and an egg yolk is also usually considered a welcome addition to the diet. Bone-meal can be given in the appropriate quantity for the size of your hound but, as with any vitamin supplement you choose to give (though with a well-balanced diet the latter should not usually be necessary), always remember that too much can be harmful. Never be afraid to mix in a few

Figure 108
Deerhound eating from a raised bowl at ten weeks

cooked, diced vegetables with the meal to add a little variety, or a tasty stock rather than just plain water can occasionally be used to soak a dried food. If giving red meat it is wise to vary the diet with white meat or fish once or twice a week as too much red meat is said to overheat the blood.

Once your hound has grown beyond the stage of his more frequent puppy meals he should be fed twice daily and to aid digestion his feeding bowls should be raised from the ground. You will find some specially made raised feeding accessories at trade stands at major dog shows, though they are less frequently seen in pet stores.

Although Sight Hounds do not appear to be heavy dogs most of them eat a substantial amount and one cannot skimp on their food. It is important, therefore, to consider the cost of feeding such an animal before deciding that a Sight Hound is really the type of dog that should be sharing your home. Hounds that are under-fed, or out of condition, will soon show this in their outward appearance.

Should you have an Afghan, Borzoi, Saluki or Whippet and feel that the coat is somewhat lacking in sheen a little good-quality oil can be added to the daily diet. Should this cause loose motions it should not be given for a few days and then only in even smaller quantities. Too much oil should be avoided.

Coat care

As the coats of the various breeds differ so much each has been dealt with in the relevant breed chapter.

Exercise

Sight Hounds do need regular exercise and this is something else which should be given careful consideration before making your final decision as to which breed to purchase. Take the advice of experts within your own breed as to exactly what programme of exercise is best to build up the muscle tone without over-exercising. You will find that opinions vary and you will almost certainly receive different advice from someone who shows their dogs than from someone who primarily works them. If you have bought from a reputable breeder then it is his or her advice you should seek initially.

The exercise programmes of all Sight Hounds, and especially the larger breeds, should be built up slowly, and as youngsters they must not be allowed to over-exercise. Exercise away from the dog's home territory provides exciting new smells and new discoveries to be made, so do not deprive your hound of his daily constitutional or you end up with a bored hound and are running the risk of having a destructive one!

Adult Sight Hounds should ideally have a combination of roadwork and free exercise each day, after which they should be allowed to relax thoroughly in comfortably warm conditions before they are fed.

Digestion

I have already mentioned that food bowls should be raised slightly off the floor as an aid to digestion and it goes without saying that if your hound is off his food for more than a day or two at the most veterinary advice should be sought. Stomach chills are not uncommon in the fine-coated breeds; these cause a loss of appetite but only for about half a day, at which time the affected dog should be kept warm and, as always, away from any draught.

Sight Hounds' stomachs are liable to slight upset if there is a sudden change of diet and so it is wise, if changing the diet at all, to do so gradually. Some hounds have slightly delicate stomachs which cause them to vomit food soon after eating but they show no symptoms of illness and the meal usually returns to whence it came within a few minutes, presumably being more digestible the second time around. If, however, your hound has persistent vomiting, most probably accompanied by thirst, veterinary advice must be sought at once to avoid dehydration. In the interim period it is wise to administer very small quantities of water mixed with glucose to keep up energy levels until help is at hand.

Distension or bloat, an acute form of indigestion, is a serious matter and can occur in those breeds that have deep briskets. The suspected causes of the original attack include excessive exercise following a meal, the feeding of too much unexpanded carbohydrate, irregular feeding times and too great a quantity of those foods which produce gases, these being primarily green vegetables. The long ligaments in the dog's stomach allow it to rotate, closing the inlet and outlet. The gas there is trapped and is joined by more as the digestive juices continue to do their work. Shock follows quickly and death can occur within a very short space of time.

In the very early stages, prior to the rotation of the stomach, vomiting can sometimes be induced by a small (pea-sized for large breeds) lump of washing soda. Bicarbonate of soda might possibly reduce the gas which is being formed. Having said that, at the onset of bloat, or even a suspicion of it, your vet must be contacted immediately and the dog taken to the surgery for what will very probably be an immediate operation. It is useful to know that the onset of bloat is usually about six hours following a meal, so it is wise to adjust feeding times so that you will be around when it might occur.

Accidents and injuries

Long-legged breeds are rather more prone to accident, I find, than the shorter, cobbier types, possibly because they run so fast. Although they are incredibly agile they can sometimes meet with difficulties along the way. Especially if you course your dog, it is wise to keep a small first-aid pack with you. This should contain bandages, cotton wool and disinfectant, and also a healing ointment and riboflavin, which is good for healing open wounds. Keep two pieces of wood with you that can, if necessary, be used as splints.

Sprains occur only too easily in fast-running dogs and exercise should, of course, be stopped at once. If your hound is too large to carry any distance, walk at a very gentle pace back to your vehicle, from which time the injured limb should be rested. This means that your hound will have to be kept in a confined space in order to keep him as immobile as possible. Cold compresses can be used at regular intervals, especially if there is any swelling, and in serious cases an elastic bandage can be used.

Toes can also occasionally be knocked up and I would suggest immediate attention by a vet to avoid long-term damage. In minor cases massage with oil may ease the problem but, in any event, exercise will have to be severely restricted for a good while. Should a toenail be broken above the quick it should be cut off as quickly as possible and bandaged to stop the bleeding. Potassium permanganate, if available, is also a useful aid to stem the flow of blood.

Any injury to the eye should be dealt with by a vet immediately for prompt attention is essential if one is to avoid long-term damage to the eye. If ointment or drops are prescribed be sure not to allow the nozzle to make contact with the eye. Should a piece of grit become lodged in the eye it can often be safely floated out with a little cod liver oil. Corneal ulcers can occasionally be caused by trauma and cod liver oil taken orally is an aid to rapid and efficient healing, although veterinary advice must, of course, also be sought as quickly as possible.

Following any accident the dog may well be in shock and must be kept warm and quiet. This is also so in cases of haemorrhage. As a temporary measure the flow of blood from a bleeding limb can be stemmed by the application of pressure between the injured limb and the body; a tourniquet can be made from any long piece of fabric such as a neck-tie or soft belt.

The tips of ears and tail are also prone to occasional accident and though not usually serious the bleeding may be profuse and will need to be controlled. In the case of a cut to the ear, a stocking can be pulled over the head to keep the ear pressed to the head. Should it be the tail tip which is damaged a little cotton wool will suffice; this may be kept on with a roll of cardboard attached by sellotape.

Stings can be painful and if they are in the mouth, on the throat, or worse still if the bee or wasp has been swallowed, they can also be dangerous. Keep the dog cool and try to keep the tongue forward so that the airway remains clear. In the cases outlined above veterinary advice must be sought immediately so that an anti-histamine injection can be administered. Anti-histamine tablets are also useful to keep handy, especially in the summer months when stinging insects abound. Should your dog suffer from a sting elsewhere (on the pad seems to be a common place), TCP will bring some relief and vinegar is specially good for wasp stings. In the case of bee stings bicarbonate of soda can be applied once the sting has been removed with tweezers.

Should your dog have difficulty in closing his mouth, be pawing at it and possibly also salivating heavily, he may well have something lodged between his teeth or across the top of his mouth, perhaps a piece of stick or bone. It may not be easy to dislodge this because of the discomfort the dog is suffering, in which case veterinary attention will be necessary for inflammation can very easily occur.

Snake bites can occasionally also be a hazard and adder bites can be lethal to dogs. Urgent veterinary treatment is essential. If the bite is on a limb, a ligature should be immediately applied above the bite to reduce the spread of venom.

Poisoning

Most frequently the signs of poisoning are sudden vomiting, muscular spasms or bleeding from an exit point, such as the gums, the latter usually being the effect of Warfarin. It is important to attempt to ascertain the poison your dog has come into contact with for the antidote used varies according to the type of poison taken. Bear in mind that the poison may not only have been in something he ate or drank, but he might very easily have walked on a toxic substance and then washed the pads of his feet, thus ingesting it. Veterinary treatment should be sought without delay. For the reasons given above, you should give him as much information as possible about the possible poison. If you have put out poison for mice or other vermin, don't be afraid to say so – your dog's health and even his life might be at stake. In your initial telephone contact with the vet take his advice as to whether vomiting should or should not be induced, for it is not to be recommended for all types of poisoning. Your hound should be kept warm, quiet and should have some fresh air.

Constipation

It is important that dogs defaecate regularly and any lack of frequency should be noted. This may be due to diet. In such cases the matter can usually be rectified by a slight change in the feeding programme. If you are feeding a dried biscuit meal, try a well-soaked meal instead, and include in the diet vegetables cooked in lightly salted water. As a temporary measure (but not as a matter of routine) you may offer a meal of uncooked liver or red meat, and this should be fed without biscuits. If you are feeding bones which, incidentally, I do not recommend unless they are marrow bones, there is a chance that a blockage may have been caused by pieces of chipped bone. A couple of teaspoons of olive oil (but only one for a Whippet) may ease the situation but if constipation cannot be cured within a day or two by these simple remedies veterinary advice should be sought without delay.

Diarrhoea

Clearly, if your hound not only has diarrhoea but is also 'off colour', lacking in appetite, or if there is any trace of blood in the motions, your vet must be consulted immediately. Having said this, there is always the possibility that loose motions may have been caused by a chill or perhaps by a change of diet. It is wise to keep the affected dog away from others and to provide warmth and, of course, be sure that any draughts are eliminated. Cooled, boiled water, mixed with a little glucose powder should be given and your hound should be starved for twenty-four hours and then kept on a diet of fish or white meat for two or three days. Arrowroot can also be used as some measure of assistance. Milk should be avoided whilst the motions are loose.

Fits and hysteria

Once a dog has gone into an epileptic fit there is little that can be done until he comes back to his senses. During a fit there is always a possibility that the dog might bite and so if it is necessary to move him from a place which is dangerous it is best to drag the hound gently by the hindquarters (not by the legs). Use of a stern voice may have some effect in bringing him round but if possible he should be kept in a darkened, confined space until recovered or until veterinary aid arrives.

Skin and coat problems

Skin irritations
These are not unusual and unfortunately are frequently difficult to diagnose and therefore often present a problem in discovering an effective treatment. In mild cases the reason might be something as simple as a slight surfeit of dairy products in the diet, too much milk, for example, or it could be that your hound is allergic to the new bedding with which you have recently provided him. With such causes the remedies present no problems. However, many skin infections seem never to be cured and are only kept under control. Serious cases in which an irritation appears to spread quickly should be dealt with by a vet just as soon as possible. A loss of coat might be due to a hormone imbalance or to ringworm, both of which need veterinary advice.

Dandruff
Should your hound suffer from dandruff or an overly dry skin, it may be that a little more fat is needed in the diet. This can be introduced by adding a little olive oil or vegetable oil to meals. Should dandruff be noticed after bathing your dog this may very probably be due to the fact that you have not rinsed out the shampoo sufficiently well, so remember to take a little more care next time.

Alopecia
This is a form of baldness in which hair drops out before the new hair has grown in. In a bitch it can happen whilst she is rearing a litter of puppies and is, indeed, often related to hormonal imbalance. It seems also to appear with some regularity during a course of steroids or cortisone. Other reasons include skin infections, parasites and, especially in the case of puppies, a thyroid deficiency. Unless the cause is hormonal due to the rearing of puppies, problems of this nature are notoriously slow to cure and so veterinary help should be sought as soon as any sign of loss of coat becomes apparent.

Parasites

I trust you will not be exercising your Sight Hound amongst sheep, but he may well run in areas where sheep have grazed and pick up the odd sheep tick, so make sure you check his coat and skin upon your return. At first glance a sheep tick somewhat resembles a dark-blue wart. This increases in size as the tick, whose head is embedded in the dog's skin, sucks his blood. The safest way to remove a tick is to apply salt directly on to the tick which will cause it to shrivel so that it can be taken off. It is essential, however, that the head is fully removed, for if left it will most probably cause an abscess to form.

It is to be hoped that your hound will not be troubled by fleas or lice, but however clean your dog there is always the danger that the odd unwelcome visitor may appear as a result of contact with another dog or with some wild animal. (Contrary to popular opinion, hedgehog fleas cannot live on dogs.) For dogs which are bathed, an anti-parasitic shampoo can be used occasionally or when you have reason to suspect that it might be necessary. If you have a breed such as a Deerhound and prefer not to bathe the coat you can use one of the flea sprays available, making sure that it does not come into contact with the eyes. It is always wise also to spray bedding and any awkward corners in the dog's sleeping-quarters.

Other problems

Abscess

Thankfully, in the shorter coated breeds abscesses can usually be noticed before they develop too far, for they can be very painful. The abscess should be bathed in a solution of hot water and salt; this will bring it to a head so that it bursts and the pus can be evacuated and drained off. The latter is important for if it heals before having fully drained the abscess will re-appear. For this reason it must not be allowed to heal up too quickly and, whilst open, should be bathed regularly in the salt-water solution. Very often the reason for the development of an abscess is a fight with another dog, or perhaps the skin being caught on a dirty object, such as barbed wire. It is therefore always wise to check the skin thoroughly after any such incident and to bathe and dress any slight puncture wound. Should it be that what appears to be an abscess does not burst, or if there are a number of them, veterinary advice should be sought.

Coprophagy

This unpleasant little habit is actually the eating of faeces and various reasons have been put forward over the years as to why it occurs. It is often said that a dog does this to compensate for a deficiency in protein, minerals or vitamins in the diet but it does seem also, occasionally, to be practised by dogs which have perfectly healthy, balanced diets. On occasion a bitch can develop the habit after raising a litter but sometimes it can happen at the puppy stage. Faeces must be removed immediately so the dog in question has no access to them and a little fat or treacle in the diet can also deter.

Should it be that, whilst exercising, your hound has the habit of devouring the droppings of other animals, such as sheep and rabbits (a seemingly tremendously pleasurable pastime!), be sure to worm regularly, not only for roundworm but for tapeworm too. Unfortunately it is not practical to remove all the sheep droppings from every field before the daily jaunt!

Ear infections

Sight Hounds are not generally prone to ear troubles but it is always wise to check inside the ear to see that it is clean and free from odour, signifying that no form of ear infection is present. Should there be canker, ear mites, or other infection your hound will probably scratch at the ear and, in severe cases hold the head on one side; the ear may also be hot to the touch. Ear cleaning aids are available but take care not to probe too far into the ear, thereby causing damage. For anything more than a simple build-up of wax veterinary attention is necessary, and do be sure to give your hound the full course of treatment in order to avoid recurrence of a problem which may seem to have disappeared before the full number of days' treatment has been given.

Heatstroke

Any owner of a dog must be extremely careful not to leave him unattended in any place where heat is likely to build up. Unfortunately, however, accidents do happen and many people are unaware of just how quickly temperatures inside a car, or indeed a wooden kennel, for example, can soar to dangerous levels. Even with windows left open, a car is not a suitable place to leave a dog, especially during the summer months, even when it doesn't appear too hot. Even if you have parked in shade it is all too easy to forget that the sun moves – and more quickly than you thought!

In cases of heatstroke time is of the essence. The dog should be placed in the cool and iced or very cold water applied both to the head and to the shoulders and neck area. Should he be unconscious, under no circumstances force him to drink. Once he has regained consciousness, however, he may be offered small quantities of glucose water or a light saline solution.

Dogs in cars can and do die, sometimes very quickly, so please keep this in mind at all times, even when the day seems only pleasantly mild. It is also worth pointing out that dogs have died, unknown to their owners, when in transit in the back of a vehicle. Heat builds up very quickly, especially if you happen to be stuck in a traffic jam, so do check on any dogs travelling with you at frequent intervals and carry with you a supply of water.

Hernias

Umbilical hernias, though not common in Sight Hounds, are usually visible from birth and can be either traumatic or hereditary. Should one purchase a puppy with such a hernia (felt as a circular swelling in the umbilical area) a vet should be asked to check whether or not surgery would be recommended in order to avoid the risk of 'strangulation'. Very occasionally a lump resembling a hernia develops following a Caesarean or similar operation. Once again veterinary advice should be sought as to whether or not surgery is advisable. The latter is usually not a true hernia but is the result of an adhesion on the original scar tissue.

Inguinal hernias are more likely to require urgent attention and often do not appear until a dog is mature. These can be located in one groin or in both and can be found in either dogs or in bitches. Veterinary advice must be sought immediately upon discovery of what will be felt as a swelling in this area. A hound suffering from an inguinal hernia should not be used in a breeding programme.

Kennel cough

Each of the many different forms of kennel cough is highly contagious and can be first noticed by the dog seeming to clear his throat, as if he has something stuck. Gradually this progresses to a hoarse cough and at this point you know that veterinary attention is essential. As it is so terribly contagious it is only fair to other dogs not to take yours into the waiting room and he must be isolated from others, not only whilst he is coughing, but for a few weeks afterwards, too, when he appears perfectly healthy. Prompt, correct treatment can seemingly bring almost immediate relief and it is all too easy to be lulled into a false sense of security. Kennel cough is most serious in young puppies, in older dogs and in those with a heart condition. It can lead to bronchitis and unfortunately can cause death. Thankfully a protective vaccine is available and is strongly to be recommended.

Kidney failure

Signs of kidney failure include excessive thirst with the consequent frequent passing of water, rapid breathing and apparent premature ageing. Whilst usually associated with mature dogs, it is possible for kidney failure to occur in young stock and problems of this nature can be inherited.

Liver diseases

Liver disorders are almost always serious and need careful attention, so at the first signs of a problem of this kind it is essential that you seek the expert advice of your vet. One of the most noticeable signs is a jaundiced yellowing of the white of the eye and of those membranes which line the eye and the mouth. Under the ear flap is another place where slight yellowing may be noticed, although this is more readily observed in daylight than in artificial light. Sickness, loss of appetite and the infrequent passing of highly coloured urine are other signs which may be noticed at the onset of such disease.

Undescended testicles

Should neither testicle be descended the correct term is 'cryptorchid', whilst if only one is descended he is a unilateral cryptorchid. The more commonly used term 'monorchid' should actually only be used if a dog only *possesses* one testicle.

Unfortunately both cryptorchidism and monorchidism are usually hereditary. I would certainly not recommend that dogs with either of these problems be used at stud, although it has to be said that in most cases they are perfectly capable of siring offspring. In cases where a testicle is retained in the body, which, incidentally, is too warm for a testicle, there is a risk of tumour, just one of the reasons why veterinary treatment should be sought at an early stage.

All the Kennel Club's Breed Standards include the clause, 'Male animals should have two apparently normal testicles fully descended into the scrotum.'

Vaccination programmes

As with any breed of dog it is important that puppies are vaccinated according to a regular programme and that boosters are kept up to date. Usual vaccines are for distemper, leptospirosis, hepatitis and parvovirus. Most vaccines now also incorporate some protection against kennel cough. Some vets send out reminders when boosters are due but most do not and it is easy to let a year or more slip by without remembering something which is a matter of course. Keep your vaccination certificate with your dog's pedigree and other important papers and make a note in your diary, just to be on the safe side. An increasing number of dog breeders now prefer to use homoeopathy as an alternative to routine vaccination.

Insurance

There are now many different companies operating insurance policies for pets although it is impossible to delve deeply into the various permutations within the confines of this book. It may well be that your vet has some leaflets in his surgery and that you could ask his advice as to which is the most comprehensive. Often one has a choice of different amounts of cover and this should be considered carefully before making a decision.

Some breeders insure puppies before they move on to their new homes. This may be something which they automatically include in the cost of the puppy or they may give the purchaser the choice of paying a little extra. Personally I feel that this is a very good idea. The cover taken out at this time usually lasts for four or six weeks, during which time the insurance company involved sends through details of how to continue the policy. Of course, you may feel that an alternative policy is better and there is nothing to prevent you changing to another should you wish to do so.

Caring for the older dog

Unfortunately for the majority of breeds described in this book, 'the larger the dog, the shorter the life-span' is a saying that holds some truth. A great many of the larger Sight Hounds are lucky if they make it into double figures, although of course some do and one always hopes one's hound will be one of them.

There are always many reasons why some dogs live longer than others but there are indeed certain things you can do which may help to give a hound a little extra time and, even more importantly, give him a quality of life he will continue to enjoy.

One of the most important things to remember is that he should not be allowed to carry too much weight, although Sight Hounds are not generally prone to this problem. Excess weight, apart from having an effect on various organs and the limbs, will, more specifically, put undue pressure on the heart, something which can often be detected by a rather unpleasant cough. Coughing can, of course, also be a sign of worms and relatively healthy older dogs should be wormed at annual intervals. Seek veterinary advice before administering a worming agent to any dog suffering from an illness or that is otherwise out of condition.

Sight Hounds seem to manage to keep their teeth well into old age but if any have loosened, but are otherwise in good order, take care as to the consistency of his food. If it is the front teeth which have loosened rather than the back ones he should still be able to enjoy his favourite crunchy foods and snacks.

A hound will usually cope relatively well with failing sight, provided he is not subjected to any drastic changes in his environment. Avoid moving the furniture around in the rooms he frequents and make sure that water and food bowls are all in their usual places. Also take care that such things as vacuum cleaners, garden hoses and watering cans are kept tidily out of harm's way.

Medical conditions can sometimes cause an old dog to lose control of his 'water works', to a greater or lesser extent, depending on the severity of the problem. Should the dog have been generally clean in the house all his life, there will almost invariably be a valid reason for this lack of control, which probably upsets him as much as you. For this reason it would be unfair to scold him; far wiser for you to make sure he is allowed outside at very frequent intervals. Even this may not entirely eliminate accidents and I am afraid you will have eventually to decide how long you can continue to cope with this set of circumstances. You may be able to prolong matters, without upsetting him too much, by confining him to a suitable area, especially during the night hours. It goes without saying that veterinary advice should be sought, for this will often be only one symptom of a much greater problem. Should your vet require a urine sample, which is highly likely, try to take a sample of the first urine of the day. Actually obtaining a sample is not always as difficult as it might at first appear, but don't expect your dog to aim straight into the bottle! Use a sterilised stainless-steel container to collect the urine and then transfer it into a suitable, sterilised bottle.

The older dog will very probably enjoy the attention he receives during grooming sessions but take care not to make them over-long, or make him stand too long in one position. Every effort must be made to avoid his getting damp or cold and if he has been bathed he should be allowed to remain indoors for a good while afterwards so that his temperature cools down slowly.

His showing or sporting days may have come to an end but this is no reason to give him any less attention than before. Because he will miss some of his outings, especially those to the race track and to shows, his interest must be kept alive in other ways. If still in reasonably good health he may enjoy the very occasional Veteran classs, possibly at a local Open Show if he wouldn't be happy travelling any great distance or if a full day at a Championship Show would tire him too much. Keep his walks fairly short and provided that his sight is still good, vary the routes so that he does not get bored.

I would be very cautious about bringing a new youngster into the household at a late stage in a hound's life but undoubtedly there are cases in which, if the situation is handled sensibly, success can be achieved to the benefit of all parties concerned. As I have already indicated, it is imperative that the older dog does not feel that someone else is being brought in to take his place and to receive all the attention that would otherwise have been bestowed on him. Neither must his much-needed sleep be disturbed by a bumptious youngster who seems constantly anxious to play. Apart from anything else, the older dog may become ill tempered if disturbed too often and you would never forgive yourself if an accident happened, essentially through no fault of either canine party. However, provided that the two are kept apart when necessary and only allowed to be together under supervision, they can certainly derive great pleasure from each other's company. I introduced a young Deerhound to a couple of ageing Afghans and I genuinely feel that the youngster's presence helped to rejuvenate them mentally. They all looked forward to their short games together and I have a sneaking suspicion that in those many hours of sleep they relived their brief frolics many times over.

Whatever you do, allow your older dog to keep his pride. Sight Hounds are proud creatures and they like to keep their dignity, even into old age.

Time to part

Thankfully we live in an age of excellent pain-killing drugs so that it is possible to keep dogs tolerably free from pain, even as their end draws nigh. Sadly, though, there comes a time when the drugs no longer have the required effect or sometimes the quality of life is such that comfort and dignity are things of the past. It is then that the decision has to be taken as to whether and when one has one's hound put kindly to sleep.

Naturally, one's hound can die a natural death and although this is usually a much greater shock for the owner it does relieve one of the painful decision of whether or not the time has really come. It is usually possible for your vet to visit your home but it is more usual to take your dog along to the surgery. I would not, however, recommend the latter if your dog is afraid of vets' surgeries, but if he is not he is likely only to think he is simply going along for another of those routine checks. Of course, in many cases, especially following injury, the decision is actually taken at the surgery.

The end is usually very peaceful with the dog going quietly and almost imperceptibly to sleep, and, provided you feel you can have sufficient control of your emotions during those final few minutes, I strongly suggest that you remain with your hound until the end. After all, he has given you loyal service and in my opinion you owe him this final favour for he will almost certainly feel more secure in your presence. On the other hand, if you know that you simply cannot avoid becoming a crumbling wreck before the end it is probably wiser to leave him with the vet.

The majority of the hounds described in this book are rather large to be laid to rest in the garden but of course this is possible, although they must be buried deeply. Should any kind of infectious disease be the cause of death cremation is the only choice open to you. Indeed cremation is perfectly normal following the death of any dog, whatever the cause, and if you prefer not simply to leave the means of disposal in the hands of the vet you may arrange with him to have your much-loved hound cremated privately. This can be done either on an individual basis or with others, the latter being somewhat cheaper. In the former case you will usually be given the choice of what should happen to the ashes; they can either be sent back to your home (usually within about ten days but I have known it to be a month) or put in a 'garden of rest'.

Whilst discussing unhappy subjects, now is the time to mention that it is always wise to make some provision for your dogs should any of them outlive you. This is not a pleasant thought but clauses can be included in your will and your solicitor will advise you of how any stipulations may be worded. The knowledge that your much-loved hounds will be cared for in the way you, their owner, consider in their best interest gives some peace of mind. As I said earlier – you owe it to them.

Histories are more full of examples of the fidelity of dogs than of friends.
ALEXANDER POPE

Selected Bibliography

Ash, Edward C., *The Practical Dog Book*, Simpkin Marshall, 1931.
—— *This Doggie Business*, Hutchinson, 1934.
Beilby, Ralph, *A General History of Quadrupeds*, Newcastle upon Tyne, 1790.
Bell, E. Watson, *The Scottish Deerhound*, David Douglas, 1892.
Chadwick, Winifred E., *Borzois*, 1971.
Compton, Herbert, *The Twentieth Century Dog (Sporting)*, Grant Richards, 1904.
Cox, Harding, *Dogs by Well Known Authorities*, Fawcett, McQuire, 1908.
—— *Dogs of Today*, A. & C. Black, 1935.
Croxton Smith OBE, A., *About Our Dogs*, London, 1931.
—— *Hounds & Dogs*, Seeley, Service & Co. Ltd, 1932.
Cunliffe, Juliette *Greyhound*, Interpet, 2000.
—— *The Encyclopedia of Dog Breeds*, Parragon, 1999.
Dalziel, Hugh, *British Dogs*, London, 1881.
Deeson, A. F. L., *Large Dogs*, G. I. Barnett & Son, 1963.
Douglas-Todd, C. H., *The Whippet*, Arco Publishing, 1961.
Drury and Others, *British Dogs*, Charles Scribner's Sons, 1903.
Edwards Clark, H., *The Greyhound*, Popular Dogs Publishing Co. Ltd, 1965.
Encyclopaedia Britannica, 1791.
Fiennes, Richard and Alice, *The Natural History of the Dog*, Weidenfeld & Nicolson, 1968.
Gardner, Phyllis, *The Irish Wolfhound*, Dundalk, 1931.
Gie, Daphne, *Afghan Hounds*, David & Charles, 1978.
Harrison, Charles, *The Afghan Hound*, Popular Dogs, 1971.
Hartley, A. N., *The Deerhound*, East Midland Allied Press, 1955.
Hubbard, Clifford L. B., *A Kennel of Dogs*, Elek Books, 1977.
—— *Dogs in Britain*, Macmillan, 1948.
—— *The Afghan Handbook*, Nicholson & Watson, 1951.
Hutchinson, Walter, *Hutchinson's Popular Illustrated Dog Encyclopaedia*, 1933–4.
Ibn al-Marzuban, *The Superiority of Dogs over Many of Those Who Wear Clothes* (translated and edited by G. R. Smith and M. A. S. Abdel Haleem), Aris & Phillips, 1978.

Leighton, Robert, *The Complete Book of the Dog,* Cassell, 1922.

—— *The New Book of the Dog,* Cassell, 1907.

Marples, Theo, *Show Dogs,* 3rd edition, Our Dogs Publishing, 1926.

Merlen, R. H. A., *De Canibus: Dog and Hound in Antiquity,* J. A. Allen, 1971.

Meyrick, John, *House Dogs and Sporting Dogs,* John Van Voorst, 1861.

Morris, Desmond, *Dogs,* Ebury Press 2001.

Niblock, Margaret, *The Afghan Hound: A Definitive Study,* K. and R. Books, 1980.

Parker, Eric, *Best of Dogs,* Hutchinson, 1949.

Russell, Joanna, *All about Gazehounds,* Pelham Books, 1976.

St John, Charles, *The Wild Sports and Natural History of the Highlands,* John Murray, 1907.

Scrope, William, *The Art of Deerstalking,* John Murray, 1839.

Sheardown, Frank, *The Working Longdog,* Dickson Price, 1989.

Sloan, A. and Farquhar, *Dog and Man, The Story of a Friendship,* George H. Doran, 1925.

'Stonehenge', *Manual of British Rural Sports,* G. Routledge, 1857.

—— *The Dog,* Longmans, Green, Reader and Dyer, 1867.

Taplin, W., *The Sportsman's Cabinet* (2 vols), London 1803 and 1804.

Vesey-FitzGerald, Brian, *The Book of the Dog,* Nicholson & Watson, 1948.

—— *The Domestic Dog,* Routledge & Kegan Paul, 1957.

Walsh, E. G., *Lurchers and Longdogs,* Standfast Press, 1978 (enlarged and revised edition).

Walzoff, Dimitri, 'The Perchino Hunt', in W. E. Chadwick, *Borzois,* fourth impression, 1989.

Watson, James, *The Dog Book,* 1906.

Wentworth Day, J., *The Dog in Sport,* George G. Harrap, 1938.

Wood, J. G., *Illustrated Natural History,* Routledge, Warne & Routledge, 1861.

Youatt, William, *The Dog,* Longman, Green, 1845.

Amongst the many journals and monthly publications used for reference the *Kennel Gazette, Dogs Monthly, Our Dogs, Dog World* and the Saluki and the Deerhound Clubs' Newsletters are worthy of particular note.

INDEX

INDEX

279